Culturally Responsive Education in the Classroom

This exciting book helps educators translate the concept of equity into the context of pedagogy in the K-12 classroom. Providing a practice-oriented framework for understanding what equity entails for both teachers and learners, this book clarifies the theoretical context for equity and shares rich teaching strategies across a range of content areas and age groups. Unpacking six themes to understand Culturally Responsive Education (CRE), this powerful book helps teachers incorporate equity into behaviors, environments, and meaningful learning opportunities. *Culturally Responsive Education in the Classroom* provides specific, practice-based examples to help readers develop a culturally responsive pedagogical mindset for closing equity gaps in student achievement.

Adeyemi Stembridge is an educational consultant specializing in equity-focused school improvement. He was the Director of the Center for Strategic Solutions at the Metropolitan Center for Research on Equity and the Transformation of Schools (Metro Center) in the Steinhardt School of Culture, Education, and Human Development at New York University, USA.

D0781744

Culturally Responsive Education in the Classroom

An Equity Framework for Pedagogy

Adeyemi Stembridge

Routledge
Taylor & Francis Group

NEW YORK AND LONDON

First published 2020
by Routledge
52 Vanderbilt Avenue, New York, NY 10017

and by Routledge
2 Park Square, Milton Park, Abingdon, Oxon, OX14 4RN

Routledge is an imprint of the Taylor & Francis Group, an informa business

Library of Congress Cataloging-in-Publication Data
Names: Stembridge, Adeyemi, author.
Title: Culturally responsive education in the classroom : an equity
framework for pedagogy / Adeyemi Stembridge.
Identifiers: LCCN 2019046441 (print) | LCCN 2019046442 (ebook) |
ISBN 9781138339385 (hardback) | ISBN 9781138339453 (paperback) |
ISBN 9780429441080 (ebook)
Subjects: LCSH: Educational equalization–United States. |
Multicultural education–Study and teaching–United States. |
Culturally relevant pedagogy–United States. |
Education–Aims and objectives–United States.
Classification: LCC LC213.2 .S697 2020 (print) |
LCC LC213.2 (ebook) | DDC 370.117–dc23
LC record available at https://lccn.loc.gov/2019046441
LC ebook record available at https://lccn.loc.gov/2019046442

ISBN: 978-1-138-33938-5 (hbk)
ISBN: 978-1-138-33945-3 (pbk)
ISBN: 978-0-429-44108-0 (ebk)

Typeset in Caslon
by Newgen Publishing UK

Shout out to all the brilliant teachers whom I've learned so much from over the years. Thank you! Thank you! Thank you!

And shout out to Hip Hop too... yes, definitely Hip Hop. None of this is possible without Hip Hop.

Contents

Preface

I'm often struck by the vibrancy even before I can determine the topic of instruction. It pulls you in – like gravity – but with personal and intentional purpose. The momentum is palpable. And though it is often the teacher leading the learning, one is able to see empowerment in the students' faces. I'm always captivated in these spaces. *They take me back to the same memory…*

It was a little theater just outside of Washington, DC, and I had come to town just to see her perform. I'd been a big-time Erykah Badu fan since her freshman album, but I'd never seen her give a live show. The venue was standing room only, and we were packed in – and yet, once the set started, I felt like Erykah was directing every syllable of sound, every sway of movement… to me. It may or may not have been my imagination that we made eye contact many times among the hundreds of other fans singing along and basking in the soul-filling rhythms that flowed from the stage. We were transfixed in her presence, but the show wasn't hers alone. The audience was anything but passive participants. In fact, we sang along and responded as she called out to us. By the end of the set, we were all equal stakeholders in an experience that had in some way changed everyone in the crowd – but I left the Filmore Theater that night certain that Erykah had developed the absolute entirety of that experience specifically for me... *and then I am eventually transported back to the classroom.*

Though the analogy may be imperfect (as are all analogies), it has become one of my favorite illustrations of what it is I envision when I describe the work of brilliant teachers. Like Badu, they draw you into an experience – and they make their audience feel as if it is designed uniquely for them. Just as with the brilliant Erykah Badu, the same is true of brilliant teachers. Their light doesn't just illuminate their own stage. It invigorates. It saturates those in assembly in such a way that they are absorbed in the brilliance themselves.

The classrooms in which these teachers operate never quite look the same, but I've learned a lot from soaking up the energy in these spaces. I will tell you straightaway that there is no simple algorithm for creating the dynamic – but one knows it when one sees it. In this way it's a lot like being in love... Love is a word that is often activated in my inner dialogue when in the presence of such brilliance. These teachers operationalize love in ways that cannot be quantified – try as we might. No external confirmation is required. Nothing is wasted. Even the most subtle of moves has purpose. (The meaningfulness of it all inspires me!) Their words detail pictures that come to life in the most profound ways. Ideas as old as civilization are re-constructed such that every kiddo has equal authorship and access to them.

I'm amazed at the prolific incarnations of understandings when a brilliant teacher is in that flow. It feels like watching Leonardo da Vinci paint the *Mona Lisa* or Marvin Gaye record *What's Going On?* It's immediately clear that something transformative is happening – and all I wish for is that the moment will last forever. I'm most enthralled by the creative choices of this brilliance that connect even the quietest (or loudest) or timid (or confident) or questioning (or certain) of students. The brilliance draws them all in like a supernova does every bit of matter in its orbit – but never, never have I seen it done exactly the same way by any two teachers. One recognizes the brilliance even as it surprises with its twists on traditional models. It feels like magic except the learning in these moments is inspirited by its relevance and realness. There is no trickery. It's authentic. It's present... and it leaves the students changed forever.

I experience something in these spaces that makes me feel hopeful and powerful. I have spent much of my career trying to unpack those moments, trying to better understand what's happening. What exactly is working for students? And just as importantly: What does the execution of that energy require of the teacher?

What Is This Book About?

This is a book about Equity – and specifically what Equity looks like (and feels like) in the context of pedagogy. Though the term "Equity" is currently a buzzword in many lecture halls and think pieces, I find that often teachers yearn for practical guidelines for its implementation; and it is, in my view, teachers who *most* need to understand the concept and its potential for application. While I have seen many elegant research studies that help to define how poorly Equity is realized in American education, a substantive understanding and interpretation of the concept is required at the classroom level. It is in classrooms where the most essential pedagogical transaction occurs – that being the social and intellectual exchanges between teacher and student.

In my work with educators, I have been trying to deepen my own understandings of what Equity is and how to build on its principles in order to improve the capacity of schools to serve the needs of the most vulnerable students. In this book, I am hoping to tell the story of my own understandings, even as they continue to emerge, about how individual schools and school systems can deliver on the original two-fold promise of American public education: (1) to sort among the various ethnic groups and social classes so as to identify and fairly position the talent of the youth to contribute to what was then a fledgling society; and (2) to prepare the youth to be responsible stewards of the American democracy. These original purposes of public schools – sullied by prejudices though they may be – have everything to do with how I conceptualize the idea of Equity as both a goal and process for thinking about the nature and design of educational opportunity. The effectual purpose of American education has largely been, however, to reinforce existing advantages and mute the voices and value of those already socially, politically, and economically marginalized. If we are to evolve as an institution worthy of the public trust, the most righteous promises of America's public schools must be re-centered as the primary foci and guiding forces for policy and practice.

In that vein, I want this book to do three things:

- First, I want to define what it is I mean by Culturally Responsive Education (CRE) – which is, in my view, a framework that is useful for closing Equity gaps in school achievement outcomes. I argue that CRE is the embodiment and the pedagogical action arm of Equity work.
- Second, I want to flesh out the intersections of Equity and pedagogy to make the argument that – at least in the context of teaching and learning, which is the central task of schools – it is insufficient to discuss one in the absence of the other.
- Last, I want to give specific practice-based examples of learning experiences that reflect what I mean by CRE to further describe and explore the essential elements of the lessons not merely so that they might be replicated, but more importantly so that teachers may effectively leverage a CRE mindset in the design of learning experiences that meet the needs of their own students.

How Is This Book Organized?

There are six chapters in this book, each following a consistent format and each advancing an aspect of what, taken together, I have come to understand as an actionable approach to CRE. Chapter 1 broadly defines Equity as a theory regarding fairness in opportunity. The premises of this book all hinge on the notion that Equity is a construct that requires that we measure fairness not merely by inputs but rather by performance, achievement, and opportunity outputs. Chapters 2 and 3 define CRE as a mental model for addressing Equity gaps and present six themes of CRE that I have found to be useful language and reference points for ensuring that the work of Equity is carried out with integrity. Chapter 4 is devoted to planning. It presents five questions that I use in the design of culturally responsive learning experiences. These questions guide the choices we teachers make in our practice that reflect our beliefs and sense of purpose. Chapter 5 builds on the classroom scenarios presented throughout the book with a description of how ten specific strategies can be employed to draw out the CRE themes; and in Chapter 6, I offer observations and summarizing thoughts about the implications going forward for policies and practices in support of more equitable learning opportunities in education.

Each of Chapters 1 through 5 begins with the story of a learning experience that illustrates the chapter's overall concept. The stories are mostly from the intermediate–elementary grades, but they range from pre-K to high school. The stories, meant to bring you into classrooms to experience how the learning opportunities are presented to kiddos, keep us focused on the true purpose for our work while providing a canvas for the topics of the chapter. The sections that follow give a description and analysis of the chapter's primary subject with a discussion of the context and mindset necessary for framing the big ideas in our teaching. Each chapter concludes with concrete ideas for how to operationalize the conceptual knowledge into classroom practices along with key points that are important to remember in doing so.

A Note to the Reader

I have had, at various points in my career, great reservations about presenting strategies without the careful effort to give them context so that they can be understood as part of a larger cohesive effort. My hesitation has been rooted in my desire to avoid contributing to any misconceptions that Equity can be achieved through some simple checklist of sorts. To this day, I am wary of those who ask for strategies without the apparent willingness to examine how their own beliefs and attitudes may undermine the effective delivery of culturally responsive instruction; but I also know that many teachers learn by doing, and that there are multiple access points into the ongoing work of improving the opportunities for all students. My caution to you the reader is to not short-shrift the effort to build the consciousness required to be a culturally responsive educator. I encourage you to think of this book as more than just a collection of strategies. This book should be used to highlight what it is about some strategies that, when leveraged with Equity in mind, are useful for creating more engaging, student-centered, rigorous learning experiences that honor your students' identities. Of all the brilliant teachers I've ever known, none were ever made effective through the use of any strategy alone; brilliant teachers have, however, always been able to skillfully use strategies in ways that are effective.

In writing this book, I am not looking to prove anything per se – nor am I endeavoring to refute anyone else. I sincerely hope to not be attached to the criticisms of the reader. Rather, I am seeking to share a paradigm about teaching and learning that has been enormously helpful to me and many persons with whom I have thought-partnered. But, in being completely forthcoming, I do have an agenda in writing this book. *I want to inspire you to do something that is really hard.* Sometimes in my presentations, particularly in more privileged spaces with predominantly White audiences, I'll perceive hostility; but frequently, I encounter a willingness to consider new ideas. In fact, when I ask people their intentions for the day, many will say something to the effect of "I'm here to keep an open mind." Sometimes that's code for, "I resent having to listen to you," but other times it is more or less a statement of truth. I've had many of those same persons come to me after the session and say something like: "You're right. This is just good for all kids…" So I ask you to have an open mind. If the text moves you, allow yourself to be moved.

Here's another thing you should know about me: I love ideas. One of the reasons I love books is because good books have good ideas in them. So when I cite scholarly literature in this book, I am not seeking to be comprehensive in my review. Rather, I'm seeking to share some of my favorite ideas and string them together into a larger narrative.

Finally, if you've ever heard me present, you probably know that I am an admirer of the artistic genius of Picasso. Picasso was a brilliant creative and also a desperately flawed person. Picasso's human failings give me a certain hope because if he could be brilliant, as imperfect as he was, then that means I can be brilliant too… and if we're being real about it, I suspect you aren't perfect either. (And by "I suspect," I mean, I know full well this to be true.) I composed a lot of this book in June and July of 2018 while travelling in Spain. After studying *Guernica* and other magnificent Picassos in person, I'm left to believe that it is possible to make a masterpiece. It is possible to be brilliant. That possibility is an essential premise to my arguments relative to Equity and CRE.

It's a remarkable thing to see how artists respond to the viewing of a Picasso masterpiece. Some are inspired, but others seem to feel something more like intimidation. They see Picasso's mastery of lines and shapes, for example, as something of an indictment against their own artistic powers. I've seen similar reactions by teachers to models of brilliant pedagogy, as well. But we are wise to remember that brilliance does not have a single expression. Brilliance is a diverse population of strategies, styles, and techniques that vary from one situation to the next. I've seen brilliance many times in the practice of teachers. It looks different in every occasion, but I know it to be brilliance all the same. The question you should be considering as you read this book is, *What kind of brilliant are you?*

We begin by defining Equity; or more specifically, we begin by defining the work of Equity.

1

EQUITY WORK DEFINED

Equity, as an education concept, is the implementation of an Equity mindset into thoughtful pedagogical design. Equity work is the sum total of the instructional and policy-developing tasks of operationalizing the values of Equity in real-time school contexts. It is, in my view, unwise to try to define Equity outside of the consideration of what the notion of Equity requires of us in terms of pedagogy. To define one minus attention to the other is problematic. Whenever we talk about Equity, we should be invoking actions, and those actions should evoke further insights – insights that support reflection, which, in turn, leads to further action.

Method Acting

Ms. Allen's fourth-grade classroom had become one of my favorite places to hang out whenever I had a little free time; and over the school year, I had developed my own relationships with her students through several co-teaching experiences. Ms. Allen and I both invest a great deal of time and energy into thinking about how we teach writing especially. We both believe that writing is one of the most powerful exercises in literacy for our students because they own such rich stories and have so much to say. The thing about fourth graders, though, is that they often have a hard time grasping the concept of revision. Revision to many fourth graders means the correcting of any mistakes specifically pointed out by the teacher; and elaboration means begrudgingly adding one or maybe two sentences at the very end of the essay. (Frequently when they submit their revision, it's with a *What do you want from me?* sort of shrug as in: *I revised...just like you asked. Now leave me alone.*)

Our problem of practice centered the question of how we can better teach our kiddos the notion of revision as a commitment to deconstruct and reconstruct their writing. We specifically wanted them to give attention to the various ways in which they could improve their clarity and also better present the tone and voice most befitting of the piece. Our idea was to have the students plan and compose a first draft of a personal narrative in the study of a specific historical event from the perspective of people whose voices are often marginalized or altogether ignored. After the first drafts were written, we instructed the students to treat their pieces like scripts and act them out – while recording themselves – so that they could observe (with the support of their peers) any disconnects between what they wrote and what they saw on the screen. In the words of Ms. Allen:

> The purpose of them being able to do that activity is for them to be able to ask, 'Is my writing conveying the message that I want my reader to see as they are reading it?' We really wanted our students as authors to be able to convey their message to their readers. We need to be able to act out the scenes, and the scenes need to be set in a way that the reader will be able to visualize what we are saying.

But in order for this to work, our students had to give dynamic and authentic screen performances of their writing or we knew they wouldn't see what could be revised. In fact, it might be more accurate to say that we wanted them to *feel* what could be revised. We needed for them to feel any difference between an authentic performance and a written piece – specifically in terms of detail, dialogue, and elaboration. If the students were shy in their performance, they might not see the possibilities for revision. The performance was key...

So we introduced the students (through YouTube) to two famous experts on the subject of acting, Lee Strasberg and Stella Adler. These esteemed acting teachers rather grumpily modeled for our students three key concepts for actors that also translate to writing: histrionics, imagination, and concentration. We needed our students to understand and apply all three into their performances so that they would best be able to discern how to revise their first draft of writing with the inspiration and direction of their own acting.

In order to get the best possible performances, we practiced several method-acting exercises. First, we drank a breakfast beverage from an imagined cup. We practiced exploring the sensory aspects of holding the cup in our hands. What does it feel like? Is it heavy? Or light? What color is it? What does it smell like? And eventually, What does it taste like? Then we fixed our hair in front of an imagined mirror making sure to get it just the way we like it. Finally, we put on our imagined socks and shoes practicing concentration and sustained attention to the task, until... a foul imagined stench consumed the room causing us to perform our stomach-churning disgust. After more than a few giggles and a few pertinent yet silly questions (e.g. "Should we pretend like someone farted?"), our students were ready to go off and act out their first drafts of the personal narratives.

Almost immediately, our students saw there were palpable differences between the texts. Said one of our kiddos, "When I'm acting, it brings out more energy than writing. So when I'm usually writing, I mostly get all the stuff that I planned about in my writing. But when I'm actually acting it out, it gets more detailed in my writing." As they experienced the gaps, they began to ask, "Can I re-write my draft? I need to elaborate more, and I need more dialogue." After revising their first drafts, we had the students record their scenes again; but this time, they shared their videos with peers. To raise the rigor further, we had each kiddo act out their own in addition to another student's writing, as well. They got to see how others interpreted their writing. If their interpretations were close, bravo! If some things were still not quite right, they knew more clearly what could be revised and how.

The students were then able to give each other feedback as they discussed strategies for making their writing better reflect the richness and energy of their acting. By the end of the unit, our students were analyzing the weaknesses of their own writing, and they were identifying their opportunities to improve what they had composed so as to more accurately capture their intent. A key to teaching revision, we learned, is to create experiences that allow the students to analyze and evaluate their own texts rather than having us evaluate on their behalf – because when they evaluate themselves, it's more likely to be understood as a personal opportunity to find the words and devices of language that best express their intended meaning with their voice. That was how we taught our kiddos tools for writing personal narratives; they learned those tools as part of a larger purpose of creating pieces that are valid expressions of their meaning. The difference is significant. By emphasizing the purpose over the tools, through a writing experience, our students *felt* like writers.

Equity as a Performative Construct

Beyond contemplating the scope and impact of Equity (or inequity) in any conceptual or statistical sense, we must get to the point where the word Equity is understood as a performative construct; and by that I mean, any utterance of the term – if the meaning is to be believed and understood – is aligned with an expression of its idea so that the utterance becomes a demonstration in and of itself.

A bit grandiose? Semantics? Maybe, but I'm offering no apologies. Let's think about it this way…

Language is a system of symbols (words and phrases) that represent ideas. Performative is a word that means the extent to which the utterance of the word (or phrase) is itself both an expression and demonstration of the idea.

It's like saying, "I love you." The language is both an expression of an idea and also a demonstration of it. Further, the way we understand the phrase, "I love you" is contextualized by behaviors. We are more or less inclined to believe we are loved by someone who has uttered the words given the corresponding behavioral evidence. Another example is the phrase, "I'm sorry," which just like "I love you" is both the expression and demonstration of an idea. In fact, we get frustrated with the people who say "I'm sorry" to us but then go and repeat the offending act. Their behavior is an outright contradiction to the words they've spoken because "I'm sorry" is nice to hear when appropriate but it can be downright infuriating when it isn't performed with a demonstration that confirms the words. The concepts of "love" and "apology" have little practical use if they aren't understood in the performative sense.

Equity, if only deliberated in conceptual terms, will be limited in its impact on policies and practices. Equity in education is a construct best understood by its performative meaning. Where "love" and "apology" are words that define affective concepts, Equity is a word that expresses a belief. The word Equity embodies the belief that we will see achievement in all student groups when all students receive opportunities that they are able to perceive as meaningful and that allow them to draw on their social and cultural literacies in order to be academically successful. Both in terms of systems and individual educators, the evidence of the beliefs about Equity should show up in practice. To speak of Equity without corresponding evidence that demonstrates how the belief lives in one's work is either an incomplete or a contradicting statement. It shouldn't be possible to claim an Equity mindset without such supporting behavioral references. Equity is an idea that is demonstrated in our work.

Beliefs

If Equity work is the performance of beliefs about Equity, then any credible discussion on Equity must center beliefs, not teaching techniques, or curriculum, or even education policy. And yet, this discussion that centers beliefs is also about all of those things because it is the beliefs about Equity that are performed through the choices we make relative to teaching techniques, curriculum, and education policy.

But really though? Why beliefs? Isn't it more practical to pen an education book specifically about strategies for teaching "at-risk" student populations? Isn't a focus on beliefs just ideological grandstanding?

No. I believe that the concept of Culturally Responsive Education (CRE) provides a template for a body of work more than a menu of isolated actions. CRE is a framework for how we define excellent pedagogy – with particular attention to gaps in performance and achievement between sub-groups. (We'll discuss that "at-risk" term later.) Though it may seem like I am using the terms CRE and Equity interchangeably, I don't intend to imply that they mean exactly the same thing. To be sure, they are closely related, but they differ in scope and purpose. My argument in this book is that CRE is a pedagogy (i.e. a theoretical framework for thinking about teaching and learning) that is most appropriate for closing Equity gaps. Equity work is the sum total of the pedagogical and systems-level tasks of operationalizing the values of Equity in real-world contexts.

Ultimately, it is wrong-headed to try to define Equity in education outside of the consideration of what the construct of Equity requires of us. The operationalization of an Equity mindset into thoughtful practices is the work of Equity. Equity cannot be effectively described without a multi-angle view of the action and the motivations that underscore the action. The actions of the culturally responsive teacher are altogether a function, product, and extension of an Equity mindset. You will have, at best, a partial understanding of the effectiveness of a culturally responsive educator without the full view; or, at worst, you'll miss the most valuable learning to be gained from the models of brilliant teaching because of a misplaced, singular focus on the technical skill. Talking about Equity in theoretical terms should invoke action in our practice, and those actions should evoke further insights which, in turn, frame choices and compel further action. As much as anything, that's my message to schools and the people who animate them.

What Equity Is Not

For some, it may be easier to understand Equity by what it is not. Equity is not equality. These are closely related paradigms, but they represent two different commitments to the notions of fairness and opportunity. The pursuit of Equal Educational Opportunity (EEO) is a central part of the larger American Civil Rights narrative (Tesconi & Hurwitz, 1974). EEO is well represented by the 1954 *Brown v. Board of Education* case (*Brown*). The landmark *Brown* decision ruled that American public schools could no longer legally segregate children based on race. Separate was deemed "inherently unequal." In other words, the goal of equality in that historical moment was to provide the same learning opportunities (at least in terms of which schools students attended) as a measure of fairness. If sameness was provided in terms of inputs, then equality could be said to have been achieved. Thus, the notion of EEO promotes fairness by giving everyone the same thing. But equality defined this way is only valid as a fair opportunity construct if everyone starts from the same place and is able to perceive the opportunity on the same terms. That is, opportunities can only be considered equal if students are similarly able to justify the investment of risk and effort required of them in order to be successful (Howe, 1989). The inputs must be equally effective in conveying the meaningfulness of the opportunity, or the opportunity itself will undoubtedly advantage some groups over others. Unlike Equity which identifies outcomes at the finish line of schooling as the measure of fairness, equality focuses on the inputs at the starting line.

Educational Equity is about fairness with a focus on outputs. Like EEO, Equity is about ensuring that students have access to meaningful opportunities. Equity, however, posits that equality isn't necessarily fair because the social, economic, historical, and political contexts in which students learn impact how they perceive and are able to take advantage of the educational opportunities available to them in school. These sociohistorical implications can create barriers to both group and individual participation that make some opportunities less accessible and less meaningful than others. This means that where equality is served by sameness, Educational Equity, by definition, compels difference – because different students need different inputs to support their fair opportunities to learn. In the Equity way of thinking about opportunity, sameness is almost inherently unfair because it assumes that everyone's potential success is equally served by identical inputs; but in the performative sense, it isn't Equity if it isn't acting in ways to close opportunity gaps. Thus I define "fairness" as the differentiating process through which Equity is achieved.

Zero-sum Game Thinking

Equity as a paradigm is challenging for so many of us educators because we've been largely indoctrinated with an equality frame of reference for understanding the concepts of fairness and opportunity. In addition, equality is (seemingly) much easier to invoke in practice. It (theoretically) requires much less of us to give everyone the same thing; but to differentiate according to need seems to be a more daunting task. To some, Equity arguments feel like we are making excuses for underperforming students and communities. To others, it feels like we are giving unfair preference to specific student populations. They ask, *But shouldn't I just treat all my students the same as everyone else? Shouldn't I just love them all equally?*

While I would never tell a teacher not to love all of their students with equal enthusiasm, it's rarely the case that we would think of sameness of love as an expectation in other parts of our lives. When giving talks, my friend and colleague Pedro Noguera will often ask: "Who in here has more than one child?" And when many hands go up, he'll say sincerely: "Look around everyone. These are the experts on Equity." We learn intuitively when it's our own children – or nieces or nephews, or grandchildren, or siblings, or parents, or grandparents, etc. – that to love someone authentically means precisely to love them knowing they aren't a carbon copy of their counterparts. Even when our own children share the same DNA, live in the same house, eat the same food, and attend the same schools – we know that we must engage in our relationships with them differently according to their individual personalities and our unique histories with them. In our personal lives, we understand that kind of love to be the highest expression of care rather than some inconceivably impossible abstraction to consider.

Our intuitive understanding of Equity is undermined by our misconceptions of what it means in practice. In recent times, Equity has been politicized as an offspring of entitlement ideologies. Equity, say its detractors, means we give something more to someone who doesn't really deserve it; and further, it's unfair to take an opportunity away from one child to give more to another. This "zero-sum game" interpretation of opportunity is especially prevalent in counter-arguments to Educational Equity. Unlike economic opportunity, which we are more likely to think of as a positive-sum construct, those who oppose the notion of Educational Equity see opportunity as a finite resource (Game theory, 2008; Mulligan, 2009; Greenhill, 2015). In matters of financial opportunity, however, most are more inclined to see it as a generative entity – meaning that where economic opportunity abounds, it creates valuable opportunities for others. When educational opportunity is thought of as a zero-sum game construct, Equity can't be conceptualized as fair because the perceived finite nature of opportunity makes it impossible to differentiate support without under-serving some part of the population. This is exactly why Equity is such a profoundly challenging concept because it is often presented to us in practice as a zero-sum game scenario.

Mindsets

To be clear, I don't believe that equality is a bad thing; but one must know when equality-inspired mindsets and practices are limited in their capacity to meet the expectations of fairness. Equality, by itself, does not ensure that all students will receive what they need to allow for them to perceive their school opportunities as meaningful and thus worthy of their engagement. Here it makes sense for us to step back and specifically define "mindset" in order to reduce the variability in our terminology as much as possible. One of the pioneers in the field of psychology, William James, defined mindsets as the abstract and/or concrete representations that precede goal-directed behaviors including decision-making (James, 1890). Carol Dweck (2008) among others similarly describe mindset as beliefs, attitudes, values, and dispositions – particularly the views one adopts of one's own abilities and intelligence – that affect the way people lead their lives in all sorts of ways. Mindsets can be learned and shared in specific social/cultural spaces often to the advantage of the group's insiders and in response to the conditions of their physical and emotional environment. Mindsets inform the ways in which groups assign meaning to social situations including the extent to which an opportunity is perceived as fair and meaningful (Barry & Halfmann, 2016; French II, 2016). Taken together, the concepts, assumptions, beliefs, methods, and notations that comprise our mindsets contribute to our subjective views of the world and are always in play at every moment of our lives.

Mindsets are neither hardwired in the architecture of the human brain nor do they invalidate the agency of human beings to act of their own volition. We can evolve our mindsets, but to do so reliably requires a conscious and focused effort. To evolve our mindsets is also difficult emotional work because it inevitably will challenge assumptions that we haven't before rigorously vetted; and upon closer examination, these are instrumental assumptions on which key beliefs hinge. The emotional investment of Equity work starts with committing to the conscious capacity for pushing one's own thinking, which means considering the evidence at all times – including the evidence of our own need to evolve. Brilliant teachers do this. Brilliant teachers are brilliant in part because they persistently pursue brilliance. They evolve because they are constantly looking to grow their practice. To pursue brilliance is to consider that there may be better ways to support all kiddos. (That commitment is, in fact, the only common characteristic I can attest to in all of the teachers whom I have ever thought of as brilliant.)

To evolve our systems and practices to be more equitable means we must be intentional about our growth with a performative understanding of Equity in mind. I think of growth (both individual and organizational) as driven largely by questioning. Individuals and organizations that grow do so because of a commitment to continually ask questions about what is and isn't working and what can further be done to fulfill the mission(s) at hand. This is the essence of what I think of when I hear the term *growth mindset*. Similarly, if Equity is to become performative, we should be thinking of Equity as a dynamic endeavor, and we should be deliberate in marrying the questions we are asking about Equity with an ongoing inquiry about pedagogy.

Equity Questions

So What Are the Questions That We Ask about Equity?

The questions we ask about Equity are about whom we teach, as in: What do our students most need to be successful? What groups of students are underperforming relative to others? How have these gaps been previously understood? What is the social, historical, and political context that frames the educational opportunities for under-achieving groups? What are the assumptions we make about students and their abilities? How does the policy- and practice environment reflect an understanding of the assets of the students and communities served by the school?

We should be willing to ask these questions in ways that lead us to rich and complicated answers, but it is critical to consider the context that shapes students' perceptions of opportunity given the sociopolitical realities of the communities served by the school. These questions lead us to a deeper understanding of the nature of the gaps in opportunity, performance, and achievement.

What Are Equity Gaps?

An Equity gap is anything that might undermine the perception of a learning opportunity as meaningful, attainable, and worthy of investment by the student – either as a function of how a student may (or may not) be positioned to take advantage of an opportunity, the design of the opportunity itself, or even the awareness that the opportunity exists. Equity gaps affect how students perceive their opportunities in school, but not all Equity gaps originate in school or classroom practices. There is much evidence of the existence (and persistence) of broad, societal inequities that subvert educational opportunities for vulnerable student populations. Here, I will not go into great depth; but in terms of education outcomes, students of color and specifically Black and Latinx-identifying students are more likely to be overrepresented in disciplinary actions, underrepresented in gifted and talented programs, and more likely to be taught by less-qualified teachers in high-poverty and racially segregated schools (Sirin, 2005; Clotfelter, Ladd, Vigdor, & Wheeler, 2007; Owens, 2016; Carver-Thomas & Darling-Hammond, 2017). These school realities can be linked to larger societal racial and income inequalities including patterns of (un)employment, health outcomes, and the disproportionately harsh conviction and sentencing of racial- and ethnic minorities in the American criminal justice system (Alexander, 2010; Stevenson, 2014; Rosenberg, Groves, & Blankenship 2016). The trends of racial-, ethnic-, and income inequity are clear and persist over time.

Equity gaps are neither surprising nor unexpected given the United States' history with race tracing back to the earliest incarnations of the "American experiment." This was characterized by the oppression, displacement, and subjugation of millions of human beings in the interest of establishing the nation as a space for European immigrants to find economic prosperity and religious freedom unhampered by the restrictions of class and intolerance from whence millions fled in distress. That these pursuits came at the expense of non-White people required an ideology to justify the mistreatment. This meant that the indigenous people of the continent were labeled savages, and the Africans brought in bondage inferior, incapable, and unworthy of freedom. While the purpose of establishing nascent nationhood was served by the effective genocide of indigenous American peoples and removal from their traditional homelands, slavery and its ideological compatriot, racism, were essential components of the original economy.

Race

Race is, of course, a difficult historical matter for us to discuss. It makes so many deeply uncomfortable; but discuss it we must because the United States of America invented a form of codified, race-based prejudice that was integral to its growth and development – and the American brand of racism continues to present an obstacle to the nation's ideals of inalienable freedom and opportunity without bias. American racism gave license to a brutal form of slavery and oppression arguably unlike any the world had seen before. Contrary to nearly every earlier form of slavery, the enslaved men and women of African descent in America were held in bondage in a society that espoused freedom and equality as its chief collective virtues. In order to validate the institution of slavery, White America justified its bondage of enslaved Africans and their descendants by rationalizing that they were sub-human and thus, unworthy of the same rights and privileges which Whites were willing to risk life and limb to protect. Racism bridged the schism between the ideals of freedom and the realities of slavery and set into motion a centuries-long conflict rooted in the effort to preserve the privilege of the powerful at the expense of those whose humanity had not been embraced in the earliest iterations of the American opportunity covenant. Racism, even after the abolition of slavery, was the energy that engendered the systemic denial of social and economic opportunities for the descendants of Black slaves as well as other non-White persons living in America (Kendi, 2016). These historical intersections of racism, economic condition, and political disenfranchisement underlie present-day realities rendering some groups more vulnerable to school underperformance than others.

We resist the discussion of race at the risk of our own peril because to seek improvement without addressing our ugliest truths is to deny ourselves access to some of the most useful insights available to us as educators. So much of the work of Equity involves facilitating learning experiences and conceptual understandings that students are able to see as meaningful and worthy of their engagement; and identity is always a prime factor in that equation. The story of one's identity is central to the perception of opportunity. If students' identities are muted (or altogether ignored) for the convenience of educators, some students will feel subjugated in ways that limit their frames of reference and capacities for accruing understandings. At the same time, we must avoid stereotyping our students based on their racial, ethnic, and other social identity markers because while everyone participates in some shared identity group, we also have individual agency that allows us to color outside of those identity-group lines. It is also true that there are a range of interpretations and opinions on race even within racial groups. Race is experienced in the context of other social classifications and identity markers so that no one can be said to have had an identical racialized experience to anyone else. Though some may try to exploit these truths as contradictions, in any number of instances, in any given school with any particular student, race may mean everything or nothing at all. We must make ourselves available for the discomfort inherently accompanying the topic of race, and we must also be prepared to dismiss everything we think we know about race to allow students to show us who they are as unique individuals with agency and their own catalogue of concepts, contexts, and lived experiences.

In my work as a coach and technical assistance provider in school districts across the United States, my task has been to support teachers in translating what the research and literature say about Equity into instructional practices. That has often been a challenge for a number of reasons. For one, I am Black, and most of the teachers I work with are White... and many White people don't like talking about Equity because they know it involves race; and many White people don't like talking about race – and especially not with Black people. There are some White people who were taught that it is improper and impolite to talk about race. There are others who have been willing but feel injured from previous efforts at engaging in discussions about race. Some White people think that talking about race means they will be personally blamed for American racism. Still others think they know everything they need to know about race, and therefore the conversation does not apply to them.

Productive Discourse on Race

For whatever the reason, talking about race can be difficult. I've developed some mental guidelines that, for me, have been helpful in creating productive spaces for the necessary and difficult discourse. For instance, I think we are wise to avoid a spirit of blame in our conversations about race. Racism is an American problem that stains our reputation abroad and impedes our greatness at home. The question of personal blame is mostly moot at this point. To every White teacher who doesn't want to be blamed for racism, I say to you that there are some problems that are not your fault, but because of position and influence, you, bearing no blame, still have responsibility because you are in a position to address the problem. To confront these issues we must engage in an honest and ongoing reflection about how race, culture, and identity impact our lives and others around us. In addition to reflection, we should also seek opportunities to listen to others whose cultural and social vantage points differ from ours. But the way I see it, these are things that decent people should be doing anyway. I do believe that this kind of purposeful disposition to growth is good for the practice of teaching, but I also think it will make you a better parent, a better bae, a better colleague, and an all-around better person. And why would anyone *not* want to be a better person?

I'm also not interested in participating in competitions for title of the most aggrieved. I feel clear that racism – and in particular the unequivocally evil institution of American slavery and the racism, culture, and beliefs that sustained its legal practice for 239 years – has had a profound impact on the lives of people of African descent in particular and people of color generally. I also feel clear that Jim Crow and other formal and informal segregation practices continue to influence the way people experience their lives and opportunities on a day-to-day basis. I think that racism has evolved in a lot of ways (though there are still some old-fashioned, hood-wearing racists in America). I believe that privilege is a real thing, and I think it's silly to argue otherwise. I believe that privilege is incredibly durable and adaptive. The thing about privilege is that the experts on privilege are the persons who don't have that privilege. For example, I am a man. While I acknowledge my male privilege, I also know that the group of people most likely to be able to discern my male privilege even better than me are those who don't have my privilege – i.e. people who don't gender-identify as men, namely women. I also know that there are many groups who have suffered at the hands of White Supremacy, and I would rather not compete with them in any Oppression Olympics. I don't want the prize of being the most impacted nor do I want to be seen as diminishing another human being's suffering in order to prove mine.

I believe the work of Educational Equity is an effort to end suffering caused by and through inadequate school experiences for kiddos and their communities. I don't want to reverse the hegemonic structures so that others will be oppressed in the ways that my community has. I don't want to improve my own ranking in the hierarchy of suffering. I want my work in education to disrupt those systems that perpetuate inequity so that we can be the great schools we need for the great nation we aspire to be. I find resolve in the hope that America can be great for everybody. My biggest concern relative to the issue of race in the discussion of Equity is that a problem can't be solved unless the parties involved are willing to deal with the problem – and not just the pretty parts, but the parts of the problem that make us most uncomfortable.

Questions about Opportunity

I say that the concept of Equity can't be separated from the work of Equity because by definition and dint of mission, Equity is an action-oriented paradigm that requires something of those who understand it. Equity work requires that we ask questions about opportunities to learn in order to highlight gaps. Once one is aware that an Equity gap exists, one must either determine to take actions to close the gap or become a defacto contributor to its persistence through silent compliance. Inequity requires inertia to maintain its status quo.

If you accept the premise that Equity is a performative construct, it must be conceded that the understanding and practices of Equity are indistinguishable from one another. That means that when we talk about Equity we should be asking questions like: What opportunities exist for our students to leverage their backgrounds and identities in the interest of school achievement? What kinds of teaching techniques work best in centering the voices and experiences of student groups historically underserved by schools? What do our racial- and ethnic-minority groups report about their opportunities to learn in schools? How are the identities of students reflected in the staffing of the school? How has the school created space and connection for partnerships with the communities served by the school? In what ways does the policy and practice environment reflect the commitment to understand, validate, and show authentic care for the most vulnerable of the learners and those historically underserved?

I have found that if we don't place our deliberation of pedagogy in the same spaces where we are giving thought to Equity, we may either leave educators unsure about how to apply the principles in their work with students or miss the chance to lean into some of the more difficult conversations relative to race and identity that are necessary for us to have in order to better understand the gaps we wish to close. In fact, the absence of pedagogy in Equity discourses consigns the work of Equity to precarious circumstances. If we talk about Equity and not pedagogy, the Equity arguments can be dismissed as pedagogically irrelevant. The problem with talking about Equity in isolation is that the discussion of Equity (like many theoretical constructs that tie together multiple concepts) has a certain tendency to stall, in that, without a practice arm, it begins to feel repetitive, irrelevant, and specious. People can legitimately (or subversively) ask: "Okay, but after studying the problem of Equity, what can we do?"

Which brings us to another critical issue.

Questions about Pedagogy

Pedagogy is the science and study of teaching and learning. It is how we think about tools, policies, and strategies for teaching. Pedagogy, though, if not focused on the needs of students (and particularly students whose growth is stagnant), fails to be progressive in the adaptations available to us. New tools emerge all the time, thus making different results possible – not because the tools change the purpose of pedagogy, but rather because the tools expand the limits of what is possible given the restrictions of previous tools and the ever-changing contexts in which pedagogy occurs. Further, if we talk about pedagogy without talking about Equity, we are more prone to rationalize the predictability of underperformance patterns because we can more reasonably say: "I've successfully taught this way for a long time. If it doesn't work now it's because something is wrong with the students and not my pedagogy."

What questions are we asking when we talk about pedagogy? We should be asking questions like: Which teaching strategies work best to facilitate rich understandings of the big ideas that matter most in the learning targets? What are the indicators we use to determine success? How will students be able to demonstrate what they know and understand? How are the instruction and assessment differentiated to best convey the understandings and to capture the evidence of all students' learning? How do my teaching practices reflect my own understanding of the social and cultural identities represented in the classroom?

What Are We Teaching?

If Equity questions are the questions we ask about *whom* we teach and pedagogy questions are the questions we ask about *how* we teach, we should also be clear about *what* it is we are teaching, as well. What is our content from the perspective of Equity?

In the internet and information age, schools must prepare students not for specific skill- and knowledge-based careers but rather for personal reinvention. By that I mean that today's students are likely to have multiple careers (and careers within careers) that require the social, emotional, and intellectual tools to update their skillsets accordingly. More than ever, schools today must prepare students to think because the capacity for lifelong learning is the essential skill for success in the modern economy (Wagner, 2008). The ability to understand complex problems, craft clear thoughts, and concentrate (on tasks or ideas) is the most valued human capital commodity in the modern American workforce. Thus, when it comes to the *what* of their learning, as a classroom teacher, I most want for my students to gain understandings – which are related to but something different than information. With the ordinary person having access to vast amounts of all sorts of data through internet-enabled devices, it is more useful and important that students are taught to be discerning consumers of information than to be able to recall even volumes of it. Discernment, analysis, synthesis, and interpretation are all tools for developing understandings, and when our students understand how to learn, they can better use these strategically in the interest of their own growth.

But what exactly is an understanding? In short, we can think of an understanding as the meaning drawn from concepts whereas concepts can be thought of as categories of words, linguistic expressions, visual images, sounds, and other stimuli taken in through the senses (Barsalou et al., 1993; Barsalou, Simmons, Barbey, & Wilson, 2003). Philosophers and cognitive scientists define a concept as a psychological representation of objects, symbols, events, or actions that are grouped together in relation to some cognitive purpose (Barrett, 2017a). Concepts are integral in the cognitive processes associated with meaning-making (Hofstadter, 2001). Thus, as it pertains to the work of Equity, I have come to think of concepts as the building blocks of understandings; they are useful and often central to a discipline and have lasting value beyond the classroom. Concepts are also a key in our ability as teachers to make a learning experience culturally responsive to any particular student or group of students. That is to say that we are more or less responsive given our capacity for teaching with and through culturally accessible concepts.

Although concepts are not exactly equivalent to meaning, they play critical roles in constructing it. Concepts are the material we use to build meaning through analogy, which Hofstadter (2001, p. 499) refers to as the core of cognition:

> One should not think of analogy-making as a special variety of reasoning (as in the dull and uninspiring phrase "analogical reasoning and problem-solving," a long-standing cliché in the cognitive-science world), for that is to do analogy a terrible disservice. After all, reasoning and problem-solving have (at least I dearly hope!) been at long last recognized as lying far indeed from the core of human thought. If analogy were merely a special variety of something that in itself lies way out on the peripheries, then it would be but an itty-bitty blip in the broad blue sky of cognition. To me, however, analogy is anything but a bitty blip — rather, it's the very blue that fills the whole sky of cognition — analogy is everything, or very nearly so, in my view.

Concepts to Establish Reference

Concepts establish reference. Concepts represent symbols and situations that provide the basis of establishing reference from its associated word (Barsalou et al., 1993; Hofstadter, 2001; Barsalou, Simmons, Barbey, & Wilson, 2003; Barrett, 2017a). As an example, the mental library of generic situations for "mother" establishes the reference for "mother" in uses of the word across utterances. These references populate "domains of reference" which then guide how individual references may be employed within specific conceptual contexts.

Once an entity is established as a referent in a particular situation, specialized frames within the corresponding generic situation provide running commentary on the referent. This transaction of thoughts within any group of persons seeking to share understandings is what allows us to update and extend our concepts, including our ability to layer and add nuance to previously conceptualized understandings. In this way, a concept is a referent used to bridge meaning; but it is also that the combination of concepts forms new concepts from old ones, specializes existing ones, and modifies existing frames. For example, when students in the primary elementary grades learn the concept of ecosystem, they understand it as a reference to physical spaces in nature where organisms live together and rely on each other to sustain an environment that is hospitable to all. This is what a cognitive scientist would call a one-entity, one-frame conceptual reference. But some conceptual combinations may warrant new frames because, though conceptually related, the updates constitute significant new types of entities. So as students reach the higher elementary and secondary grades, the conceptual reference of ecosystem can be employed in combination with other conceptual frames of reference to support the understanding that democratic governing systems, for instance, are intended to support the well-being of many cooperating groups of people in a way that sustains the freedoms and opportunities for all in the environment. A democracy then can be understood as a kind of political ecosystem for humans.

Enduring Understandings

I am a big fan of the work of Wiggins and McTighe (Wiggins, McTighe, Kiernan, & Frost, 1998) who, among others, have centered Enduring Understandings in the design of learning experiences. They've defined Enduring Understandings as "statements summarizing important ideas and core processes that are central to a discipline and have lasting value beyond the classroom" (p. 10). These Enduring Understandings synthesize the concepts students should regularly center and revisit in the study of a particular content area. Importantly, an Enduring Understanding should impact behavior. Understandings are performative in the sense that they are confirmed by how people act differently given the depth of their understandings. Thus, it is fair to say that an understanding qualitatively changes you.

In the information age, in order for students to see their learning opportunities as meaningful, I've found that there is little profitable application in the recitation of facts. Concepts are what allow us to bring order to the information available to us – and through concepts we make meaning that resonates for students. Therefore, concepts are the substance, the essence – the basic unit of understandings – and what we truly want to teach in the modern school.

Even what may seem to be simple concepts often have much more complex constructions than we might think at face value. If we are able to get inside of our concepts, we can better identify the underlying structures, which then allow us teachers to better leverage concepts to close Equity gaps in the opportunities for students to learn. I discuss this further in Chapter 4, but it's important now to distinguish that concepts can be described both in perceptually objective terms (i.e. object-focused) and also in goal-oriented terms (i.e. goal-focused).

Object- and Goal-focused Concepts

Let's take for example the concept of a phone. Depending on your age and the part of the world in which you were socially and culturally indoctrinated, when you think of the concept of a phone, you might think of a plastic and metal device that sits on top of a desk with a moveable handle into which you speak, which is connected to the base by a flexible cord which is connected to the wall (and the hidden telephone lines that connect to poles and circuits in the beyond) by a cable of some sort. Sometimes a phone has a base but no cord to connect the handset to the base. Sometimes it is more plastic than metal and other times the opposite. Many of today's students have a very different concept of a phone, which is some variation of the smartphone family of electronic devices. When most American teenagers today think of their phone, they are likely to envision a mobile device that isn't connected to any cables unless the phone requires a charge, in which case the phone isn't connected to the hidden universe of telephone lines but rather to an electrical outlet for power. Many students would think of a rectangular-shaped device with a screen that might be touch sensitive that can fit into a pocket or a purse which rarely ever leaves their possession; but there are many objective instances of phones that can fit into the category. There is no single prototype instance that represents that concept, and in fact, some of the devices that fall under the category of phone do not have all of the features of the other objective instances of phones.

Goal-focused concepts, on the other hand, are flexible and adaptable to situations given the purpose for which the object-focused concept is to be employed (Barrett, 2017a). So for example, if we were to consider a purely mental concept such as "Things that Distract Students from Learning," a phone might be one of the first things that comes to mind. Other instances in that category might include stress from home, gossip among peers, an acne breakout, or a new budding romance with a fellow student. These instances share no perceptual features; this category is entirely a construction of the mind. Yet, our brains group all of these instances together to populate the category. Though these all have different perceptual elements, and it would be highly unlikely to describe these in any way that is objectively similar, they each satisfy the goal-focused conceptual criteria of serving as potential distractions to students' learning.

Our understanding of the world and everything in it is conceptual in nature – either in the objective, descriptive sense or in the goal-oriented sense (Barrett, 2017a). A single object can be part of different goal-focused concepts. A phone does not always have to serve the goal of making a telephone call. In fact, for many of our students, making a phone call isn't among the first things that they say when asked to consider the goals of a phone. Sometimes a phone is used to communicate with people but it may not be through a telephone call but rather a video call or text messages. Or a phone may be indicative of a status symbol, or a phone may be a tool to access social media, or to surf the internet, or to watch videos on YouTube, or even to play games.

The Life of Concepts

But it is important to note that concepts, though represented in the mind with certain prototypes, are an amalgamated grouping and interpretation of multiple object- and goal-focused instances. Not every instance of a concept need have every feature of the conceptual prototype to be recognized as an instance of the concept. This means that every time we draw on a concept to make meaning of anything, we are encountering a unique instance that is unlike any other we've ever before encountered (Hofstadter, 2001; Hofstadter & Sander, 2013; Barrett, 2017a). Even more importantly though is the notion that different individuals and groups of people have different instances populating their conceptual references; and different spaces may evoke different domains of reference relative to specific concepts from others. This means that though there is seemingly a great deal of shared understanding of concepts among the general population, every one of us has our own unique relationship with and understanding of concepts, and those understandings are a function of the range of instances from which we draw and the social and cultural indoctrinations which have informed how meaning is constructed relative to those concepts.

Since concepts do not objectively equate to meaning, concepts do not have universal meaning. As such, the construction of the meaning of concepts is a function of both our lived experiences and also our social and cultural indoctrinations, which include cultural knowledge. We learn these concepts from birth through our relationships and the customs and habits we are taught. Invariably, and here is a really important point for our consideration: the concepts we learn are fraught with bias. As we learn concepts, we are taught what is right and wrong, good or bad, appropriate or inappropriate in the context of the conceptual prototypes. We see others who share similar conceptual frames of reference to us to be more "normal" than others whose concepts differ in some ways we perceive as significant. In fact, one way to think about identity is in terms of concepts shared with other persons in specific spaces. If unchecked, we are more likely to discriminate against those whose concepts differ greatly from our own because we see them as either odd or inferior (or dysfunctional or derelict); and because we learn concepts from/in the social/cultural spaces in which we are indoctrinated, we tend to hold firmly to them as sacred and true. Alas, many social conflicts result from a perceived clash among concepts.

Yet, the life of concepts in the human brain is anything but static. In essence, every new encounter we have with a concept updates the cognitive database of instances, thus informing the prototypes we associate as conceptual references and benchmarks. In a very real sense, your brain categorizes and arranges references – experiences, objects, actions, senses, and events – to create meaning by uniquely drawing on concepts. And further, when your brain needs a concept, it can construct one by re-organizing references to fit the occasion.

Brilliance

Brilliant teachers have always approached their practice in ways that operationalize an unyielding belief in their own capacity for leveraging deep and powerful understandings and supporting students' academic identities. In this book, I admiringly refer to pedagogy that engages all students in rigorous thinking while providing opportunities that empower kiddos to use their social and cultural fluencies in the interest of learning as… brilliance. (And I think of brilliance as fluid because I've had moments in which I am brilliant, and others in which I am definitely not.) I know I had my own brilliant teachers who are my personal superheroes for how they invested in me. In fact, I became a teacher because, though I knew I'd never be able to repay mine for their influence on my life, I wanted to play a supporting part in other people's success stories. My teachers lit a passion in me to develop the academic identity that justified the necessary investments in order to be more successful in school. As a young teacher, I struggled. I later came to realize very few don't. Now, I especially love working with teachers because it keeps me close to kids – which is why we do what we do, right? That's what we say all the time… "It's about the kids." Well, if it really is about our kiddos and what they need, then an Equity – not equality – mindset is a much better fit for our work with young people.

And thus we are back to the essential point of this chapter and a foundational presupposition for this book. Equity, as a theoretical construct, is made performative through CRE. Equity work is the design of pedagogy, and the systems in support of it, that are responsive to the needs of students and their communities in order to provide fair opportunities to learn – or a Culturally Responsive Education. This is done, in part, by prioritizing the teaching of understandings and giving consideration to the concepts and conceptual frames of reference we use to structure the pedagogical and policy environment. At the very least, CRE means the responsibility to acknowledge the conceptual diversity that contributes to the differences in how students experience school and the content to which they are exposed therein.

Further, Equity work is grounded in the positive-sum belief that all students benefit from thoughtfully developed learning experiences – meaning that the highest-performing students should receive meaningful opportunities to accelerate and expand their learning while the most vulnerable students receive supports that are just as meaningful and also intentionally aligned with their specific needs. And since the achievement gaps are most predictive by zip code and race (Tienken, 2016; Tienken et al., 2016), that means that Equity in pedagogy insists on the importance of rigorous and engaging learning experiences for everyone – students of color, low-income students, and also affluent kiddos and White children, as well. *Everyone.*

The Challenges of Equity and Pedagogy

Going forward, there are a few key implications from this chapter on which my further arguments in this book rely. I can best describe these in terms of the challenges they represent.

Social Injustice

First, there are many social injustices and inequities that make life profoundly unfair for a lot of our kiddos. We should object to those inequities because that's what conscious people of good will and integrity do in a multicultural, pluralistic democracy. But I am clear that the single most radical commitment that a teacher can make in the interest of Equity is to be brilliant with our kiddos every day. That is a herculean feat, and I know teachers who do it. I've learned from them. I've taught with them. They're awesome!

I say this to say that I am certain that thought-life and mindset matters in teaching. The things we think about and how we think about those things have a lot to do with the fruit of our labor. The quality of our teaching is, in large measure, a product of the quality of our thinking. When Descartes said, "I think therefore I am," he wasn't just stating a philosophical truth; he was giving us the keys to a difference-making career. Brilliant teachers are thoughtful. Sometimes, they're so good that it almost seems like they're improvising the whole thing, but in my experience, that's almost never the case. These brilliant teachers are thinking – and the ones who are most often brilliant regularly and rigorously *think about their thinking*. They accept the challenge of investigating some of those deep-seated beliefs that are so embedded in our subconscious they evade anything less than our most rigorous contemplations.

Bias

At this deep level of our consciousness, our biases and other automatic assumptions, if unchecked, can corrupt even the best lesson plans. Bias shows up in our conscious and nonconscious choices because our choices are filtered through our concepts and the attendant biases we've inherited with them. At this deep level of consciousness, you are using the lens of your concepts to make predictions about what you will see and how you should interpret the environment around you. That's actual science by the way (Barrett, 2017b). Many of the myriad steps that go into creating powerful learning experiences occur at the level of nonconscious thought, engaging unarticulated beliefs and assumptions about the structure, nature, and expectations of pedagogy. To be brilliant in our most challenging schools, we need lots of people thinking deeply about the intentions of their practice.

Let me be blunt, however. If among your biases (because we all have biases) is the feeling that all [fill in the racial/ethnic group of choice] are characteristically [fill in the stereotyping trope of choice], your struggles with students are to be expected. You have the responsibility to seek out your problematic attitudes around racism, and any other marginalizing mindsets you bring to bear. The responsibility to address and redress your explicit biases is solely your own. No book on teaching is going to help you if you don't do the work of building your own awareness of race and identity. It is hard work, but it is essential to the greater task at hand.

Every day, an individual teacher makes hundreds, maybe thousands of micro-choices – choices that show up in all sorts of interactions with students. When I'm coaching teachers, I pay careful attention to their pedagogical choices. We teachers create with our choices. We have choices of what to teach and how to teach it. The inspiration of these choices is a function of both mindset and purpose. We must see ourselves as agents of Equity if we expect our efforts to yield opportunity-gap closing results. We must accept the responsibility of our choices and commit to using them wisely and in the interest of fairness.

The Challenge of Tools

A challenge of Equity in pedagogy that confronts every teacher revolves around the question of when to stick with familiar tools and models, and when to reach out and embrace those that offer new possibilities given the nuance of unique and changing contexts. The answers in practice to these questions are as much a function of tools as they are of one's beliefs. Teachers are like curators of art gallery exhibitions in that we make inspired choices based on what we want the viewers of the art to experience. Teachers curate spaces with their strategies and their intentions for the learning experiences of students. Through careful attention to and reflection of one's craft, the tools of the most brilliant and culturally responsive teachers become an extension of their own intentions. There is no checklist, however. These tools and methods are expressions of our convictions about the purpose of education and the capacity for teachers to effect the desired end(s). We have choices in what to teach (content) and how to teach it (pedagogy). The strategies we choose in teaching should reflect the needs of our learners (Equity), and the inspiration for those choices is a function of our clear-eyed view of the purpose of American public schools. If the public purpose of schools in a multicultural, pluralistic society is lost, and the individual benefit is prioritized in developing the policy and practice environments of schools, we will have relinquished the moral high ground that justifies the investment of all Americans into the institution. Brilliant teaching is a performance of the commitment to Equity, and I think of the work that happens at the intersections of Equity and excellent pedagogy as Culturally Responsive Education.

The Challenge of Outcomes

And lastly, we cannot say that we have achieved anything remotely resembling Equity until we are confident in asserting that rigorous and engaging learning experiences are available to students in the communities traditionally marginalized due to factors of race and class. Statistically this means that we cannot say Equity has been achieved until neither the identities of students – particularly their racial and ethnic identities – nor their socioeconomic status are reliable predictors of school achievement and performance. Until those trajectories of school success are disrupted, there is Equity work to be done.

OPERATIONALIZE THIS!

Create Community Through Learning Experiences

In the method-acting unit, Ms. Allen and I wanted our students to feel inspired to deepen their understanding of the critical literacy concept of revision while engaging as part of a writing community. In fact, we think of this as their right. In community, members of the group share experiences that further clarify and define their collective identity. The idea of community was fleshed out experientially when we had the students use their video recordings as texts for conferencing with their peers. Students watched and discussed what they saw in the videos, receiving support in clarifying how their writing could be improved. What they saw (or didn't see) in the videos was translated to what was present (or not present) in their writing. The technology was an instrument used to capture another representation (or draft if you will) of the writer's intent. It was a medium through which the disconnect between the writer's mechanics and meaning could be more explicitly uncovered.

We feel like our students should have the opportunity to develop their tools as writers by learning with and from other kiddos whose skills and understandings are part of a whole, functioning supportive system in which every member gets to contribute something that is valuable to others. We think of this as a goal for every content area, but especially literacy in which the skills of communication are developed. Most writers benefit from the support of a community built on camaraderie and common goals. We think it's our students' right to build these skills in community because identity is a function of relationships, and our kiddos are best served in constructing their identities as writers inside of a community of writers. We think it's patently unfair to ask students to invest themselves in such a demanding task as solo actors.

Equity isn't possible without the element of connection. Our students and the communities we serve must feel connected to us, and we are better teachers when we are connected to them. The method-acting

learning experience itself allows for us, their teachers, to better understand our students as writers and deepen our relationship with each
individual kiddo while they are also able to receive support and feedback from each other as they think rigorously about their writing.
These goals of meeting the needs of our students through community
complement their own relationship with writing, their identities as
writers, as well as their technical understanding of writing concepts
such as voice. They enjoyed the deep conversations about their writing,
and they had a clearer sense of what they needed to do to more effectively deliver on their intent. Ms. Allen always works hard in the classroom, but her efforts in this unit were magnified through the support
she gave to each kiddo, which in turn reverberated throughout the
entire writing community as students acted on their understandings
and incorporated them into the feedback they gave to each other.
It was a splendid illustration of a positive-sum learning experience
where the resources effectively support *everyone's* opportunities to
think rigorously and not just a select few.

Challenge Your Learners to Stretch Beyond Their Comfort Zones

In this unit, our students' engagement needed to be driven by a sense
of productive dissatisfaction. We wanted our kiddos to find under-
developed meaning and technical limitations in their pieces. We
wanted them to feel greater agency than we had seen prior in both
their commitment to and stamina for revision because with the experience of effectively communicating their meaning to an audience, they
would know first-hand the power of the writer. But a student isn't a
writer until they internalize a command of the tools of composition in
the direction of their own goals for a piece. That sense of connection
to the writing process cannot be manufactured by anyone outside
of the writer themselves, though good teaching can facilitate such
encounters.

Success in this learning experience meant that our students would
emerge with a deeper conceptual understanding of revision, knowing
it's less about correcting mistakes (though it is about that too) and
more about an undertaking in which they visit and revisit their text to

confirm, deconstruct, and rebuild the piece until it matches their intent in meaning and style. In the production of any writing piece, revision is a complex problem, and like any complex problem, it doesn't rely specifically on simple algorithms to solve. It requires creative approaches. We wanted our students to find a greater commitment within a peer group of fellow writers to the task of revision than what we had previously seen, and we needed to create new pathways for our kiddos to understand how to present their thoughts in clearer terms.

Revision is, by definition, an inherently challenging endeavor because each piece requires something different of us as writers in order to develop it effectively. As such, revision always challenges our abilities as writers in ways that are unique to both the writing task and our identities as writers in any given moment. Through this experience, our students were also able to learn some of the "soft" skills necessary in effectively giving and receiving feedback. No one can know everything, and thus we are all assisted by being able to participate in networks within which we can share support.

Design Inter-disciplinary Units for Richer Learning Experiences

The academic content of the personal narrative piece itself fell within an inter-disciplinary (writing and social studies) unit on the westward movement. We wanted our students to learn about the events of the expansion of the United States farther toward the Pacific Ocean – but we thought it essential that our students were able to understand these historical events from multiple perspectives, including those of the indigenous peoples who had lived in what is now the continental United States for thousands of years prior to the arrival of European explorers. Our personal narrative writing required that students developed their pieces from the perspective of an indigenous person. To be effective, their writing had to leverage empathy for a historical point of view frequently overlooked, which meant they had to cohesively bring together multiple themes (historical, geographic, social) into a piece that could have reasonably been told through the experience of one individual. We wanted our students to write from a sense of personal connection and inspiration. They had to first think like their protagonist before they could tell their story in writing. The students had to be strategic about the presentation of their voice. In this way, their writing choices extended beyond the mechanical and into something more imaginative and adaptive.

In the language of our fourth-grade curriculum, we wanted students to "show, not tell" – which is the term used to describe the writer's use of techniques and tools that allow the reader to experience the story more vividly through actions, thoughts, senses, and feelings rather than trite exposition, summarization, and description. We especially emphasized the writer's tools of dialogue and elaboration. Taken together, this is a pivotal conceptual understanding for fourth-grade writers because it requires that they rigorously consider the audience for their writing outside of themselves. To think beyond one's own interpretation of the piece in order to anticipate the interpretations of an audience is an inherently rigorous way of composing because it requires that students critically analyze (and predict) the impact of their author's craft (literary devices, viewpoint, dialogue).

The first draft of their writing was about what we expected with none of the pieces from even our strongest writers meeting our hopes for showing and not telling. Before giving our kiddos any feedback on the pieces, we introduced them (through a YouTube video mash-up) to the extra-prickly Stella Adler and Lee Strassberg. We got a few giggles from the students as these iconic acting teachers cantankerously directed their students to find deeper inspiration for performances. As we listened to Adler and Strassberg encourage their students to use their emotion to create greater histrionics in their acting, we highlighted the themes of imagination and concentration along with histrionics as three essential elements and goals for our kiddos' writing, as well. Our Equity mindset informed our pedagogy through the use of our tools and techniques. We wanted our students to push their thinking around the idea of revision; and we wanted to do it in a way that they would be able to see the classroom community as a viable resource in support of their growth as writers. Our pedagogy was designed specifically to support our students through the uncertainty of composition.

References

Alexander, M. (2010). *The new Jim Crow: Mass incarceration in the age of colorblindness.* New York: New Press.

Barrett, L. F. (2017a). *How emotions are made: The secret life of the brain.* New York: Houghton Mifflin Harcourt; London, England: Macmillan.

Barrett, L. F. (2017b). The theory of constructed emotion: An active inference account of interoception and categorization. *Social Cognitive and Affective Neuroscience, 12*(11), 18–33.

Barry, C., & Halfmann, K. (2016). The effect of mindset on decision-making. *Journal of Integrated Social Sciences, 6*(1), 49–74.

Barsalou, L. W., Yeh, W., Luka, B. J., Olseth, K. L., Mix, K. S., & Wu, L. (1993). Concepts and meaning. In L. Barsalou, W. Yeh, B. Luka, K. Olseth, K. Mix, & L. Wu (Eds.), *Chicago Linguistic Society 29: Papers from the parasession on conceptual representations* (pp. 23–61). Chicago, IL: University of Chicago.

Barsalou, L. W., Simmons, W. K., Barbey, A. K., & Wilson, C. D. (2003). Grounding conceptual knowledge in modality-specific systems. *Trends in Cognitive Sciences, 7*(2), 84–91.

Carver-Thomas, D., & Darling-Hammond, L. (2017). *Teacher turnover: Why it matters and what we can do about it.* Palo Alto, CA: Learning Policy Institute.

Clotfelter, C., Ladd, H. F., Vigdor, J., & Wheeler, J., (2007). High-poverty schools and the distribution of teachers and principals. Retrieved from http://scholarship.law.unc.edu/nclr/vol85/iss5/5

Dweck, C. S. (2008). *Mindset: The new psychology of success.* New York: Ballantine Books.

French II, R. P. (2016). The fuzziness of mindsets: Divergent conceptualizations and characterizations of mindset theory and praxis. *International Journal of Organizational Analysis, 24*(4), 673–691.

Game theory. (2008, November 23). *The Economist.* Retrieved from www.economist.com/node/12669299

Greenhill, R. (2015, January 20). Is the world zero-sum or win-win? *World Economic Forum.* Retrieved from www.weforum.org/agenda/2015/01/win-win-world

Hofstadter, D. R. (2001). Analogy as the core of cognition. In D. Gentner, K. J. Holyoak, N. Boicho, & B. N. Kokinov (Eds.), *The analogical mind: Perspectives from cognitive science* (pp. 499–538). Cambridge, MA: The MIT Press/Bradford Book.

Hofstadter, D., & Sander, E. (2013). *Surfaces and essences: Analogy as the fuel and fire of thinking.* New York: Basic Books.

Howe, K. R. (1989). In defense of outcomes-based conceptions. *Educational Theory, 39*(4), 317–336.

Kendi, I. X. (2016). *Stamped from the beginning: The definitive history of racist ideas in America.* New York: Nation Books.

James, W. (1890). *The principles of psychology*. New York: Henry Holt and Company.

Mulligan, C. B. (2009, March 23). The job market isn't a zero-sum game. *The New York Times*. Retrieved from https://economix.blogs.nytimes.com/2009/03/23/the-job-market-isnt-a-zero-sum-game/

Owens, A. (2016). Inequality in children's contexts: Income segregation of households with and without children. *American Sociological Review*, *81*(3), 549–574.

Rosenberg, A., Groves, A. K., & Blankenship, K. M. (2016). Comparing black and white drug offenders: Implications for racial disparities in criminal justice and reentry policy and programming. *Journal of Drug Issues*, *47*(1), 132–142.

Sirin, S. R. (2005). Socioeconomic status and academic achievement: A meta-analytic review of research. *Review of Educational Research*, *75*(3), 417–453.

Stevenson, B. (2014). *Just mercy: A story of justice and redemption*. New York: Spiegel & Grau.

Tesconi, C. A., & Hurwitz, E. (1974). *Education for whom? The question of equal educational opportunity*. New York: Harper & Row.

Tienken, C. H. (2016). Standardized test results can be predicted, so stop using them to drive education policymaking. In C. Tienken & C. Mullen (Eds.), *Education policy perils: Tackling the tough issues* (pp. 157–185). Philadelphia, PA: Routledge.

Tienken, C. H., Colella, A., Angelillo, C., Fox, M., McCahill, K. R., & Wolfe, A. (2016, December 5). Predicting middle level state standardized test results using family and community demographic data. *Research in Middle Level Education*. Retrieved from www.tandfonline.com/doi/full/10.1080/19404476.2016.1252304

Wagner, T. (2008). *The global achievement gap: Why even our best schools don't teach the new survival skills our children need – and what we can do about it*. New York: Basic Books.

Wiggins, G. P., McTighe, J., Kiernan, L. J., & Frost, F. (1998). *Understanding by design*. Alexandria, VA: Association for Supervision and Curriculum Development.

2

THEORY OF CHANGE: CULTURALLY RESPONSIVE EDUCATION

Culturally Responsive Education (CRE) is a mental model that is useful for identifying themes and tools of practice for closing Equity gaps. CRE provides a conceptual context for policies and practices that focus on Equity without marginalizing some students relative to others. It actively enlists the awareness of culture, race, ethnicity, gender, ability, and other social identity markers that shape the perceptions of educational opportunities in the interest of and effort to provide meaningful learning experiences for all students.

Family Narrative

It started with an off-hand comment by Mrs. VanNess while we were recording a podcast to highlight what we'd learned in a literacy unit we'd planned together for her fourth graders. She admired the studio-quality microphone we were using and said, "This makes me think about having my students use a cool mic like this to interview their parents!"

Hmm, I thought. That's an interesting idea.

Fast forward to the next school year, and in collaboration with Mrs. VanNess' grade-level team, we decided we would design a learning experience to teach a theme that had the students explore the narratives of their own families – because our kiddos are better human beings when they feel connected to the amazing stories which they inherit through family (Baumeister, & Muraven, 1996; Fivush & Nelson, 2006; Reese, 2013; National Scientific Council on the Developing Child, 2015). With the whole team, we designed a month-long unit that revolved around interviews that students conducted with a family member. The interviews became our texts which the students used to identify and write about the themes they uncovered in some episode of their family's narrative. The students first saw video models of interviews – starring the interviewer (and only co-starring the interviewee) while we focused our attention on the types of questions that were most likely to yield the richest responses.

We then did a Question Formulation Technique (QFT) activity to generate questions that the students could use to start their interviews, and we practiced their interviewing skills in the classroom. *What is an open-ended question? What is a closed-ended question? When would you choose to use one rather than the other?* Mrs. VanNess interviewed her mother in front of her class. Her kiddos thought that was the coolest thing! She modeled her interviewer skills so well that she learned something new about her mother's story of immigrating from Japan to the United States, captivating the kiddos as they saw it all transpire before their eyes. There and then the kids were hooked on the idea of discovering something equally interesting and unknown about their family members too!

We sent the students home with devices over the weekend so they could video record their initial interviews, which we then watched back in the classroom in small groups. The students received feedback and thought-partnership about what seemed to be the most promising threads for a follow-up interview with the family member. The table-talk was dynamic. It sharpened curiosities for what to bring up in the second round of interviews. *Where was there the greatest potential to uncover a theme? What kind of question – open-ended or closed – would best get the answers sought?* Most importantly, the students were coming to understand their own agency in excavating the themes of particular interest to them.

The kiddos took the devices home for another weekend and conducted their follow-up interviews which were more focused on specific storylines than their more general first-efforts. The students then received another round of support from their peers to further clarify the themes which they would present in their final project. One day, while walking through the building on my way to another classroom, one of Mrs. VanNess' fourth graders stopped me to thank me for working with his teachers on the project. "It's bringing me closer to my Dad," said this 9-year-old kid, as I held back the tears forming in the corner of my eyes. It was an experience that bonded us all together.

We gave the students several assessment options to portray their themes, each with a writing component. Their performance on the assessments were powerful indications of their growth as writers; the kids were so excited and in charge of their discoveries! They then recorded video reflections to summarize their experiences. Said one of Mrs. VanNess' fourth-grade girls:

> I had fun writing. We didn't just do the project. We learned that we have grit. Because if you want to be writers – like how I'm reading about Malala... Like, I could learn how to write a book!

"See Better"

In the first scene of the first act of Shakespeare's King Lear, the king is confronted with a dilemma of his own creation. He has called for a public gathering in which his three daughters are tasked (by the king himself) to proclaim their love for their father. The stakes are high. The daughter who's able to give the most flattering expression will receive the largest share of the kingdom which Lear plans to soon bequeath.

We learn that of his three daughters, the two oldest, Goneril and Regan, are more interested in protecting their inheritance than they are invested in true fondness for their father. Only Cordelia, the youngest, truly loves and honors her father; and yet, it is her public expression that least pleases the king.

CORDELIA:
...I am sure, my love's
More richer than my tongue.

KING LEAR:
To thee and thine hereditary ever
Remain this ample third of our fair kingdom;

No less in space, validity, and pleasure,
Than that conferr'd on Goneril. Now, our joy,
Although the last, not least; to whose young love
The vines of France and milk of Burgundy
Strive to be interess'd; what can you say to draw
A third more opulent than your sisters? Speak.

CORDELIA:
Nothing, my lord.

The king is highly annoyed. He speaks forebodingly, "Nothing will come of nothing."

In private chambers, the Earl of Kent, one of Lear's most trusted advisors counsels the angry king. In a volatile exchange which ultimately results in his banishment from the royal court, Kent implores the king to more rigorously read the situation with two words: "See better."

King Lear is an amazing piece of literature to engage with adolescent kiddos because of its powerful and timeless themes of loyalty and integrity – two concepts which resonate exceptionally well in classrooms largely attended by students of marginalized and otherwise vulnerable communities. But as in much of Shakespeare's work, King Lear is also threaded with the motif of insight. Lear lacks it, and that ultimately is the source of the play's tragedy.

I have often used this scene summary to begin conversations with groups of teachers to make the connection between Lear's dearth of insight and the remarkable ability of brilliant teachers to *see better*. If there is one single element of practice that separates brilliant teachers from the rest, it is the ability to see something deeper and more meaningful than others inside of a seemingly innocuous scenario. It is this insight that allows for powerful connections – in a myriad of ways.

To see better is a heightened perception of the profound humanity of teaching and learning. To see better in teaching and learning is to have clearer sightlines for the different needs and motivations brought to bear by students in learning experiences. To see better means to have a greater capacity for recognizing the depth and range of investments (behaviorally, emotionally, and cognitively) asked of students (and also of teachers themselves). This better sight allows teachers to make more precise teacher moves – both in planning and in real-time instruction – that enhance the likelihood of meaningful student engagement. Ultimately, this is the essence of what it means to be responsive.

What Is Responsiveness?

I think of the work that happens at the intersections of Equity and excellent pedagogy as Culturally Responsive Education, and the idea of responsiveness is essential for understanding the CRE themes and approaches that I advocate for in order to close Equity gaps. Broadly speaking, responsiveness is the capacity for providing access to powerful understandings along with meaningful supports for learning. It's when instruction becomes most personal and therefore most engaging. It's those moments when students feel that the learning experience is designed with their specific needs and interests in mind, when their background and language is leveraged, and when the understandings from previous learning are connected in ways that highlight pathways to even further engagement.

Responsiveness facilitates trust – which is essential for our most vulnerable students to be willing to take the risks associated with rigorous learning. Trust is a function of interpersonal connection, and responsive instruction can be the galvanizing element of learning communities in which all feel as though they are a capable and contributing part of the whole. A true and authentic sense of community fortifies identities in ways that are otherwise impossible outside the context of spaces in which one can be led to believe – through experience and meaningful affect – that they themselves have the tools and ability to be successful (Boaler, 2008; Boaler & Dweck, 2016).

It's important to make a distinction between responsiveness and relevance. The idea of CRE has evolved over at least three decades, and during that time the "R" in CRE has represented "relevance" in some circles and "responsive" in others. They are related but different. In my view, relevant means that cultural symbols are embedded into learning experiences; these symbols are intended to support the conceptual connections we hope for students to make. These symbols of relevance are not bad, but, in the context of instruction, they are more surface and static in nature than responsiveness. While it is important for teachers to seek cultural intersubjectivity (Boykin & Nogeura, 2011) with students, it isn't possible (nor essential) that teachers will share the exact same cultural frames of reference and understandings with them. It matters far more that teachers are willing to see their students as sources of knowledge, full of concepts, and bearers of information (Moll, Amanti, Neff, & Gonzalez, 1992). When we see our kiddos in the light of their assets, we can more responsively leverage their identities and backgrounds in order to give students the opportunities to bring their own cultural references and fluencies into learning spaces (Yosso, 2005). In this way, responsiveness requires an openness of teachers and the persistent deepening of our own understanding of content so that we can support students in making the connections through which greater understandings are forged.

What Are the Elements of Responsiveness?

I have found the work of social psychologist Harry Reis (University of Rochester) to be instrumental in my own understanding of the meaning and purpose of responsiveness in CRE. Reis, who has written and researched extensively in the study of relationships, defines "responsiveness" in this way:

> Responsiveness is rooted in the personalities, goals, and relationship-history of interacting persons, grounded in the elements of their interaction, and revealed in their perceptions of those interactions. It contributes to the growth and well-being of relationships, or, in its absence, to their decline and dissolution; likewise, responsiveness fosters the growth and well-being of individuals, or, in its absence, their stagnation and discontent. Because it is a fundamentally interpersonal process with intrapersonal origins and consequences, responsiveness highlights the centrality of relationships for understanding individuals.
>
> *(Reis & Gable, 2015, p. 67)*

There are two key threads that run through Reis' work that are especially pertinent to this discussion of CRE: First, even more than just "responsiveness," we should be thinking about "perceived responsiveness" as being shaped by both interpersonal and intrapersonal forces. That means it matters at least as much that our actions and interactions are perceived as responsive as it does that we teachers are acting in ways that we intend to be responsive to students. Ultimately, the success of our relationships with students is determined by their assessment of us as either responsive or not. They are the final judges of the matter. Second, one's perception of responsiveness in relationships with persons in the position to be supportive affects one's capacity to self-regulate (Reis, 2014). In terms of students, this means that where kiddos perceive the adults and relationships in school spaces as responsive, they are more likely to have a higher subjective opinion of their well-being and greater likelihood of seeing the opportunities therein as meaningful and worthy of their investment of time and energy, thus contributing to choices that more productively lead to successful school (and life) outcomes.

Further, Reis describes responsiveness as having three core components – understanding, validation, and care:

> Responses are likely to be perceived as responsive to the extent that they possess three qualities: (a) Understanding, or whether the partner is believed to have accurately and appropriately "got the facts right" about oneself. Understanding matters because it fosters a sense of authenticity and also because the next two factors are predicated on it. (b) Validation, or the belief that partners value and appreciate one's abilities, traits, and world view. Validation matters because it conveys the partner's liking for and acceptance of the self which supports belongingness and felt security. (c) Caring, or the confidence that partners will provide help when it is needed, which demonstrates their concern for one's well-being.
>
> *(Reis, 2014, p. 259)*

Thus, the goal of responsive instruction is to be perceived by students as an experience of understanding, validation, and care – because human beings are more willing than not to invest ourselves in whichever spaces and communities we find this support and connection.

The CRE Mental Model

So much of responsive instruction is a function of our being fully present. Brilliant teachers *see better* because they are present and devoted to their purpose. It goes without saying, but you really have to want to be great for our most vulnerable students, and being great is often a product of that clear-headed focus on why we're doing what we're doing, which allows us to be more perceptive readers of what's happening in the moment.

There are many challenges in being culturally responsive including sometimes that our students themselves don't always seem to appreciate our efforts in the ways and on the timelines that we would prefer. On behalf of every kiddo who may have appeared to rebuff your honest effort to understand, validate, and show care, let me say, "thank you." Let me also offer some advice: Rather than spend energy bemoaning the kiddo you perceive as unappreciative of you and your efforts, I find it eminently more useful to give careful attention to my own presence – and specifically my own behavioral, affective, and cognitive engagement. CRE always starts with being present.

I define CRE as a mental model useful for identifying themes and tools of practice for closing Equity gaps. In order to advance our understanding of what CRE looks like in the classroom, let's clarify exactly what is meant by the term "mental model."

What Is a Mental Model?

A mental model is a way to think about the world that more likely ensures that our choices reliably and consciously reflect our preferred mindset. First postulated by the American philosopher Charles Sanders Peirce, mental models are psychological representations of real, hypothetical, or imaginary situations which examine and diagram the state of things in order to solve problems (What are mental models?, n.d.).

The best way to define mental models is by explaining what they do. Mental models support processing and decision-making through the clarification of the variables and consequences of our thinking in order to direct our subsequent actions. It's a good bet that you've encountered mental models at some point even if they weren't explicitly referred to as such. Some of the best known include: backward chaining; falsification; inversion thinking; probabalistic thinking; and the Feynman technique. One of my favorite mental models was popularized by Jeff Bezos. He calls it the *Regret Minimization Framework*, which is activated through the asking of a simple question: In (X) years, will I regret not doing (blank)? This is famously the process he undertook when making the decision to leave his position on Wall Street to start an internet book-selling business that eventually became Amazon.

Using the CRE Mental Model to See Better

CRE, as I define it, is also a mental model. The CRE themes are the tools we use in our design and discovery. To see better is the goal – and also the true challenge of culturally responsive teaching. Many educators enter conversations about CRE with the intention to find answers (generally in the form of strategies) for solving the problems of practice that contribute to Equity gaps; but the process of problem-solving is most effective when it is consistently capable of generating the right questions in support of our design of strategies to address novel circumstances in ways that align with our values and beliefs about fairness and opportunity. It is essential that we are able to recognize the limitations inherent in the search for strategies compared to the far more rigorous task of elevating our awareness in order to see better. The question of "what to do" can actually be a limiting question because it potentially constrains one's capacity for creative design and concentrated presence. A sense of purpose is greater than a laundry list of strategies; but there are some principles and guidelines that give form and context to our responses and designs.

Reis (2014) and many others speak to the importance of authenticity in relationships and responsiveness. I absolutely concur; but authenticity, by definition, can't be scheduled on any program. It's real or it's... inauthentic. I've found that our students measure authenticity over time. The more vulnerable the student's circumstances, often the longer it may take to be perceived as authentic. Thus, the work of Equity requires patience and emotional maturity. This work of Equity is challenging for us. I know it is for me. I've been cursed at, ignored (my least favorite), and joked-on by the most clever kiddos. (They say I look like Frozone from *The Incredibles* – I can't understand why anyone would be offended to be called Frozone because he's only one of the [literally] coolest superheroes currently saving the world from movie-screen doom! *Where's my super suit?*)

Authenticity is a must for our students. One of their assets is that they can spot frauds at great distances. Harry Reis talks about authenticity being a function of understanding. Our students perceive the adults in their lives who understand them as authentic. (That's just one of the reasons why it's so important to make the effort to become familiar with your students' lives outside of school.) Some adults in their lives offer fraudulent relationships, the kind based on false or stereotyped pretenses. For many of our students, their ability to spot frauds is essential to their well-being. They are wise to be careful. Authenticity is perceived through consistent understanding – which is not to say that we endorse bad behaviors as we seek to earn students' trust. As long as the behaviors aren't a danger to anyone, the goal of our efforts should be to have the student to feel fully understood because it's only from a place of understanding that behaviors can change.

In the next chapter, I explain how six themes inform authentic pedagogy and how I and other teachers bring the concept of CRE to life in real classrooms. While the themes are not a self-contained universe of concepts and language, when utilized, this mental model both shapes behaviors and sets our approaches to solving problems of practice. In this way, the CRE mental model gives direction to our Equity thinking, and our pedagogy that follows. Themes that inform practice, however, must be understood in the larger context of purpose – or they will likely be reduced to a simple checklist by those who wish to manualize Equity. Rather, it's important to consider this work within the larger narrative of American democracy so as to properly calibrate our consideration.

The Purpose of American Schools

The revolutionary idea of providing free and public education to every child of every class and category of White ethnic groups was as essential to the identity and development of the young America as was the notion of the separation of church and state. (The course-correction that would broaden the mission to include the education of non-White students would come later.) From the onset, the institution of American public education had both egalitarian and utilitarian purposes. In the egalitarian sense, common schools were intended to be an equalizer and mediator in the distribution of opportunity. In the utilitarian sense, schools were designed to prepare students for productive citizenship. Our conceptual context for understanding Equity is still to this day informed by these purposes of schools in the culturally pluralistic democracy of the United States. The original premise for public (common) schools is to nurture the talent of all students in service of the greater interests of the public (common) good. This purpose is a mandate for American education which precedes and guides all others. To underperform with regard to this original and abiding objective is to betray the only measure that truly matters in the assessment of its efficacy as a uniquely American institution.

In the egalitarian sense, the defining proposition of the free and public education narrative is its intended role in equalizing the distribution of social and economic opportunities in American society. Education was seen as a direct and reliable pathway to being accepted as fully American. In its earliest iterations, "Equality of Opportunity" (in theory) meant that all White, male, land-owning members of the young American society would have equal chances to pursue wealth and enter any occupation and/or social class that their work ethic and skillsets allowed. Schools were to serve the role of a merit-based sorting mechanism of talent among students. Thus, schools are a major actor in the nation's original and continuing pursuit of freedom and opportunity for all. American education is a project that evolved directly from the nation's earliest imaginations and incarnations of the American opportunity ethic. This ethic was, of course, designed with specific attention to and consideration of White, land-owning men – but the ideal has been extended (through sustained and intense social-activism and a long sequence of legal battles) to women and non-White people, as well.

The legacy of the tensions between the ideals and execution of American education continue to confound the conversations about race, ethnicity, ability, and opportunity that are still difficult, though necessary, for us to have. I say these conversations are necessary because a democratic society like ours, established and connected by an ideal more so than a religious, racial, or ethnic identity, evolves relative to its conflict. It is in conflicting interpretations that shared concepts are re-focused and new commitments forged. The original framers of the Constitution of the United States, the document bearing forth the concept of America to those who would inherit the responsibility of protecting it, shared a noble idea of freedom and opportunity for everyone. *I so dig that idea!* The problem is that the framers didn't resolve to extend the full concept of freedom and opportunity to all which they should've known would ultimately undermine the freedom and opportunity of everyone, their heirs included.

Over time, the identity of an American was available to anyone with White skin without the hinderances of ethnic bias. Germans could be American, as could Frenchmen, as could Spaniards, as could Irishmen, as could Italians, as could Englishmen – as could anyone of European ancestry with the will and ethic to pursue opportunity in the "American way." That's essentially how America became famous. America was a whispered dream in the cellars of inequities throughout Europe. (I doubt that even one Black African person or an indigenous person on the South American continent would have thought it hopeful and inspiring to go and pursue the American dream between 1619 and 1865.) But, in a society that espouses freedom and opportunity for all, there can be no state-sanctioned denial of liberty that doesn't threaten the national sovereignty. The good news is that schools are a magnificent space to build better understandings and practices for what Equity truly looks like. It is in schools that we can learn from the tensions involved in the distribution of opportunity. It is in schools where we can pursue the American dream of multicultural and multi-racial pluralism. We are a better nation because of the debate and efforts to improve the execution of the ideal of American public schools. Some ideals, though imperfectly executed, are so profoundly noble that they warrant the continued effort to realize.

History of Culturally Responsive Education

CRE has a rich literature base with hundreds of contributors, and in a way, I'm sure *everything* I've ever read – from Jerome Bruner to A.N. Whitehead to Maya Angelou to Chaucer to Thich Nhat Hanh – has informed my understanding of CRE. But the work of four scholar-practitioners in particular – Gloria Ladson-Billings, Lisa Delpit, Geneva Gay, and Sonia Nieto – has had specific and enormous influence on my theoretical and practical understandings of the concept. While it is clear that elements of what we call CRE have been embodied in master teachers' pedagogy throughout antiquity, these four women have each made distinct contributions that together form the essential baselines from where I began my own discovery of what it means to be a culturally responsive educator.

The Four CRE Matriarchs

Gloria Ladson-Billings has been studying the practices of successful teachers of African American students since the 1980s, and in the tradition of Freire, she challenges the idea of pedagogy as culturally neutral in its advantaging or disadvantaging of students (Ladson-Billings, 1992a, 1992b, 1994). Her work encourages a more robust insightfulness from a pedagogical perspective into the racial achievement and performance gaps that were then first being uncovered quantitatively through the analysis of standardized test scores (Ladson-Billings, 1995b; Ladson-Billings, 1995c). I've often used her article, "But that's just good teaching! The case for culturally relevant pedagogy," to highlight the key criteria that Ladson-Billings employs to distinguish Culturally Relevant Teaching:

> a pedagogy of opposition not unlike critical pedagogy but specifically committed to collective, not merely individual, empowerment. Culturally relevant pedagogy rests on three criteria or propositions: (a) students must experience academic success; (b) students must develop and/or maintain cultural competence; and (c) students must develop a critical consciousness through which they challenge the status quo of the current social order.
>
> *(Ladson-Billings, 1995a, p. 160)*

Lisa Delpit's (1995) work is a call to teachers to better understand the scope and influence of the cultural power they hold. Over three decades, she's explored how both larger societal power imbalances and cultural conflicts replicate within classrooms and impact the ways in which students are able to access educational opportunities.

She argues that our reflection on education inequities should center the power imbalances and cultural conflicts within classrooms which reflect broader societal inequities. Says Delpit (1995, p. xiv): "The culprit in these situations is not simply racism, though it certainly plays a part. It is the reluctance of people, especially those with power and privilege, to perceive those different from themselves except through their own culturally clouded vision." This inability is particularly destructive in classrooms where teachers view low-income and minority children as 'other' and "see damaged and dangerous caricatures of the vulnerable and impressionable beings before them" (1995, p. xiii).

Teaching that is fair and meaningful, writes Delpit, accepts students for who they are but also takes responsibility to educate without blaming them for the inadequate economic and educational opportunities dictated by the prevailing power structures. She thinks of this as a more complicated process than merely the replication of a specific bank of teaching techniques and tools:

> My charge here is not to determine the best instructional methodology; I believe that the actual practice of good teachers of all colors typically incorporates a range of pedagogical orientations. Rather, I suggest that the differing perspectives on the debate over "skills" versus "process" approaches can lead to an understanding of the alienation and miscommunication, and thereby to an understanding of the 'silenced dialogue.'
>
> *(Delpit, 1993, p. 123)*

Geneva Gay defines Culturally Responsive Teaching as employing the cultural characteristics, experiences, and perspectives of ethnically diverse students as conduits for more effective teaching (Gay, 1995, 2002). She describes five essential elements of Culturally Responsive Teaching: (1) developing a knowledge base about cultural diversity, (2) including ethnic and cultural diversity content in the curriculum, (3) demonstrating caring and building learning communities, (4) communicating with ethnically diverse students, and (5) responding to ethnic diversity in the delivery of instruction. Learning opportunities in school, argues Gay (2000), are more personally meaningful when academic knowledge and skills are situated within the frames of reference of students. Gay's work compels educators to carefully investigate their own social and cultural identities in order to better understand how they impact (positively or negatively) the success of racially and ethnically diverse student populations:

> Scholars, like classroom teachers, are ethnic and cultural beings. Their attitudes and values are nested in their writings, research, and teachings. These need to be revealed and then analyzed to better understand their particular positions and points of view. Learning to discern how the 'positionality' of authors affects their analysis of educational issues during their preparation programs may become a habit that teachers take into the classroom and pass on to their students. Furthermore, it is an excellent way to dispel the notion that scholars are infallible or the only ones with legitimate claims to expertise. In the process of revealing the constraints of one's positionality, the power of another's perspectives is unfolded. The intellectual give-and-take that results is a compelling illustration of the social construction of knowledge in action.
>
> *(Gay, 2000, p. 225)*

Sonia Nieto's work reminds us that Culturally Responsive Pedagogy is adaptive, rigorous, and inclusive. It neither follows a one-size-fits-all, pre-determined curriculum, nor is it based on pre-packaged strategies targeting specific populations of students. Rather, Culturally Responsive Pedagogy offers learning experiences that challenge students and provide opportunities for them to draw on their own cultural fluencies in order to reach the goals for successful learning (Nieto, 1999, 2002). Culturally Responsive Pedagogy requires that we all regularly consider in the most meaningful ways how our own values, biases, strengths, and limitations can potentially affect our effectiveness with students of diverse backgrounds. Culture, says Nieto (2003), is hugely impactful in the ways students experience their identities in specific learning spaces:

> More recently, the term culturally responsive pedagogy has come into use and been advocated persuasively. An outgrowth of multicultural education, culturally responsive pedagogy is founded on the notion that – rather than deficits – students' backgrounds are assets that students can

and should use in the service of their learning and that teachers of all backgrounds should develop the skills to teach diverse students effectively.

(Nieto, 2003, p. 6)

Nieto further warns against the over-simplification in our understanding of these issues related to Culturally Responsive Pedagogies:

> Despite my great support for these philosophies, however, I am also concerned that they can be used in simplistic ways that fail to address the tremendous inequities that exist in our schools. For example, to adopt a multicultural basal reader is far easier than to guarantee that all children will learn to read; to plan an assembly program of ethnic music is easier than to provide music instruction for all students; and to train teachers in a few behaviors in cultural awareness or curriculum inclusion is easier than to address widespread student disengagement in learning. Although these may be valuable activities, they fail to confront directly the deep-seated inequalities that exist in schools. Because they are sometimes taken out of context and isolated as prepackaged programs or "best practices" – multicultural education and culturally responsive pedagogy can become band-aid approaches to serious problems that require nothing short of major surgery.

> *(Nieto, 2003, p. 7)*

What We Can Learn from the CRE Matriarchs

I saw Robert Farris Thompson, a professor of art history at Yale University and an authority of African diasporic art philosophy, give a quote in a fantastic documentary on the life of Jean-Michel Basquiat (The Radiant Child, 2010), articulating what the brilliant artist himself understood about influence. Basquiat, said Thompson, never mindlessly copied the work of other artists and that, further, the notion of "influence" was misunderstood. Basquiat didn't copy, said Professor Thompson, but rather he "improvised revisions." Basquiat understood that "influence is not influence. It's simply someones's idea going through my new mind." Similarly, the overarching and interconnected themes in the research and scholarly works of the CRE matriarchs contextualize my understandings of CRE and provide the grounding needed to act with a focus on principles beyond just a catalogue of specific practices. These ideas became the baselines for the themes I use to position CRE as an actionable philosophy for teaching that is a starting point and framing device for the planning and implementation of responsive learning experiences for all students.

From Ladson-Billings, we learn that the mindset and beliefs of the Culturally "Relevant" Educator should be operationalized in pedagogy, and that Culturally Relevant Teaching is a practice of critical and cultural consciousness that prepares students for participation in a multicultural, democratic society. From Delpit, we learn that systems that produce inequitable outcomes are replicated and reinforced by education that doesn't challenge and empower students to push back against societal inequities. From Gay, we learn that Culturally Responsive Teaching assumes that academic knowledge and skills situated within students' lived experiences have higher interest appeal and are therefore learned more easily and thoroughly; and further that teachers must come to terms with their own social and cultural identities as contributing to (or detracting from) the performance of students. And finally, from Nieto, we learn that the Culturally Responsive Pedagogy mindset fundamentally honors and appreciates the students' cultures, experiences, and histories, and reflects that respect through curriculum and rigorous pedagogical approaches which cannot be reduced to a boiler-plate list of "best practices."

The concept of CRE provides a multi-disciplinary framework with myriad implications for practice rather than a mere checklist of individual and specific actions. I use the term "Culturally Responsive Education" to build on the cumulative body of work of Gloria Ladson-Billings, Lisa Delpit, Geneva Gay, and Sonia Nieto (among many others not named) to refer to the construct that is useful for identifying themes and tools of practice for closing opportunity gaps. While I think of the "R" as a reference to "responsiveness" – which is in my mind a substantive difference from "relevance" – I too will sometimes use the words "teaching," "pedagogy," or "education" interchangeably. I most often say CRE because education is a broader term that includes pedagogy and also other aspects of the work of schools, including that which is considered in policy and pedagogical planning spaces. Thus, the CRE mental model provides a conceptual context for policies and practices that focus on Equity without marginalizing some students relative to others. It actively enlists the awareness of culture, race, ethnicity, gender, ability, and other social identity markers that shape the perceptions of educational opportunities.

The Purpose of Culturally Responsive Education

The purpose of a CRE mental model is to create fair (in terms of Equity, not Equality) and meaningful learning opportunities for all students. CRE is an approach to the design of learning experiences that centers the goals of responsive instruction. CRE is not a collection of strategies. Many strategies, used with the goals of responsiveness, can be tools of the brilliant teacher; and the same strategies, used without the mindset and intentions of responsiveness, can fall utterly flat. The goal in the selection of any strategy should be to create circumstances in which the students will find the learning opportunity to be responsive and meaningful. Too often, however, we teachers choose strategies based on our familiarity with them and the ease with which the strategy can be implemented.

When responsiveness is the goal of instruction, the expectations for educators differ from traditional notions and practices of schooling – especially in the current era of high-stakes standardized testing. The goal of responsiveness doesn't assume student engagement; rather, responsiveness accepts that student engagement is a function of well-designed learning experiences. A lot of teachers find this to be altogether objectionable. They feel that students should come to us already fully prepared to engage regardless of the quality of our instruction. If there was ever such a time when that was true, I'm sorry (not sorry) to say that day has passed. It is now unequivocally the responsibility of good instruction to be responsive to students' needs and the specific contexts in which they learn. Responsiveness yields greater engagement.

In a culturally responsive learning experience, the true purpose of school is realized in that our students have the opportunities to build their capacities for rich thinking and productive action within the context of networks of others who are also invested in those same capacity-building efforts, with each and every kiddo afforded the meaningful opportunities to bring in aspects of their cultural identities and fluencies to further the learning experience for themselves and others. When we are successful, our kiddos invariably feel more deeply connected to school because it is a place where they are able to predict how they can engineer successful outcomes for themselves without compromising the integrity of the social and cultural identities which in many ways define the core of their being.

OPERATIONALIZE THIS!

Design Learning Experiences that Students Will Be Able to Perceive as Responsive

The goal of Culturally Responsive Teaching is to create lessons that students can perceive as experiences of understanding, validation, and care – because human beings are more willing to invest ourselves in the spaces and communities in which we find support and connection than otherwise. That spirit of responsiveness was embedded throughout the design of the Family Narrative unit. In order for kiddos to be successful, they each had to become the master storyteller of a narrative that holds significance for them and their families. Our job as teachers was not to legislate what story to tell but rather to facilitate the structures and supports students needed to be able to invest themselves in the story and connect it to a rigorous learning outcome. Our students were able to use their cultural fluencies in order to grasp the themes of their family texts and be able to translate those in ways that could be understood and appreciated by others in the classroom community. By using tools of their cultural identities to mine the rich themes in the stories of their family members, our kiddos had opportunities to experience academic success through the leveraging of their out-of-school identities. Responsiveness redefines the purpose of learning for students. It gives clarity and charts the course through which authentic engagement is achieved. Responsiveness is dynamic. Responsiveness is emotional. Responsiveness is personal… Responsiveness is the essence, action, and performance of brilliance. In the practice of a brilliant teacher, responsiveness is at once a mindset, an action, and also a product.

In the Family Narrative project, we sought to design a learning experience that would allow us to see our students better – in more vibrant, multidimensional, multigenerational terms – by having them create texts that we would analyze and interpret as a community of thinkers and writers. Together, we extended the thread of those texts further into other content; and by doing so, our students felt competent precisely because of their cultural fluencies and the stories they were able to mine from the rich lived experiences of their loved ones. In this learning experience, we saw our students' families as having great worth, and our students saw the storylines in their own family narratives – the storylines that they inherit from the previous generations – as themes that could be related to the literature learned about in school. Thus, our students' relationships with family members and the knowledge and identities therein were central elements of the learning targets.

It's important that our kiddos saw each other as resources in the writing process. Their own interview questions were developed with the support of the classroom community as tools for uncovering the themes that they most wanted to examine. Our 21st-century students need to be able to manufacture and identify questions that will guide their own thinking. In the internet age, where information is freely and abundantly available via the World Wide Web, the fundamental role of the teacher is changed from what it was when I first entered the classroom more than two decades ago. Then, the role of the teacher was more or less to be the "expert-knower" in the room. Our job as teachers was to be the mountains of knowledge, and the students were responsible for coming to the mountain. But the advent of the smartphone changed all of that! Our students now consume more information through their handheld devices than was imaginable when I first started teaching, and that reality has ushered in a paradigm shift in the purpose of teaching. Rather than being the expert-knower, the essential skill of 21st-century teaching is expert-facilitation of others' knowing. Having our students generate their own questions using the Question Formulation Technique, for example, was an essential step in their engagement because we wanted students to feel an authentic sense of ownership of the themes they would identify from the interviews with their family members; and that means they had to discover the threads of these themes themselves. We wanted them to feel responsible for the quality of the narratives they were able to report. We discussed what it means to "go deeper" with questions, how to pursue a detail in a response in search of a larger and even more interesting find. In our students' reflections, many of them talked about wanting to ask more probing questions, realizing how their inquiry had the power to excavate rich and nuanced narratives of their family members' experience. Many of the kiddos found the stories they wanted; others had a rigorous learning experience through realizing how they could pursue the project differently the next time. In the words of one of Mrs. VanNess' kiddos: "I would talk more to my mom about how she met my dad because she didn't give me all the juicy details, she just gave me some."

Center Instruction on Rich, Meaningful Understandings

I always start my planning with time to think carefully about what I want my students to understand and feel. This is in many ways the marrow of responsive pedagogy. (These and the other strategies I use in planning for culturally responsive learning experiences are covered in greater detail in Chapter 4.) Our clarity regarding targets for students' understanding and what and how we want them to feel gives us the direction and the insight that we need during instruction to know when we're close and/or to recognize when we need to go in a different direction to secure the experiences we most hope for students. Through this intentionality, we are much more likely to be able to successfully leverage everything we know about who our kiddos are – their assets, their vulnerabilities, their cultures and identities – in order to support the true learning target which is something much deeper than just a content standard.

Many of our students have experienced trauma and disrupted family structures in their home lives, and some of our students do not have biological family members to interview, in which case we supported them in clarifying another key understanding which is that they are free to define "family member" as anyone – whether of blood relation or not – who provides counsel and care that the students see as reliable. Multiple studies have identified the availability of at least one stable, caring, and supportive relationship in the life of a child as a protective factor that supports resilience (Crosnoe & Elder, 2004; Cicchetti, Rogosch, & Toth, 2006; Hartling, 2008). We have great compassion for our kiddos, and we also know that in order to support them well and prepare them for a successful future, they are much more bene- fited by developing tools and an empowered awareness for how to manage their own well-being than they are merely by our sympathies. In order to survive, our students have to learn how to command a sense of mastery over their life circumstances. Research on resilience says that "those who believe in their own capacity to overcome hardships and guide their own destiny are far more likely to adapt positively to adversity" (National Scientific Council on the Developing Child, 2015). We must fight for a world with fewer injustices and also pre- pare our students to live in it without having their own sense of agency destroyed. An important understanding we wanted for our students even at such a young age is that they will need to develop tools that allow them to identify trustworthy persons and enlist their support in much the same way that other students are able to find within their families. It is enormously unfair and equally unfortunate that some of our students have such a massive responsibility in constructing their own social networks, and we their teachers empathize with them; yet, we also know that they must be taught the competencies they need to construct their own systems for support. This is an essential skill for their future well-being, and in this learning experience, that effort yields both an emotional and an academic return.

The idea of theme is such an important concept for students to understand. In the older grades, our kiddos who struggle most with literature often lack the know-how for identifying themes (beyond plot) in complex texts. In this learning experience, we wanted students to understand that they are the beneficiaries of rich narratives in their own families, and these narratives have important themes and life- lessons with which they should be familiar. Further, the extent to which they were able to convey the richness of the family narratives with the rest of the class is a function of their own ability to ask questions that get to the heart of their family stories. Beyond merely the surface- level understanding of this, we wanted our students to feel inspired and empowered in the act of their discovery. Through this experience, our kiddos built on their abilities to uncover important themes, but they also were able to explore stories and historical events that hold important insights which they can refer to at later points in their own lives. In doing so, students thought rigorously in terms of analyzing original sources of evidence and complex, abstract themes, perspectives, and concepts. They were able to compare and contrast the themes in their own family narratives with the themes found by their peers, and they were also able to synthesize the pieces of their interviews (i.e. texts) in order to articulate a theme which captured new knowledge or a nuanced perspective to which they were previously not acquainted. Through this learning experience we hoped our students would feel more secure in the expression of their academic identities through formal research, writing, and presenting following the guidelines and using the conventions of standard academic language.

Incorporate Technology to Further Leverage Engagement

The use of video to capture students' reflections was also an important aspect of this learning experience. I personally find it exhilarating to see a room full of 10-year-olds sprawled out on the floor and under tables thoughtfully recording their reflections while enveloped in the background of a symphony of engaged voices. Community is defined in large part through reflection. The narratives that bind social groups are reinforced through the replaying of events. Reflection is the process through which group narratives are constructed. With the technology of video, our students had opportunities to reflect together on both the narratives they collected through their interviews with family members and also what we all learned together about what it means to ask good questions and glean from interviews the themes that we can further explore. It is often the case that students most vividly realize their agency in learning in their reflection of the learning experience, and video is an excellent tool to incorporate for that purpose.

We thought it especially important that our students had the opportunity to conduct multiple interviews so that they could coordinate their interpretations of their texts with the consultation of their peers. We want our students to understand that writing is an iterative process, and that there are many discoveries available to the thoughtful writer throughout the various stages of inquiry and composition. To shortchange one part of the writing process limits the possibilities for the fullest expression of the themes in which we hoped our kiddos would feel a meaningful investment. Because they were exploring themes in their own social networks, and also because they were responsible through their interviewing for exposing what is interesting, their investment was greater than what we would typically see in a more traditional research project. This investment for our students was personal and emotional, which then evoked stronger cognitive engagement, as well.

References

Baumeister, R. F., & Muraven, M. (1996). Identity as adaptation to social, cultural, and historical context. *Journal of Adolescence, 19*(5), 405–416.

Boaler, J. (2008). Promoting 'relational equity' and high mathematics achievement through an innovative mixed ability approach. *British Educational Research Journal, 34*(2), 167–194.

Boaler, J., & Dweck, C. S. (2016). *Mathematical mindsets: Unleashing students' potential through creative math, inspiring messages and innovative teaching.* San Francisco, CA: Jossey-Bass.

Boykin, A. W., & Noguera, P. (2011). *Creating the opportunity to learn: Moving from research to practice to close the achievement gap.* Alexandria, VA: ASCD.

Cicchetti, D., Rogosch, F. A., & Toth, S. L. (2006). Fostering secure attachment in infants in maltreating families through preventive interventions. *Development and Psychopathology, 18*(3), 623–649.

Crosnoe, R., & Elder, G. H. (2004). Family dynamics, supportive relationships, and educational resilience during adolescence. *Journal of Family Issues, 25*(5), 571–602.

Davis, T. (2010). *The radiant child.* Hollywood, CA: Curiously Bright Entertainment Films.

Delpit, L. D. (1993). The silenced dialogue: Power and pedagogy in educating other people's children. In L. Weis & M. Fine (Eds.), *Beyond silenced voices: Class, race, and gender in United States schools* (pp. 119–139). SUNY series, Frontiers in Education. Albany, NY: State University of New York Press.

Delpit, L. D. (1995). *Other people's children: Cultural conflict in the classroom.* New York: New Press.

Fivush, R., & Nelson, K. (2006). Parent-child reminiscing locates the self in the past. *British Journal of Developmental Psychology, 24*(1), 235–251.

Hartling, L. M. (2008) Strengthening resilience in a risky world: It's all about relationships. *Women & Therapy, 31*(2–4), 51–70.

Gay, G. (1995). A multicultural school curriculum. In C. A. Grant & M. Gomez (Eds.), *Making school multicultural: Campus and classroom* (pp. 37–54). Englewood Cliffs, NJ: Merrill/Prentice Hall.

Gay, G. (2000). *Culturally responsive teaching: Theory, research, & practice.* New York: Teachers College Press.

Gay, G. (2002). Preparing for culturally responsive teaching. *Journal of Teacher Education, 53*(2), 106–116.

Ladson-Billings, G. (1992a). Culturally relevant teaching: The key to making multicultural education work. In C. A. Grant (Ed.), *Research and multicultural education: From margins to the mainstream* (pp. 107–121). Washington, DC: Falmer Press.

Ladson-Billings, B. (1992b). Reading between the lines and beyond the pages: A culturally relevant approach to literacy teaching. *Theory Into Practice, 31*(4), 312–320.

Ladson-Billings, G. (1994). *The dreamkeepers: Successful teachers of African American children.* San Francisco, CA: Jossey-Bass.

Ladson-Billings, G. (1995a). But that's just good teaching! The case for culturally relevant pedagogy. *Theory Into Practice, 34*(3), 159–165.

Ladson-Billings, G. (1995b). Multicultural teacher education: Research, practice, and policy. In J. A. Banks & C. A. M. Banks (Eds.), *Handbook of research on multicultural education* (pp. 747–759). New York: Macmillan.

Ladson-Billings, G. (1995c). Toward a theory of culturally relevant pedagogy. *American Educational Research Journal, 32*(3), 465–491.

Moll, L. C., Amanti, C., Neff, D., & Gonzalez, N. (1992). Funds of knowledge for teaching: Using a qualitative approach to connect homes and classrooms. *Theory Into Practice, 31*(1), 132–141.

National Scientific Council on the Developing Child. (2015). Supportive relationships and active skill-building strengthen the foundations of resilience. Working Paper 13. Retrieved from https://developingchild. harvard.edu/resources/supportive-relationships-and-active-skill-building-strengthen-the-foundations-of-resilience/

Nieto, S. (1999). *The light in their eyes: Creating multicultural learning communities.* New York: Teachers College Press.

Nieto, S. (2002). *Language, culture, and teaching: Critical perspectives for a new century.* Mahwah, NJ: L. Erlbaum.

Nieto, S. (2003). Profoundly multicultural questions. *Educational Leadership, 60*(4), 6–11.

Reese, E. (2013, December 9). What kids learn from hearing family stories: Reading to children has education benefits, of course—but so does sharing tales from the past. *The Atlantic.* Retrieved from www.theatlantic. com/education/archive/2013/12/what-kids-learn-from-hearing-family-stories/282075/

Reis, H. T. (2014). Responsiveness: Affective interdependence in close relationships. In M. Mikulincer & P. R. Shaver (Eds.), *Nature and development of social connections: From brain to group* (pp. 255–271). Washington, DC: APA Press.

Reis, H. T., & Gable, S. L. (2015). Responsiveness. *Current Opinion in Psychology, 1*, 67–71.

Shakespeare, W. (n.d.). *King Lear*. Retrieved from http://shakespeare.mit.edu/lear/full.html

What are mental models? (n.d.) Retrieved from https://mentalmodels.princeton.edu/about/what-are-mental-models

Yosso, T. J. (2005). Whose culture has capital? A critical race theory discussion of community cultural wealth. *Race Ethnicity and Education, 8*(1), 69–91.

3

THE SIX THEMES OF CULTURALLY RESPONSIVE EDUCATION

The six themes of CRE don't tell any teacher or school administrator specifically "what" to do. Rather, these six themes give context, language, and direction for how responses to behaviors, circumstances, and the tasks inherent in a wide range of teaching scenarios are best leveraged with clear and unambiguous sight of the underlying challenges and opportunities for facilitating meaningful learning experiences for students.

Memes for Meaning

Mr. Vaughn and his human geography class were having a hard time finding their mojo on a regular basis. His class of mostly high school sophomores didn't engage as much as we liked, and we wanted to see if there was something different we could do to light a fire for all of us. Mr. Vaughn and I planned a lesson around different governing ideologies, but we knew his kiddos wouldn't want to hear a lecture – at least not one without some kind of personalized context...

So we planned a learning experience for them using memes. We had the kids read short statements on several types of governing authorities – but to show us they understood, they had to make memes to represent each approach to government – because the universal language of teenagers at this point is essentially the language of memes and gifs! The kiddos quickly got the hang of it. We discussed the appropriateness of images to use and how we don't need to "punch down" to make a point if we have a credible argument. (A big part of what we wanted for students in this experience was to have the opportunity to share ideas absent the threat of name-calling or attacks from those with countering perspectives. To disagree in anger in a classroom discussion is a betrayal of human civility. The very forum exists to communicate so there is no reasonable need for hostility in doing so.)

As the students created memes, Mr. Vaughn and I moved around the room to listen in on their thinking and nudge them in a better direction if they seemed to be off-track. We reviewed the memes, one governing philosophy at a time, projected them onto the interactive whiteboard for the whole class to see, and had each group explain the concept for the meme they used – with "mini-lectures" sprinkled throughout from Mr. Vaughn who responded directly to each meme, making connections and adding conceptual clarity.

After several cycles of meme sharing, we went into a Philosophical Chairs activity with prompts written to generate debates about the merits and flaws of the different theories of governing we'd defined. The key, of course, to a successful Philosophical Chairs activity is to write the prompts in such a way that they can be reasonably agreed or disagree with. During the experience, if there is a side that is under-supported relative to the other, just jump in and make a super-strong point yourself. Get some students to change their mind and join your side of the debate. That always kick-starts the conversation!

We kept the ninth and tenth graders engaged for the full block period, hearing voices which we had hardly heard from all year. We learned (once more) that when we center the learning experience in the language and assets of the students themselves, we give them more meaningful opportunities to engage for their individual good and the overall benefit of the whole learning community.

The Story of the Six Themes

In Chapter 1, I discussed the importance of considering Equity and pedagogy in the same spaces, and the risks of losing focus on one or both if we do not. In Chapter 2, I defined Culturally Responsive Education (CRE) as a mental model (a way to think about the world that more likely ensures that our choices reliably and consciously reflect our preferred mindset) useful for identifying themes and tools of practice for closing opportunity gaps. It gives a conceptual context for policies and practices that focus on Equity without marginalizing some students relative to others by actively enlisting the awareness of culture, race, ethnicity, gender, ability, and other social identity markers that shape the perceptions of educational opportunities. Mindset – a function of our beliefs, values, and attitudes – can be thought of as an individual's capacity to ask themselves challenging questions so that their thinking and practice (and their thinking about practice) remain productive and forward-moving.

If CRE is to be operationalized beyond theory, it must be performative in our pedagogy, and the only way to do that is to bring more conscious awareness of our mindset into our practice. I've come to identify six themes to support our thinking at the intersections of Equity and pedagogy. Taken together, these six themes are an effective framework for putting language to the mindset and practices that close Equity gaps for students. Specifically in terms of Equity and CRE, we've got to ask good questions to make our practices more responsive for students. In the description of the six themes that I use to understand and operationalize CRE, I share guiding questions to support our inquiry-based approach to Equity in pedagogy.

The thoughtfulness that underscores the questions we ask ourselves about our mindset and practice is difficult work. Unfortunately, not every teacher I work with wants to do the hard work of crafting a culturally responsive mindset. Many would prefer to reduce our understanding of CRE to a simple recipe. For them, it seems easier to think exclusively in terms of strategies. In this way, they think they can understand the practice of brilliant teachers on the same rational level as that of less brilliant teachers. Strategies become a sort of impartial metric, as in, *I will measure my effectiveness against brilliant teachers by comparing my strategies with theirs.* They think strategies can equate to mastery, but I've stopped thinking of mastery as the goal – which is why I prefer to think in terms of brilliance – because, in my mind, the idea of brilliance represents a more dynamic, continuously evolving concept than mastery. Brilliance is the exercise of understanding the whole rather than completing a finite task. The CRE themes (and the whole they represent) must live inside of us. It must become part of us, our teacher essence. It must develop into an *inside-understanding* of Equity. In my work with teachers, I use these themes to think ourselves inside of complex teaching and learning scenarios. When we approach our craft in this way, we are not attempting to merely present an effective lesson; rather, we are bringing an experience to life that incarnates our Equity mindset. It is a way of being that produces action which is greater than an index of actions.

These CRE themes will not support your improvements in practice unless you offer a consistent effort to internalize them. Look for connections between the themes and make them your own by finding ways to put these themes into practice. But I feel compelled to say explicitly here that the themes do not constitute a checklist. I repeat: This is not a checklist. Rather, this is a lens I use to draw meaning from the learning experiences that most powerfully engage students and to anticipate the elements likely to work well in the future. The six CRE themes give a conceptual context for describing how pedagogy and policy support Equity in teaching and learning. It's the language we use to articulate the elements of good practice. Taken together, these six themes provide us with vocabulary and tools for understanding the ways in which some students may feel alienated or under-supported by school pedagogies and structures and how teaching can be more effectively organized to mitigate the Equity gaps that persist in such scenarios. My goal here is to provide some baseline definitions that may serve as the foundation for continued exploration of the CRE themes.

The CRE Circles

My friends and former New York University colleagues, Chemay Morales-James and Roey Ahram, and I devised a representation of CRE that we came to call "the CRE circles." I've found it to be a useful illustration of the CRE concept, especially in terms of moving us away from any checklist notions relative to our thinking about Equity. The search for simple checklists is especially dangerous because it can easily contribute to deficit-thinking about students. For example, if a specific strategy has been seen to be effective with one group of students and it

CRE requires that schools be really smart about culture.

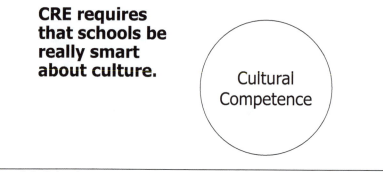

Cultural Competence

Figure 3.1 Cultural competence

is applied with other students without careful attention to the underlying themes that support trust and a meaningful sense of community, the strategy is less likely to be productive, which could in turn lead to blaming students as in: *You see how broken these students are? I used the same strategy that was successful with those other students, but it still didn't work.* Rather, the circles put our use of strategies into a larger context of cultural competence and mindset.

The CRE circles start with a single circle which represents cultural competence (see Figure 3.1). In some of the schools where I've spent significant time, there are literally dozens of cultures represented among the student population. In these cases, with students coming from all over the world with all sorts of cultural backgrounds and indoctrinations, it is likely impossible that any one person will be able to have mastered all of the cultural fluencies of the students; and yet, CRE requires that schools be really smart about culture. The question of how cultural difference might influence students' perceptions of opportunity must always be in play. We should always be making the effort to understand more deeply the fluencies that inform the cultural lens of our students; and though schools may not be able to house an exhaustive cultural expertise of all the groups represented, there must be a commitment in place to identify and understand differences in cultural perspectives.

While cultural competence is critical, it isn't sufficient by itself. Cultural competence informs culturally responsive habits of thinking (see Figure 3.2). Culturally responsive habits of thinking are patterns

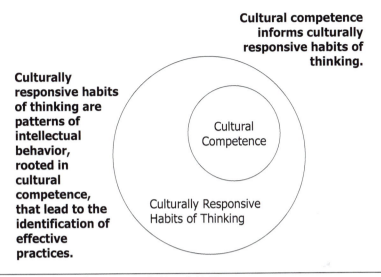

Cultural competence informs culturally responsive habits of thinking.

Culturally responsive habits of thinking are patterns of intellectual behavior, rooted in cultural competence, that lead to the identification of effective practices.

Cultural Competence

Culturally Responsive Habits of Thinking

Figure 3.2 Culturally responsive habits of thinking

of intellectual behavior, rooted in cultural competence, that lead to the identification of effective practices. When I think of culturally responsive habits of thinking, I think of mental qualities such as (but not limited to):

- viewing teaching and learning as a journey and not a destination;
- regularly thinking about one's thinking;
- listening/observing with understanding and empathy;
- questioning and innovative problem-posing;
- designing learning experiences with a focus on engagement; and
- mining actionable data from students' learning experiences.

Though by no means a comprehensive list, these are indicative of the qualities of recurring behaviors among teachers most likely to effectively leverage responsive practices. At first glance, these may seem to be less focused on Equity than pedagogy, but a deeper look reveals otherwise. To view teaching and learning as a journey requires that one is perpetually mindful of the potential for growth and willing to make adjustments in one's practice. It means that we define good practice by the ability to evolve in relation to the needs of one's current students. To regularly think about one's thinking is to ensure that we are evolving with intention and relative to our beliefs and values about fairness and not in a random or thoughtless response to the policy environment. To listen and observe with empathy literally means to imagine what it feels like to be someone else, which requires the consideration of their full identity – race, gender, and all. Questioning and innovative problem-posing demands the re-centering of one's assumptions regarding cause, effect, and correlation. True innovation isn't possible unless one is willing to acknowledge that they themselves – their attitudes and behaviors – might be the key inhibiting factor. The constant focus on engagement entails a user-centered approach to design which elevates the awareness of students' humanity; and the mining of actionable data calls for the thoughtful deliberation of the range of relevant evidence through which students may demonstrate their understandings.

But, That's Just Good Teaching

The rest, as Gloria Ladson-Billings (1995a) told us more than 20 years ago, is just good teaching – i.e. good practices (see Figure 3.3). While I am a strong proponent of the contemplation and isolation of specific obstacles to opportunities for particular groups, it is terribly wrong-headed (and intellectually lazy) to think of some specific strategies as being uniquely suited to serving the needs of some specific groups. I don't believe that there is a "Black boys toolkit" for example. I believe that there are good strategies that, if properly employed in a suitable context, can have great success with even the most vulnerable students. We are wise to understand the barriers to opportunity, but the goal of our work isn't to develop race-/ethnicity-/gender-specific strategies. Rather than limiting our students to one dimension of their identity for our pedagogical convenience (and loaded with our stereotypes and biases), the goal is to compassionately see each student as fully human, the same way you would want for a teacher to see your own child or a child you love dearly. Our goal isn't to shrink our toolkit. We want to sharpen our perception and capacities for leveraging strategies in ways that are most beneficial to students in need of specific support. Context always matters, and a significant part of Equity work is the task of interpreting context.

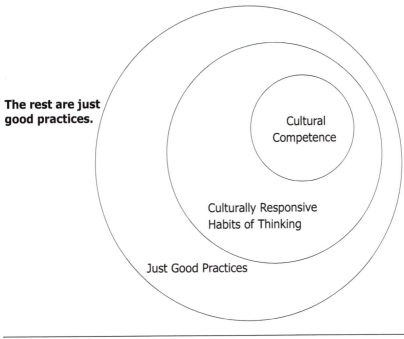

The rest are just good practices.

Cultural Competence

Culturally Responsive Habits of Thinking

Just Good Practices

Figure 3.3 Just good practices

The Six CRE Themes

Over several years of working with teachers, school and district administrators, and school support staff, I came to realize, however, that even the conceptual representation of the circles required additional thematic context in order for the idea of CRE to be operationalized into policies and practices effective for closing Equity gaps. I first started using the themes (see Figure 3.4) as sub-sections of professional development trainings. It was a helpful paradigm for chunking out a broad conversation. In time, I came to see the six themes as essential for the bridging of Equity and pedagogy. I think of them as a web of interconnected ideas that can be labeled initially as separate components; but they are ultimately defined in context relative to the whole as an interrelated ecosystem of intellections. The themes are:

- Engagement;
- Cultural Identity;

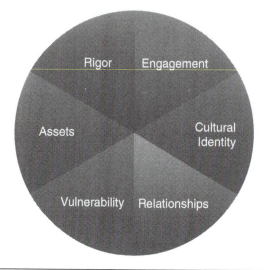

Figure 3.4 The BIG six themes

- Relationships;
- Vulnerability;
- Assets; and
- Rigor.

I continue to deepen my understanding of the themes everyday. These are the tools I use to make sense of how to draw from my pedagogical toolkit in any given context. They guide my understanding of my purpose in instruction and the strategies I can employ to achieve that purpose. My goal in these following sections is to present each of the six themes and give them an independent definition; but in practice and in any kind of sophisticated understanding, these themes aren't meant to exist outside of their relationship to the whole. They are each intricately connected to every other theme. The lines that divide each are permeable, allowing all of the themes to blend in with the others. You can start with any one of the themes and move forward by choosing any other as a next stopping point in your deliberation. Taken together, the themes are a lens. They are the language and references for considering the context and methods for teaching and learning that are most likely to close Equity gaps.

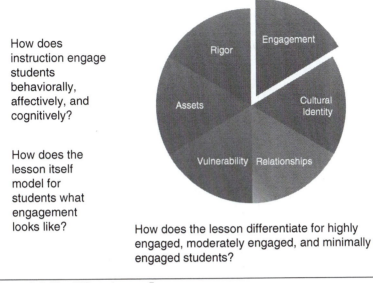

How does instruction engage students behaviorally, affectively, and cognitively?

How does the lesson itself model for students what engagement looks like?

How does the lesson differentiate for highly engaged, moderately engaged, and minimally engaged students?

Figure 3.5 The BIG six themes: *Engagement*

Engagement

Engagement (see Figure 3.5) is both a theme and a goal for CRE. I think of it as a theme because brilliant teachers have a deep and nuanced understanding of student engagement, but engagement is also an interconnected function of a larger purpose-driven experience for learners (Wood & Bandura, 1989; Ryan & Deci, 2000). There are two overarching points I want to make about the theme of engagement: First, we must be clear and specific when discussing the indicators of engagement because it is a concept with (at least) three dimensions; and second, engagement is a function of identity, and if we can understand and leverage engagement well, we are in effect supporting students in the cultivation of identities that will allow them to justify the effort necessary for success in school. In terms of the former point, I often talk about Engagement as the moneyball of education by drawing on the moneyball philosophy in baseball because if engagement is present, then everything else about the learning experience has a greater likelihood for success.

At one point, the moneyball concept was co-opted by a wing of educators who thought it could be applied to a hyper-focus on statistics drawn from high-stakes testing – but I think they are misguided. It is not that I am opposed to statistics; it's that their attempts to measure some things with quantitative tools lack a certain understanding of the qualitative nature of engagement. Moneyball is a concept in baseball that governs how games are managed and teams are put together. First, there are a few key premises that should be made explicit in order to understand the moneyball philosophy, such as there is no clock in baseball. The game is played in the time-frame of innings... An inning consists of both teams having an opportunity to take at-bats on offense. An inning ends when both teams have made three outs while in their at-bat portion of the frame. Therefore, the most valuable statistical commodity in baseball is an "out" – meaning it is finite and final. It can't be recovered. The winning team must record 27 outs and have scored more runs than the opposition in order to secure victory.

The moneyball philosophy says the ideal scoring strategy is that which puts runners on base without causing outs. Moneyball thinking seeks to put base runners on the base paths in whatever way possible – whether it's a bloop single, a base on balls, or even a batter who is hit by a pitch... and a home run is not worth much if the home-run hitter is more prone to strike outs and empty plate appearances than other players, thus causing more outs in the long-run than their home runs offset. The players who get on base without causing outs, regardless of how they do it, are the players most valued according to the thinking of moneyball (Lewis, 2003).

I call engagement the moneyball of education because like "outs," I think of students' engagement as the most valuable commodity in the interest of learning. If a student checks out during instruction, we can't teach them anything until we re-engage them (Brewster, & Fager, 2000; Bandura, 2002a; Henry, Knight, & Thornberry, 2012). As long as students are engaged, we have a chance to teach them. If we can keep kiddos on the base paths, we know that we will eventually score. Engagement, however, can be an elusive target, and so we must often innovate and explore to locate the most appropriate strategies. It is important to keep in mind that strategies for engagement are neither universally nor objectively nor culturally neutral in how they are defined. They are always defined in context. The techniques that work to support engagement with one group of learners may need to be applied differently from one classroom to the next. The design of highly engaging learning experiences requires a keen sense of context because human beings are a highly social species and interpersonal and cultural contexts matter.

The moneyball metaphor (like all metaphors) is an imperfect illustration, but it helps to reveal a simple but significant truth: our students can only learn when they are engaged. Therefore, students' engagement is a central goal for any instructional design. (In Chapter 4, we'll talk more about how we can mindfully incorporate our understandings of engagement in the design of learning experiences.) Engagement is a term that is used often in education and frequently without sufficient depth of thought to truly give the idea its just due. We are wise, however, to calibrate our definitions so that we can be certain that we are conjuring up the same goals and understandings when we use the word *engagement*.

Another way to think of engagement is as if it's the output resulting from the commitments and/or investments that students make in learning. Highly engaging learning experiences are developed on a premise(s) that addresses the question: Why should students invest themselves? When we seek engagement, we are asking for an investment(s) from our students – either behaviorally, affectively, and/or cognitively. The output of engagement is in large part the function of how worthwhile students imagine the investment in learning to be. The idea of investment implies that there may be qualitative differences in the level or degree of engagement.

It's useful to have specific language to describe the engagement that we see in our students. I've had the experience of going into classrooms with educators and seeing engagement that others see as disruption, or at other times, I've seen disengagement that others see as compliant engagement. To reconcile our views, we must ensure that our terms and the categories we assign are precise. There is an article I like to use as an anchor for the vital definitions of engagement written by Jennifer A. Fredricks, Phyllis C. Blumenfeld, and Alison H. Paris (2004). It decomposes the general term Engagement into three types (behavioral, affective, and cognitive) which can be defined apart from each other though they should not be regarded as mutually exclusive.

Behavioral Engagement can be thought of as the physical investments that students make in their learning. In the simplest terms, behavioral engagement entails the student's willingness to follow the rules and accept the behavioral guidelines offered in instructional spaces. It is generally thought of as positive, respectful conduct, particularly toward the authority figures in school. With adherence to the expectations for demeanor, behavioral engagement requires a good-faith effort to contribute to the actions associated with success by complying with the norms for teaching and learning. These are all minimal and baseline expectations, however, as a student could theoretically be behaviorally engaged and more or less apathetic to the outcomes of school. As with any investment, behavioral engagement bears risk for the student. The risk of behavioral engagement is it may betray their own authentic expressions of self (Bandura, 1977, 1989; Fredricks, Blumenfeld, & Paris, 2004).

Affective Engagement can be thought of as the emotional investments that students make in their learning in ways that yield greater care on their part regarding outcomes and, thus, a greater likelihood for sustained interest in the learning beyond the assessments given by teachers. Affective engagement is evidenced in students' self-driven effort, persistence, concentration, and attention to learning tasks. In classrooms, it looks like interest (versus boredom), active (versus passive) learning, and the students' feeling of belonging to the school community (versus a sense of isolation). Affective engagement is often experienced through interpersonal connections with teachers and peers in school. These relationships are generally indicative of how much students care about their role and their sense of self-efficacy in school communities. The risk of affective engagement is heartbreak and disappointment if the output doesn't match the effort. Hard work that doesn't pay off in the ways students might anticipate when they are emotionally invested can be demoralizing (Bandura, 1977; Elliott & Dweck, 1988; Zimmerman, Bandura, & Martinez-Pons, 1992; Bandura, 2002b; Fredricks, Blumenfeld, & Paris, 2004; Stevens, Olivárez, & Hamman, 2006; Orth, Robins, & Widaman, 2012).

Cognitive Engagement can be thought of as the intellectual investments that students make in their learning. It speaks to the extent and intensity of self-regulation in attending to one's own learning, and also the willingness and ability to be strategic in the building of understandings and completion of tasks. It is the acceptance of difficulty in achieving short- and long-term academic goals. As Fredricks, Blumenfeld, and Paris (2004, p. 64) note, the "conceptualization of cognitive engagement includes flexibility in problem solving, preference for hard work, and positive coping in the face of failure. Other researchers have outlined general definitions of engagement that emphasize an inner psychological quality and investment in learning, implying more than just behavioral engagement". The risk of cognitive engagement is that students may experience vulnerability in revealing that they "do not know" the sought-after answers.

One way that we can think of academic identity is by its expression through engagement. In other words, engagement is both a function of and metric for academic identity. Students are more or less engaged in school to the extent that their academic identity supports the investments necessary to be successful. Think of it this way. The spaces where you are most willing to consistently engage, to take risks, to invest yourself fully, are also the spaces in which you have the strongest sense of identity. You have more in the way of relationships on the line with other persons who share similar identities and also with the activities and rituals within the spaces where you are most comfortable and confident in your identity. In those spaces where your identity is most strongly developed and supported, you are more motivated to persist and take on difficult challenges than where you don't feel as meaningful a connection. Engagement inspires and is inspired by motivation. When students feel committed to and invested in their learning, they are more likely to be able to sustain that engagement over longer and more focused periods of time.

The theme of Engagement clarifies several goals of the culturally responsive educator. (It's also important to note that it's very difficult to engage students if you, the teacher, aren't engaged yourself.) Though all the different dimensions of engagement are important, our highest goal is cognitive engagement because with cognitive engagement comes a self-directed and empowered authority over one's participation and outcomes in learning. In that regard, a learning experience is most successful when the students are not reliant on the teacher for their sustained intellectual investments. When they are autonomously motivated in this way, they are in full control of the learning experience (which, though we teachers say we want engagement, can be a terrifying experience for those of us accustomed to being the centerpiece of teaching and learning). Further, the theme of Engagement reveals the false dichotomy we are often guilty of making between the academic and non-academic needs of students. This model of engagement shows us that when students are affectively engaged, for instance, they are more likely to be cognitively and also behaviorally engaged, as well. Our students' humanity isn't neatly divided by academic and non-academic partitions. Their academic selves are also intimately connected to the motivations, aspirations, and vulnerabilities of the other parts of their selves. And finally, teaching self-regulatory behaviors and traditional academics simultaneously isn't a burden but rather an entirely reasonable expectation of instruction. Our students learn best how to manage their own engagement when they are taught (and given support in constructing) the tools and techniques to engage in productive and disciplined ways. There is no such thing as a purely academic lesson because any effective lesson conveys both content and tools to manage one's own investment in the learning.

The questions we can regularly ask of ourselves to ensure fidelity of our thinking with the design of learning experiences include but are not limited to: How does instruction engage students behaviorally, affectively, and cognitively? How does the lesson itself model for students what engagement looks like? How does the lesson differentiate for highly engaged, moderately engaged, and minimally engaged students?

Cultural Identity

I have a thought experiment that I like to use in introducing the theme of Cultural Identity (see Figure 3.6) that I think facilitates a deeper understanding of the significance of identity and how we perceive spaces and opportunities in our daily lives. It begins with a question (and you should think about it too): *Where in the world are you most comfortable?* Before committing to an answer, there are a few caveats for the response. First, the place you identify must be specific, meaning it must have a GPS coordinate. So if you love the atmosphere of coffee

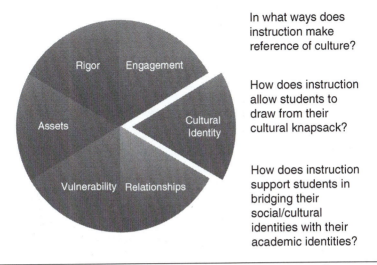

In what ways does instruction make reference of culture?

How does instruction allow students to draw from their cultural knapsack?

How does instruction support students in bridging their social/cultural identities with their academic identities?

Figure 3.6 The BIG six themes: *Cultural Identity*

shops like me as an inspiration for your thinking, you have to name a particular coffee shop for which you could provide the name and address. Second, it has to be a social environment – i.e. an environment where there are other people and you have to have some interaction with them. (That rules out the cottage on a private beach somewhere on a South Pacific island.)

Thinking about this particular place where you are most comfortable in the whole world, consider what specifically it is about that environment that makes you comfortable. Be as precise as possible because there are valuable clues in those details about your identities. After thinking about the particular elements of the environment that support your comfort in that space, think about what would have to change about that environment in order for you to feel less comfortable. It is in these answers that insights are available to us about the essence of our cultural identities.

I have heard a range of responses to this thought experiment. I personally have several ways I can answer the question myself, but my favorite is probably Yankee Stadium. I am an unapologetically obnoxious, die-hard fan of the 27-time World Champion New York Yankees! (This feels like a good time to remind you that the Yankees have won more championships than your favorite team, so ponder that for a moment before you continue reading...) I've loved the

Yankees since I was a kid growing up in the Bronx, but as an adult, one of the reasons that Yankee Stadium makes my list is because I have gone to countless games with my son; and there, together, we have had some of our most important and intimate conversations. In Yankees Stadium, we are surrounded by people like us who share the same passion for the Pinstripes, and we have a tremendous amount of familiarity not only with the routines and customs of a Major League Baseball game, but we also share a distinct historical perspective with our fellow Yankee fans. At Yankees Stadium, I can talk to almost anyone because there is a shared text available for us, and as Yankees fans, we all have a perspective that we can reasonably expect to resonate with others.

For my son and I in particular, I feel most like a Dad at Yankee Stadium, and I know my son feels his identity as a son especially saliently there, as well. I make no apologies for essentially brainwashing my kid to be a Yankees fan. Some of his earliest memories are of us wearing our matching Yankees jerseys and hats to watch a game together. A large part of the blueprint for our relationship was sketched at Yankees games, and now – even in his early 20's – that is one of our most cherished pastimes together. I've given some of my best fatherly advice at Yankees Stadium, and I've done some of my best listening there too. We've gone to games together when our relationship was not functioning very well, but Yankees Stadium is the place where we could always get back on the same page. I now believe that our sense of certainty in what we can expect from the space is a strong facilitating factor in that.

You may have answered the question differently. I've heard many people talk about book stores or churches or dog parks. The most frequent answer I get – especially from women – is home. I'll usually look for the chance to push the specificity of their reasoning by asking for a particular event or time when one could come to their home and observe their comfort. Many people will tell me about weekend dinners when their family is gathered. When further asked why they feel so comfortable in those weekend dinners at home with their family (or in any place they've named), the answers are worded differently but remarkably similar in essence. In the spaces that people name as their most comfortable places in the world, people say they are comfortable because they know the rules. They know how people are expected to show up, and they feel as though they can act like themselves without having to worry about being judged unfairly. If you think about the spaces where you are most comfortable, you may feel similarly. If so, you likely understand context and subtext in those spaces differently than an outsider might because you are familiar with the specific and unique history of the space. That means you get the meaning of the conversation there on levels beyond merely the literal. If you think about it, that means that you are smarter and funnier in those spaces. This is where you share threads of inside jokes so much so that you often don't even have to explicitly deliver a punch line to draw laughter from others. You are smarter here not only because you feel "less judged" but because you are more familiar with the concepts shared by others who have identities also anchored in those spaces. In your most comfortable place in the whole world, you have greater cultural fluency, and your familiarity with the "social reality" is more finely developed. We feel most like ourselves in the spaces where we have the strongest connections to the social realities and the constructions of our selves (i.e. our identities) therein.

When I ask people what would have to change for them to feel less comfortable in the spaces they've named, the answer I most often hear is something about a person who isn't familiar with the norms joining the social space or someone who enters the space with real or perceived hostile intentions. (Many women have mentioned that a visit from their mother-in-law to a weekend dinner might make them less comfortable, in which case they would feel more judged. That's no shade to mother-in-laws around the world. I'm just reporting the data I've collected.)

Cultural Identity is the feeling of belonging to a group. It is part of a person's self-conception and self-perception and is related to race, ethnicity, religion, nationality, language, gender, social class, generation, locality, or any kind of social group that has its own distinct cultural norms (Bransford, Brown, & Cocking, 2000). It's important, however, to level-set our definitions of both culture and identity as separate constructs before we come back to understanding how the theme of Cultural Identity informs our Equity work. Let's start with culture.

Culture

Edward B. Tylor (1832–1917), considered to be the one of the founders of the field of anthropology, was quoted as saying that "Culture is that complex whole which includes knowledge, belief, art, morals, law, custom, and any other capabilities and habits acquired by man as a member of society" (Tylor, 1871, p. 1). In the present day, culture is commonly understood to mean the shared norms, values, habits of living, customs, beliefs, and ways of knowing that moderate human interactions and are transmitted from one generation to the next. As the term and our understanding of it has evolved in the various social science fields, culture has come to be recognized as the very lens through which we experience our humanity. Your perception of the world, your capacity for meaning-making, the very ways in which you recognize and understand truth is a reflection of your cultural indoctrinations (Browne, 2008).

In defining culture, it is probably better that we think in terms of that which is cultural (e.g. cultural norms; cultural spaces; cultural understandings; cultural references, etc.) than to try to confine our definition to a static, rigid entity. We experience culture as a dynamic, meaning-making process that informs us as to what is and is not appropriate (in terms of language, behaviors, and beliefs) in any given social space. It is a process through which we trade on previously developed concepts and understandings in the social spaces we inhabit to interpret meaning in the interactions we have with other human beings. Culture is an idea that must be handled with great responsibility or it can otherwise become easy to dismiss another's cultural vantage point because of one's own cultural sense of judgment of right and wrong or good and bad. In the effort to understand how culture influences the work of Equity in schools, I find it helpful to think of culture in terms of narratives, scripts, and affects.

Cultural Narratives are shared accounts of connected events – real or imagined – presented either in written or spoken language, images or tropes that hold meaning for members of a cultural group. Research from both the social sciences and the cognitive sciences suggest that humans in all cultures come to cast their own identities in recognition and alignment with some sort(s) of narrative themes and/or form (Fireman, McVay, & Flanagan, 2003; Collins, 2015). In both the literal and figurative sense, narrative is a form of storytelling. Narratives give context to consciousness by directing our understanding of how to perceive events and personality types. Our conscious experiences are subsumed by the narratives we construct with other humans and employ as frames of reference for meaning-making, memory, and self-identity. Cultural narratives illustrate values and convey life-meaning through morals and the portrayal of certain character types. Narratives function as conduits for concepts and are well known in specific cultural spaces. The familiarity with their themes and characters become tools and signals in the expression of cultural fluency. To the extent which one is familiar with the narratives of a cultural group, the more or less legitimate their identity under that cultural banner is thought to be.

Cultural Scripts are patterns and styles of speaking characteristic of a given speech community which cannot be satisfactorily described (let alone explained) in purely behavioral and/or linguistic terms; rather, they constitute a tacit conceptual system of "cultural rules" that embody norms governing specific groups' forms of communication (Goddard & Wierzbicka, 1997). In addition to the transmission of literal meanings, the norms of communication within any given speech community reveal what cultural insiders see as core values and beliefs commonly held among those sharing the identity. The validity of a cultural script depends on its symbolic power, accuracy, and enactment to cultural insiders. Understanding the cultural scripts of groups with which one lacks fluency can be challenging because it requires that you are able to suspend the narratives and scripts with which you have been culturally indoctrinated.

Cultural Affects inform our perception and expression of emotion in specific social contexts. Though all humans are emotional beings, the ways in which we demonstrate our emotions are a function of our social and cultural indoctrinations, which means that our expression of emotions is neither culturally neutral nor socially objective. Mary Helen Immordino-Yang's (2010) research considers the neurobiology of social emotions and helps us to better understand how emotion underscores human social interactions including cognitive processes such as how one might regard the human qualities and identity traits one finds admirable (Immordino-Yang, McColl, Damasio, & Damasio, 2009; Azevedo, Macaluso, Avenanti, Santangelo, Cazzato, & Aglioti,

2013). Our biology and sociality intertwine to shape the perceptions of our experiences. There is growing agreement within the cognitive science community that the expression and even the construction of emotions are not hardwired cognitive processes preloaded from birth into the human brain but rather the result of social and cultural indoctrinations within social groups (Bandura, 2002b; Immordino-Yang & Fischer, 2009). We learn how to feel; and we are socialized into a social and emotional understanding of how others are likely to feel given the ways in which we read the social environment and make unconscious predictions through our brain's categorizing of concepts and precepts filtered through our prior experiences. We also know every human thought, conscious and nonconscious, elicits emotion. Affect informs every aspect of our thinking (Barrett, 2017b) including the ways in which we infer the mental states of others, language, memory, cognitive representations of the self, and face-recognition (Rule, Freeman, & Ambady, 2013).

Nearly everything about how we as humans think and feel is molded by and through our cultural indoctrinations, which literally starts at birth when the brain is besieged by a world of new information that is calibrated over time to calculate and regulate one's interpretations of the meaning of the social environment and the appropriateness of one's expressions therein. If culture is the set of norms and shared understandings that govern human interactions in specific social spaces, cultural fluency is the ability to understand how signals will be read and registered in various social settings by cultural insiders. Cultural fluency is one's ability to send signals that can be read with accuracy and understanding by others with similar cultural fluencies (Rule, Freeman, & Ambady, 2013). Tapping into cultural fluencies is a function of one's familiarity with cultural narratives, scripts, and affects.

The Iceberg Metaphor

My colleagues and I at New York University's Metropolitan Center for Research on Equity and the Transformation of Schools regularly referred to Edward T. Hall's Cultural Iceberg Model (1976; see Figure 3.7) to describe the construct of culture because it is too often understood in a narrow and biased light. Any oceanographer will tell

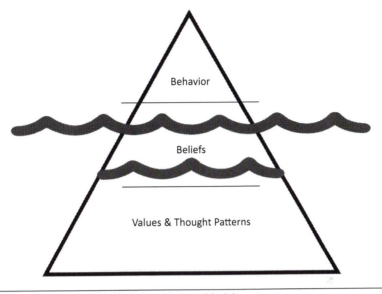

Behavior

Beliefs

Values & Thought Patterns

Figure 3.7 Edward T. Hall's Cultural Iceberg Model

you that only about one-eighth of an iceberg is visible above the water line. The iceberg metaphor is useful because it helps to illustrate that culture is both a matter of styles and surface appearances, and also much deeper ideologies that form the basis of core belief systems. Similarly, the scope and depth of our cultural identities are not easily defined through the characteristics immediately observed by sight and sound.

At the tip of the iceberg, we think of the three F's: food, fashion, and festivities... This is the surface aesthetic of culture. These include things like dress, music, visual arts, drama, crafts, dance, literature, language, and games. These are aspects of culture that are explicit, visible, and taught fairly easily. These elements of culture are fun and interesting, but if we limit our understanding of culture to the surface domain, we run the risk of subscribing to a *heroes and holidays* approach to cultural awareness. That's cool, I guess – but it's thin and ultimately unfulfilling. I call this surface level the *symbolic domain* of culture because it is the home to the symbols of culture though the full meaning of those symbols may not be apparent to the uninformed eye.

Just below the surface of the cultural iceberg is the space of unspoken rules. This is the area where implicit understandings influence behaviors. I call this area of the cultural iceberg the *comportmental domain* because it's where the interpretations of and social metrics for mediating conduct and expressions within the range of human emotion are developed. In other words, this is the space where the significance and meaning of interpersonal behavior is defined. Notions like courtesy, conversational patterns, concepts of time, personal space, rules of conduct, facial expressions, nonverbal communication, body language, touching, eye contact, concepts of beauty, courtship practices... are all social notions that are familiar to people from every cultural group in every kind of cultural space on the planet – but the ways in which these are operationalized and the understanding of the preferred and appropriate expressions of each is absolutely cultural. The behaviors and the beliefs that underscore them are an expression of these notions in the *comportmental domain* and defined by the group's social norms.

At the deepest level of the iceberg metaphor are the unconscious rules of culture. These are the habits, assumptions, understandings, values, and judgments that we know but do not or cannot articulate. I call this the *visceral domain* of culture because it's where social group members are indoctrinated to feel certain ways based on beliefs and thought patterns that have been shared over many generations within the group. It isn't easy to explain this deepest level of the cultural iceberg, but I often think in terms of the "Nana test" to help define how these beliefs inform our identities. The "Nana test" is when you refer, consciously or nonconsciously, to your sense of whether Nana (your beloved grandmother) would approve of a thought or behavior. The "Nana test" draws on our deepest understandings of right and wrong, good and bad, acceptable and unacceptable. At this level of the cultural iceberg, we consider notions like tone of voice, preference for competition or cooperation, attitudes toward elders and dependents, concept of cleanliness, notions of maturity and adolescence, nature of friendships, patterns of group decision-making, conceptions of past and future, and definitions of obscenity. These are the attitudes and ways of thinking that we see as representative of cultural groups' indoctrinations.

Taken together, these dimensions of culture – symbolic, comportmental, and visceral – provide the prism through which we make sense of the world and our lived experiences. One's perception of opportunities, one's capacity for meaning-making, one's sense of self in relation to others is a function of social and cultural indoctrination. Culture reflects the ways in which people give priorities to goals, how they behave in different situations, and how they cope with their world and with one another. People experience their social environment through their cultural lens – meaning our understandings of fairness, and how we're received, our perceptions of others as being kind or unkind, and whether or not we view an opportunity as worthy of our physical, emotional, and intellectual investment are all a function of cultural indoctrinations. Further, and this is important, culture is fluid and dynamic; and we are all multicultural beings in one way or another. We read cues in different social spaces that guide us as to what aspects of our cultural identities are useful in demonstrating competencies and belonging. While it may be argued that there are abiding shared experiences and characteristics of specific cultural groups, all cultures evolve over time. The evolution is most easily seen in the styles expressed at the surface level, but change occurs at every level of the iceberg.

The Responsible Use of Culture

The subject of culture, in order to be a useful tool for supporting the design of learning experiences that close Equity gaps, must be handled with a certain responsibility. If, for example, your goals in understanding culture are to isolate the deficits of specific groups so as to teach more effectively, you are unlikely to be as successful as you will if your intentions are to learn more about the habits and attitudes that support the well-being of cultural-group insiders. Another culture can only be understood from one's own cultural perspective, and the examination of cultural others with an eye toward deficits is more likely to yield stereotyped notions and discourses that classify the problems of opportunity and achievement gaps as endemic to specific cultural groups – though we are generally unlikely to associate such deficits with an immutable, inherent characteristic of our own social groups. And further, through a deficit lens, there is a tendency to conflate culture with condition – as in the myth of the culture of poverty, a long-debunked assortment of stereotypes that explains generational poverty as a function of the habits, attitudes, and beliefs of low-income people (Gorski, 2012). The inclination to understand culture through a deficit lens doesn't uncover promising practices for rigorous and engaging pedagogy. Rather, it will feed deficit ideologies and the misdirected policies that further exacerbate race- and class-based inequities in America's public schools.

Chimanade Adiche (2009) gave a brilliant TedTalk titled "The danger of the single story" – a must-see for all interested in this work – in which she warns against minimizing the identities and indoctrinations of others when they seem unfamiliar to our own. I understand Adiche's counsel to also mean that we teachers should be careful to not try to use culture as a predictive tool. Predictions about the behaviors and beliefs of others based on an assumed understanding of cultural ways of being is dangerous. It leads to thinly constructed narratives of what are in reality rich, multi-layered stories. While culture should not be employed as a predictive device, it is a powerful descriptive tool, one that can be used to understand the nuanced ways in which people interpret and experience their environments. Students who feel reduced to a single story are unlikely to trust us enough to engage in the risk of truly rigorous learning. The greatest risk, of course, with relation to stereotypes is the fear of confirming others' worst possible assumptions about one's own identity groups.

In our work with students, we need to be able to understand how culture mediates a continuum of perspectives; and yet, we must also remember that all human beings have individual agency to color outside of the cultural lines. I've found it helpful to think of culture as a tool that doesn't so much anticipate how people will act... rather, it's more about what themes, references, and experiences – individual and shared – inform peoples' perceptions. The key to using culture as a tool in engineering powerful and effective teaching and learning experiences for students is to embrace nuances, explore the breadth of stories within the group, and actively avoid unintentionally restricting the expression of students' identities with our own limiting stereotypes of them.

Identity

Because culture affects how people learn, remember, reason, solve problems, and communicate, it is part and parcel of students' intellectual and social identity development; and thus understanding how aspects of culture may vary within and between student populations sheds light on variations in how students learn. A deep knowledge of cultural identity helps us to understand how behaviors are constructed and interpreted given the baseline beliefs and experiences – personal and collective – that inform them. With this understanding, we are ultimately better able to provide students with the tools and learning experiences needed to fully develop themselves as productive thinkers.

In the simplest terms, identity is one's sense of and perception of self. Identity is determined both from within and without – meaning that as a species, humans have come to self-perceive on conscious and nonconscious levels by how the world responds to us and the characteristics that come to most frequently describe us. Cultural identity includes such measures as race, ethnicity, sex, gender, age, class, language, and ability; but it isn't rigidly limited by them. All of these parts of ourselves are always present, and they guide how we consciously and nonconsciously deduce meaning from the events and circumstances of life. Cultural identity is a function of the experiences we've had individually and the perspectives we are likely to share with persons of similar cultural backgrounds. Our cultural identities are formed in the context of our social group memberships (Alexander, 2012). It is who we are in specific social spaces. It encompasses the social tools and mental devices (i.e. thought patterns, familiarity with cultural narratives) we use to engage the opportunities available to us in those spaces. If you accept the premise that identity is a function of what you can do, where you do it, and with whom it is done, we can see that all of us are in some way multicultural beings. We are constantly reading the cultural signals of the social environments we're in to determine the meaning of things happening around us while we also mediate the manner in which we can communicate our meaning (Nisbett, 2003; Chiao, & Ambady, 2007).

I've discussed how engaged learning always bears some risk. Learning means, quite literally, opening ourselves to new ideas and new ways of thinking which might undermine some certainties we hold relative to others. In order to invest oneself in any social space, one must trust that the effort given will not betray one's core values and also that the risks taken are likely to yield some beneficial end. Thus, learning depends on trust that the ground will not give way beneath us, trust that effort is worthwhile, trust for teachers, and trust for our fellow learners in a learning community. We all draw on our cultural fluencies and emotional concepts to determine when and with whom we feel safe enough to trust another person. Importantly, trust is a two-sided coin; where you feel as though the persons around you are trustworthy, you too are more trustworthy to others. Trust and agency are symbiotic: they allow for metacognition, relationships, rigor, engagement, and the development of academic identity. I've observed that brilliant teachers possess a certain kind of *trust literacy* – meaning they are able to read the emotional economy in their classrooms so that they can earn and employ the trust of students in the interest of their engagement. Many teachers know and do this intuitively, but it should be an explicit goal of effective instruction because trust is an enormous consideration of Equity.

Some students, given their social and cultural backgrounds, come with fluencies and capital that are more likely to be steeped within the dominant indoctrinations of the hegemonic authority and thus more highly regarded by the school. These students, given the social and cultural consistencies between their social background and the environs of school, are more likely to trust the processes and adults in schools and are more likely to be seen as trustworthy themselves in turn. And let's not shy away from an explicit reference to race on this point. If/when one's racial identity seems to be an obstacle to trust and/or in conflict with the pursuit of academic achievement, the effort necessary to perform successfully is fundamentally and profoundly undermined. If/when someone believes that they must mute their racial- and/or ethnic identity in order to be successful in school, then even if/when someone accepts those terms, they can never be as brilliant as they might otherwise because they are only drawing from limited aspects of themselves in the effort to achieve.

Cultural Identity is a massive and fluid concept. By dint of mission, the practices of Culturally Responsive Education should affirm students' sense of selves by bridging their cultural and academic identities. In learning experiences that are culturally responsive, students should not have to choose between the two. This is an essential goal of CRE because if a student does not experience these parts of themself as being in synch – or worse, if they experience their cultural-self to be in conflict with their academic-self, it will be more difficult for them to make sense of the opportunities available to them and further to justify the investments which school asks of them (Norton, 2005). When leveraging the theme of Cultural Identity in the consideration of learning experiences for students, I ask questions like: In what ways does instruction make reference of culture? How does instruction allow students to draw from their cultural knapsack? How does instruction support students in bridging their social/cultural identities with their academic identities?

Relationships

Shortly before her death in 2013, Dr. Rita Pierson gave a classic TedTalk that magnificently captures that indomitable spirit of great teachers, that undeniable chutzpah which insists through persistent beliefs and good practices that students sign on to the highest view of themselves. It's something we all want to do for our students. In terms of Relationships (see Figure 3.8), I've been struck many times by the language that students use when describing the teachers they trust. They'll say things like: "I don't do Ms. So-and-So's work, but I do my

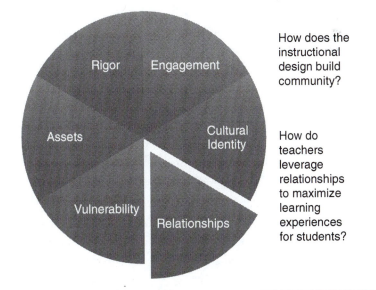

Figure 3.8 The BIG six themes: *Relationships*

work in Ms. So-and-So's class." Have you ever heard that before? What has been increasingly clear to me in my experiences in schools and with students – which also bears out in the research – is that students exposed to the risk factors most predictive of academic underperformance are much more likely than their less-impacted peers to use language which indicates that they learn *for* their teachers as much as they learn *from* them (Skinner & Belmont, 1993; O'Connor, Dearing, & Collins, 2011). It makes sense that relationships are especially vital for students with more exposure to the elements of social, economic, and educational disadvantage because these are the children for whom school is more likely a hope in the unseen rather than a realistic life-goal supported by the resources and experiences of parents and other adults in their out-of-school lives. For them, relationships are the channel through which their investment in school is personalized.

Relationships draw from our authenticity as educators. Interpersonal relationships involve dynamic social exchanges that occur between teachers and students and among students and their peers (Ryan, Stiller, & Lynch, 1994). The most effective teachers leverage dynamic social exchanges best by incorporating their relationship-building efforts in the context of teaching and learning – which affirms for students that they have the right to school, that their school identity can co-exist peacefully with their social, ethnic, racial, and gendered identities, and that meaningful relationships with individuals in school can extend to relationships with academic content, as well.

When I think of Relationships, I envision a triangle (see Figure 3.9). More often than not, we think of the two points representing students and teachers as of paramount importance. The lines between these points represent the reciprocal and interpersonal relationships between students and teachers, the two bound together as part of a larger teaching and learning community. Similarly, we also think of the relationships among students, the sense of shared identity as part of a group engaged in learning facilitated by the teacher. The third point to the relationship triangle also deserves attention – the element of content – or that which we want students to learn. Every credible educator I know would prefer that their students develop deep understandings and mastery over content rather than mere rote memorization for the purpose of immediate recall. This depth of learning

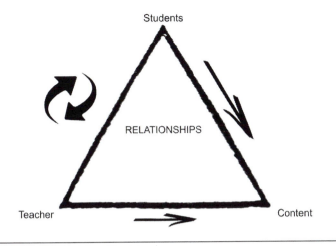

Figure 3.9 The CRE relationships triangle

requires that students enter into a meaningful relationship with the content itself. By that, I mean we want students to think like scientists, historians, and mathematicians. We want students to be able to embody literacies beyond the preparation of essays. We want students to develop a rich appreciation for the creative arts... and so on. In this way, students will be able to transfer and extend the understandings they gain in one content area into multiple others. This is often most profoundly facilitated through the modeling of a relationship with content by teachers. It's why some of the best teachers are the persons who don't hide their unyielding love affair with their content. Students often tease them, but the passion these teachers have for their content is compelling. They are living examples for students for what it means to be lifelong learners.

There is a wealth of research that describes the impact of relationships on the achievement and performance of students. The research on Teacher–Student Relationship Quality or TSRQ shows that teachers who are aligned with the same core values, popular culture, and family traditions are better able to create meaningful learning in the form of personal relevance, prior knowledge, personal experiences, and interests. I don't take this to mean that educators must believe all that our students' communities espouse, but we have to be seen as giving the effort to understand without judgment. The research has shown repeatedly that relationships promote deep understandings, higher-order thinking, the reduction of school-performance anxieties, effective and efficient information processing, and long-term retention in learning (Pajares, 1996; Battistich & Horn, 1997; McLaughlin et al., 2005; Lahey, 2014). The evidence is clear. Relationships matter. Relationships support trust, and while many of us educators harken back to the "good ol' days" when trust in schools was largely assumed, today's students require that we earn their trust through the demonstration of competence, fairness, and integrity – and the best way to do so is through the pathway of relationships (DeSteno, 2014).

To be clear, I am not asking you to be friends with all of your students. I don't even like all the adults I work with... much less the students! But I can assure you that when a student senses your personal dislike for them or your lack of investment in the effort to improve your relationship, they are much less likely to trust you and thus unlikely to work *for* you. Yes, there is emotional labor involved in doing this; and yes, you will have to forgive students in the effort to build relationship. You're a grown-up. You can do it. I often advise teachers to engineer a success for your most reluctant learners that allows for you to reflect with them on how they acted in concert with you and your instructions that led to a win. I want to be forthcoming that this counsel I give to teachers is much less about the actual win than about the opportunity to reflect with students about the win. When done authentically, this can be an effective strategy for renewing unproductive teacher–student relationships. When your students recognize that your guidance and their partnership with you led to their success, they are more likely to invest, or at the very least, they are more likely to reveal the impediments to their success – which then allows you to employ protective factors more meaningfully.

And in some cases, you aren't responsible for the breakdown in relationship between student and school – but if you want to see the student have greater success, you are responsible for restoring what isn't working. In my experiences, these efforts can have a landslide effect, especially when coordinated among adults working in tandem. Success yields future success... and once students internalize through supportive reflection what they have done to contribute to their improved performance, they are much more likely to buy into our vision for them as successful students.

Ultimately, effective instruction is defined by its capacity to support the academic identities of students and also a healthy and productive sense of community for learners. In order to ensure the relevance of the theme of Relationships in the design of learning experiences for students, I give attention to questions like: How does instructional design and coordinated support affirm relationships between students and teachers? Among students? Between students and content? How does the lesson and instructional design further build community in the classroom? How do teachers leverage relationships with (1) highly engaged, (2) moderately engaged, and (3) minimally engaged students to maximize learning experiences?

Vulnerability

In essence, I am concerned with two aspects of our educator practice when I consider this theme of Vulnerability (see Figure 3.10). The first aspect of my concern comes in the form of a question: How do schools become meaningful protective factors for our most vulnerable students? The second aspect of my concern with regard to the theme of Vulnerability is of a more personal nature for each of us as educators. It pertains to our individual willingness to engage our profession whole-heartedly – which in my view requires the deep-seated commitment

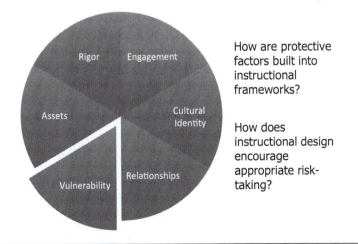

Figure 3.10 The BIG six themes: *Vulnerability*

to confront our own limitations in skill and understanding so that we may evolve into better educators.

Let's first look at the question of, *How do schools become meaningful protective factors for our most vulnerable students?* I have heard lots of well-meaning educators use the language "at-risk" to describe populations of students most statistically likely to underperform academically. I, myself, used to use similar language, but over time, I've come to see the term "at-risk" as problematic for a couple of reasons. My first concern is that it squarely locates the risk within the student, and when we accept the notion that the risks leading to school underperformance inhere in the student, we disavow ourselves of the responsibility and potential for re-directing problematic trends in our schools and society writ large. My second concern is even scarier in that "at-risk" thinking may stain the self-esteem of our most vulnerable students, unwittingly convincing them that they are hopeless and helpless, and thus resigned to a lifetime of disappointment and failure.

I think it's more appropriate to think of risk as a universal human condition. Risk is something to which we are all exposed. Further, all risk is relative. The same circumstances for one person may not qualify as the same level of risk for another given the relative access to supports and resources which may otherwise buffer the impact of the risk. The "at-risk" paradigm, well-meaning as it is, may be interpreted as permission to release schools and society from certain responsibilities in serving children. If we believe that the risk inheres solely in the student, then we aren't responsible as much as they are for the support necessary to improve performance. Further, the at-risk way of thinking may lead us to focus on what we may think of as cultural impediments to school achievement rather than a careful examination for how school and societal structures stack the odds in favor of some and against others. For these reasons, I try to refrain from using the term "at-risk" and rather I will refer to students' "exposure to risk factors." When I'm intentional about referring to risk as something that exists as a function of students' lived experience and not as a result of their own deficit, I am better able to ask and answer what is the most important question: *What protective factors can be provided to mitigate the risk?*

This, of course, begs the question: What are risk factors? Generally speaking, risk factors are circumstances and conditions that we think of as having a mitigating effect on the likelihood for school success. In defining risk factors, I tend to draw from the social science literature which qualifies risk as (1) family background – specifically low education and income level of parents; (2) limited access to social networks that hold economic, relational, and experiential resources; and (3) inconsistent access to high-quality schools and educational services (Centers for Disease Control and Prevention, n.d.).

Family background is a strong predictor of stress and stability or instability within the home environment. Studies have shown repeatedly that the strongest predictors of student success are the mother's educational background and the family's zip code (Wentzel, 2003; Dearing & Tang, 2010; Fan & Williams, 2010; Calarco, 2014; Tang, Davis-Kean, Chen, & Sexton, 2016). Educational background within the family is not only a strong indicator of economic well-being, but more highly educated parents generally have more resources to support their students' learning needs.

Social networks are also an important element in the discussion of Vulnerability. Robert Putnam, in his book *Our Kids: The American Dream in Crisis* (2015), makes a compelling argument that poverty and social disadvantage in America today are increasingly experienced in socioeconomic isolation and segregation. For example, when low-income and/or racial-/ethnic-minority children attend schools largely enrolled by other low-income and/or racial-/ethnic-minority children and also live in communities with very little racial, ethnic, or economic diversity, their social networks and access to resources are severely compromised. They have fewer opportunities to access social networks that hold economic, relational, and experiential resources which allow families to engage social safety nets when threats to school success surface. Further, in our increasingly segregated society, students who go to schools largely attended by other students from high-poverty, low-resource backgrounds are exposed to fewer rigorous and less meaningful learning opportunities with less-qualified and less-experienced educators (Resnick, Bearman, & Blum, 1997; McLoyd, 1998; Yoshikawa, 2013; Putnam, 2015). These schools have higher discipline occurrences and they tend to levy harsher consequences for school behaviors, not uncommonly leading to criminal charges. The schools are often overwhelmed under the circumstances, which further causes students to fall behind their peers in more affluent and better-resourced communities.

Clearly, risk factors confound school achievement, but we shouldn't think of risk as a list of isolated circumstances. Rather, risk is a function of a cross-current of circumstances affecting some groups differently and disproportionately relative to others; and risk exponentially enhances the impact of other risk, so that one risk factor in the presence of a second risk factor is far more impactful than the mere presence of one (seemingly) isolated risk (McGee & Spencer, 2013; Spencer & Swanson, 2013). So Black and Latino students, for example, in America are statistically more likely to live at or below the poverty level, but increasingly we are seeing a growing gap in achievement trends within specific racial and ethnic groups when we control for economic background relative to these identity measures. So while being Black, for example, has historically qualified as a risk factor in school achievement, to be economically poor and Black qualifies as compounded risk when we look to see which factors correlate most strongly with school achievement (Spencer et al., 2006).

Protective factors are a bit easier to explain than risk factors because protective factors are anything that has the potential to effectively mitigate risk. Among the most common mistakes we make in education is the indiscriminate application of what we think are protective factors to risk circumstances that we don't understand well. When we do this, we not only waste time and resources with ineffective supports, but we also further deficitize our students out of frustration when the poorly conceived protective factors miss the mark. We say things like, "these kids don't want to be helped. They won't help themselves." Or, "they don't value education enough to take advantage of the opportunities." These are the frequently referenced arguments of persons who lack the compassion and insight to uncover and engineer protective factors that honor and empower the students and communities we seek to serve. Don't mistake me. I'm not saying it's easy work, but it's the work we've signed on for.

The second aspect of the theme of Vulnerability is of a more personal nature for each of us as educators. It pertains to our individual willingness to engage our profession wholeheartedly – which to me means embracing our own uncertainties and insecurities in the interest of creating the safest and most authentic learning spaces possible for all of our children. To be vulnerable also means to be willing to take the risks to remain a vigilant learner in one's own professional development. The absolute most self-destructive attitude in the profession of teaching is the "I already do that" attitude. It's a poor mental habit that will halt one's growth. Brilliant teachers are consciously vulnerable in their craft because they know that vulnerability begets vulnerability and neither trust nor learning is possible without vulnerability. I am a big fan of Brene Brown's work on vulnerability. You can read and watch any book or talk of hers and be a better human being afterward, but I specifically take her work to mean that when we have personal courage in our willingness to be present and are deliberate in our own growth trajectory, and when we can treat ourselves and others with compassion, we are in a much better position to see better those opportunities we have to facilitate connections for and with students in school. At times these connections are interpersonal and at other times they are conceptual. Whatever the case, connections facilitate engagement.

The task of teaching is to find methods to support students from a range of backgrounds; the notion of risk invites us to consider what circumstances and conditions would otherwise interfere with the instructional support of students. The questions we ask about Vulnerability include: What environmental risk factors does this student face? What protective factors are (or could be) in place to mitigate those risks? How does the lesson and instructional design encourage appropriate risk-taking?

Assets

The theme Assets (see Figure 3.11), as I define it, carries with it an inherent responsibility for the teacher in the 21st-century classroom. This responsibility is two-fold and applies to *every* teacher and particularly those with cultural backgrounds that differ from their students. It is to first actively put in the thoughtful observation and effort to recognize the assets of all of your students, and second, to leverage those

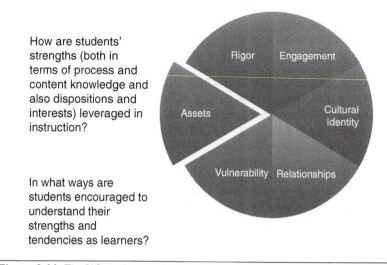

How are students' strengths (both in terms of process and content knowledge and also dispositions and interests) leveraged in instruction?

In what ways are students encouraged to understand their strengths and tendencies as learners?

Figure 3.11 The BIG six themes: *Assets*

assets of your students into the design of learning experiences. Very few people would disagree with that sentiment (and if you do, you are probably a terrible person) but the operationalization of that mindset may seem a bit beyond our sense of self-efficacy.

I would argue, however, that this is well within the skillset of competent teachers; but it requires a mindset that is the result of thoughtful and focused intentionality. Let's begin by defining assets first because it is a much more sophisticated and subjective notion than we may initially assume. I have two ways that I like to think of assets. The first is based on the Habits of Mind, and the other is based on the social science framework of Cultural Capital. Both models work together. The Habits of Mind are a kind of entry point to the consideration of Assets, and the Cultural Capital model is an extension – but both are effective constructs for supporting more deliberate thinking in terms of what we consider in the discussion of students' assets.

In the most general sense, an "asset" is something that is regarded as valuable and accessible for satisfying debts, commitments, or opportunities. In the financial sense, an asset is defined as a resource with economic value that is owned and controlled with the expectation that it will provide future benefit. Assets are accumulated or created to increase the value of the owner's endeavors and operations. An asset can be thought of as something that has the potential to generate currency-earning opportunities in the future, regardless of the nature of any specific industry. The ability to successfully engage students is enhanced through the knowing of their assets and needs in the context of the learning targets and the classroom environment. Importantly (and remember Gloria Ladson-Billings here), brilliant teachers calibrate their pedagogy to maximize engagement without lowering their expectations for students' learning.

The Habits of Mind are a model for thinking about "what intelligent people do when they are confronted with problems, the resolutions to which are not immediately apparent" (Costa & Kallick, 2008). Costa and Kallick explain Habits of Mind as follows:

> A Habit of Mind is a composite of many skills, attitudes, cues, past experiences, and proclivities. It means that we value one pattern of intellectual behaviors over another; therefore, it implies making choices about which patterns we should use at a certain time. It includes sensitivity to the contextual cues that signal that a particular circumstance is a time when applying a certain pattern would be useful and appropriate. It requires a level of skillfulness to use, carry out, and sustain the behaviors effectively. It suggests that after each experience in which these behaviors are used, the effects of their use are reflected upon, evaluated, modified, and carried forth to future applications.
>
> *(Costa & Kallick, 2008)*

I use the 16 Habits of Mind as a teaching tool for both teachers and students. With teachers, I like to use the Habits of Mind to support our planning and reflection of the ways the various aspects of students' personalities show up to support successful performance in school. I also use these Habits to convey directly to students how their gifts and abilities come in a range of attitudes and behaviors. The Habits of Mind remind adults that some of the very attributes that can sometimes annoy us (e.g. humor) are the same qualities that students rely on to support their engagement in difficult learning tasks. Through the Habits, teachers are better able to conceptualize our students' behaviors as expressions of engagement which allow us to know them better as learners. In addition, when students have greater command of their own Habits of Mind, they are more likely to sustain their engagement and also build new Habits more thoughtfully and with intention. The Habits work well within the more general definition of assets as something useful and/or valuable in the effort to meet social and performance commitments.

I am also a fan of the work of Tara Yosso, and in particular, her writing on the Cultural Capital of marginalized communities. When referring to the work of Yosso, I tend to frame assets in the fiscal terms of tools and acquisitions. If assets are resources used to accumulate goods and services, then we can interpret our students' assets more accurately if we consider them as a function of how they're used to accomplish meaningful transactions. (The students, in this case, are of course the arbiters of what is considered meaningful.) Yosso's often-cited article, "Whose culture has capital? A critical race theory discussion of community Cultural wealth" (2005), gives a useful model for conceptualizing the various forms of capital that students from marginalized communities bring with them to school. If we are not thoughtful, these can be dismissed or altogether overlooked by educators and education systems. Yosso identified six types of capital – familial, social, resistance, linguistic, navigational, and aspirational – each with a strong and distinct tradition within communities that have experienced historical oppression and opposition in the collective and individual pursuit of freedom and opportunity.

Yosso reminds us to be mindful of how school norms for the expectations of attitudes and behaviors are situated against a White, middle-class norm. The notion of Cultural Capital, then, if not clarified and discussed thoughtfully, could be weaponized against non-White communities as assertions of cultural deficits. In her words:

> This interpretation of Bourdieu exposes White, middle class culture as the standard, and therefore all other forms and expressions of 'culture' are judged in comparison to this 'norm'. In other words, cultural capital is not just inherited or possessed by the middle class, but rather it refers to an accumulation of specific forms of knowledge, skills and abilities that are valued by privileged groups in society.
>
> *(Yosso, 2005, p. 76)*

In Yosso's model, for example, resistance may be thought of as a form of Cultural Capital if the resistance is framed in a social narrative of historical oppression and marginalization. Resistance can be understood in the context of cultural tradition as agency and an unwillingness to endorse systems that have been effective largely in producing inequality. (I've found this awareness immensely useful to me in responding to disruptive classroom behaviors. It makes it much easier for me to not take the offending behaviors personally and to place them in a larger narrative.) Yosso's six types of capital, and also the Habits of Mind, can be thought of as currencies in the classroom. They are the tools, attitudes, and skillsets that students use to successfully participate in life and learning transactions; and just like in the financial sense, capital is an asset, and assets are used to successfully participate in transactions, both financial and social.

Our students use their assets to be successful in school. If a student is not invested in the purpose of school (i.e. they don't find formal education to be meaningful), they are likely to use their assets to disengage from or even disrupt the proceedings of school. Seeing their assets, however, rather than merely seeing that which you perceive as their deficits, is essential for being able to facilitate an enduring investment in their academic identities. It is difficult for anyone to sustain an investment in any social space or in developing any part of our identity if we are unable to see how the assets we've already accumulated can be useful to our well-being in new territories. Our assets show up most clearly when we are seeking to participate successfully in some (social, financial, or other) transaction. Thinking about it this way, it can be argued that the best times to learn about students' assets – and especially our most vulnerable students' assets – is when they feel as though they are in conflict. I have learned in my work with kiddos of all ages that I am much more likely to be successful in my transactions with them when I make the decision in my own mind that they are asset-filled beings and much more than what I may perceive as the sum total of their deficits. This doesn't mean I ignore their risk factors and vulnerabilities. Those are real considerations in my thinking as well, but I am much more inclined to secure effective strategies from my toolkit when I set the intention to see my students as being capable and competent in specific ways (Moll, Amanti, Neff, & Gonzalez, 1992; Sternberg, 2000). In terms of planning, a nuanced understanding of my students' assets allows me to build in opportunities for them to use their tools and strengths to deepen their engagement in learning experiences. We get more from our kiddos when we plan with their assets in mind.

But there is a caution. It has two facets. The first is that we must be careful to not stereotype. Race and ethnicity are big parts of a lot of Americans' identities; and yet, no one person is exclusively understood in terms of either race or ethnicity. The theme of Assets reminds us to see students as unique while also allowing for the space to think about how race may be a contributing factor to their perception of opportunity. Given that we Americans are all products of a society that was established on the premises of White supremacy ideologies, I think it's wise to avoid the outright dismissal of race and racism as a contributing factor at the level of root causes for any pattern or particular instance of underperformance (Hanley & Noblit, 2009). Yet, our students are not beholden to any single racial template for their identity. Everyone has the agency to determine their own relationship with their race/ethnicity.

The second caution is that our ability to recognize the assets of others is a function of our own cultural fluencies and indoctrinations. As cultural beings, we learn concepts by comparing them to concepts with which we are already familiar (Barrett, 2017a; Hofstadter, 2001; Hofstadter & Sander, 2013). We all learn this way. We understand new concepts either through direct experience or from our ability to analogously combine and/or extend previously developed conceptual understandings to comprise a newly constructed understanding. If we think of assets as a type of concept, that means that our students may hold or express some assets that fall beyond our own scope of cultural understanding. I use a few examples to illustrate this point in my work with teachers. My favorite one is based on the Oxygen Network show *Snapped! Snapped!*, in its 23rd season at the time of writing, which is a true-crime television series that is nearly always about women who murder (or arrange for the murder of) their husbands, boyfriends, or lovers. Whenever I bring the show up in professional development spaces, I like to pause to see the (often simultaneously guilty and gleeful) look of recognition in the faces of women in the room. Some people have never heard of the show while others are enthusiastic (issuing out high-fives) when I ask for someone to describe for the rest of us the *Snapped!* premise.

I use *Snapped!* to make a point about perspective in the recognition of assets. Most (nearly all) women will agree that murder is a bad behavior – even when it comes to an ex-lover. And yet, the experience of being a woman – in a patriarchal society where sexism impacts the lives of women as a group and individually – creates certain common frames of reference for people who share the cultural identity of women. Most women (nearly all) have experienced the micro- and macro-assaults of misogyny. Most women (nearly all) have been made to feel unsafe in the presence of a man. Most women (nearly all) have had the experience of having their ideas dismissed or diminished by a man. Sometimes in my presentations, I will ask women if they can think of one really confident and really stupid man who objectifies or treats them as if they are inferior in some way. I ask them not to name names but it almost always appears to me as though all of the women are able to grasp the concept (though many men in the room often seem to want an expedited point forthcoming at this juncture).

The experience of being a women under patriarchy makes the premise of the show *Snapped!* possible. The show can only draw viewers if the weekly protagonists' humanity is relatable. Otherwise, it would be a show about monsters, and it would terrify us to know that these sociopaths live among us killing enough men to provide the producers of *Snapped!* with more than 20 seasons' worth of murderous content! The show only works because the primary viewing audience (which I assume to be mostly women) collectively draws from a set of concepts, experiences, and a shared identity that doesn't endorse the bad behavior of murder but is informed by a frame of experiential and conceptual reference that allows a person to reasonably understand the protagonists' thought processes. A woman is likely to watch that show and say: *She shouldn't have murdered him... but why do men do such ugly things?* And in other cases, we may even see the act of murder as defensible, but only if we relate strongly enough with their social perspective to see how the accused was, in effect, drawing on assets to achieve some meaningful end.

We contextualize in these ways all the time, and it shows up in how we consciously and nonconsciously measure the assets of our students. If we share a common frame of reference – that is, similar cultural fluencies and indoctrinations – we are more likely to understand their actions and the motivations for their actions. When you have a greater capacity for understanding, you see better how assets may be applied (or misapplied). We are wise to remind ourselves that our perceptions of our students' assets are centered around our own experiences, indoctrinations, and fluencies. The awareness of this makes us more competent in our interactions with students. In order to give appropriate consideration to the theme of Assets, I like to consult questions like: How are students' strengths (both in terms of process and content knowledge and also dispositions and interests) leveraged in instruction? In what ways are students encouraged to understand their strengths and tendencies as learners?

Rigor

While all of the CRE themes build on and support each other, I especially think of Rigor (see Figure 3.12) and Engagement as sister (or maybe bookend) themes in this framework. It is not possible to effect authentic rigor without engagement; and conversely, it is not possible to say that students are authentically engaged – especially not cognitively engaged – in the absence of rigor... and yet, rigor is often misunderstood by educators. As a theme, the essential importance of Rigor

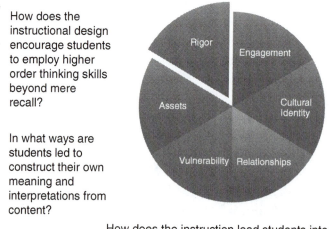

How does the instructional design encourage students to employ higher order thinking skills beyond mere recall?

In what ways are students led to construct their own meaning and interpretations from content?

How does the instruction lead students into stretching their understanding of content?

Figure 3.12 The BIG six themes: *Rigor*

is clear. Whatever we do in instruction with students, whatever ways in which we frame and deliver their opportunities to learn – what we offer in the content of the experience must be substantive and meaningful. It must be relevant and it must be rigorous. Learning that is rigorous is more interesting than that which is rote.

Though I loved teaching high-school English and I experienced success as a classroom teacher, I do not hesitate in admitting that my understanding of rigor then was limited. (I'm admitting that knowing that I am far from alone). Many conflate rigor with "difficult," but that can't possibly be true because I can make any learning experience more difficult for students simply by giving them incomplete or incoherent directions. Others misunderstand rigor to be a function of volume. That too fails in its explanation because to give students many opportunities to learn without ensuring that their thinking will yield the most desired understandings actually defeats the instructional purpose by reinforcing misconceptions.

I've used a few tools to facilitate discussions about rigor in my work as a technical assistance and professional development provider. All of these tools have value. The two resources I used to use most were Norman Webb's Depth of Knowledge (DOK) and Bloom's Taxonomy. But then I found the work of Karin Hess, and I became a much more effective communicator of the concept (Hess, Jones, Carlock, & Walkup, 2009a; Hess, Carlock, Jones, & Walkup, 2009b). Bloom's Taxonomy is standard learning in just about every graduate school teacher-training program. It does exactly what taxonomies do: it categorizes. In this case, it categorizes types of thinking or the mental processes through which we expect students will learn. It helps us to consider how students will be asked to think in terms of remembering, understanding, applying, analyzing, evaluating, and creating (which is represented as the pinnacle of the taxonomy). Norman Webb's DOK wheel is a great tool too. It speaks to the complexity of thinking we want for students inside of learning experiences. It highlights four "levels of thought" (i.e. DOK levels); these levels are (1) recall, (2) skills and concepts, (3) strategic thinking, and (4) extended thinking. In the descriptions of these levels, words like "design, critique, and prove" are the guidance offered for teachers in terms of what extended thinking should look like in the learning of students.

Both Bloom's Taxonomy and Webb's DOK levels have well-known graphs which represent the big ideas behind the models, but I've found that when teachers study these graphs without also reading the accompanying literature, the tools end up lacking a certain clarity and direction for implementation. Hess' Cognitive Rigor Matrix (CRM) is a happy (research-based) marriage of Bloom's and Webb's work with a graphic that effectively captures the integrity of the ideas in play. That isn't to say that teachers shouldn't read the literature which introduces the CRM, but through the CRM graphs, it's made clear that rigor is a function of both type and complexity of thought. Specifically, in the CRM, the type (Bloom's) of thought targeted is also aligned with a level of complexity (DOK) so that teachers can plan for both as targets for students' thinking.

Rigor is a CRE theme because it allows students to extend their understandings in rich and complex ways so that they are able to leverage their in- and out-of-school competencies in deep learning. It is often a paradigm shift for teachers, but we must think more specifically of rigorous instruction to mean that students will be able to own their learning in such a powerful way that teachers themselves can't even predict exactly where it will go – and that must be the goal of rigor, or it isn't an exercise in rigor but rather one in regurgitation.

Let me make the point this way: Do a Google search for the article "What exactly do 'fewer, clearer, and higher standards' really look like in the classroom?" (2009). The article itself explains the rationale for the CRM and also describes a study of the evidence of rigor in a survey of students' work. In the article, Hess et al. (2009b) present the original version of the CRM. In any cell on the matrix, the description of the task represents a corresponding type and level of thinking. Look at the far left column of the matrix and take note of the descriptions of the Bloom's Revised Taxonomy of Cognitive Process Dimensions. Then look at the listing of Webb's DOK levels across the top row. Now carefully read a few of the boxes in the DOK level 4 column, extended thinking. Skim up and down the fourth column. Study closely one or two of the boxes you read, and think about your own students or students you know well... What would it look like, sound like, and feel like if your students were thinking just as described in those DOK level 4 cells?

In any case that I can imagine, if my students are thinking in the ways described in the DOK-4 column, they are cognitively engaged. And what's more, if they are thinking in these ways, they are in the unique position to extend their understandings of the academic content and concepts by finding meaning through and/or with concepts that they have previously learned – either in school or social spaces. That means they are able to construct their understandings and also perform them based in part on how they represent what they are learning through some combination of the academic and cultural concepts with which they are already familiar. If we are able to develop learning experiences in which students can further bridge their concepts, that means all students are given fairer opportunities to draw on previous domains of reference for building and extending understandings. This is inherently more equitable than learning experiences that fall short of this goal.

This is a vitally important element of the CRE mental model. In so many classrooms, teachers are inclined to bring less rigor to instruction in the effort to make the learning more accessible, and too often students seem to be more manageable behaviorally when we ask them to do less difficult work. Our students can become conditioned to low-rigor expectations. This is the "I did my work" mindset of our students. When students don't have strongly developed academic identities, they will often offer mindless compliance in exchange for lessons that don't seem too hard to do. But Rigor is a CRE theme because when students have meaningful opportunities to bring what they know to support new learning, they have more dynamic cognitive experiences. My contention (which is based in and backed up by cognitive science) is that the go-to approach for creating greater engagement in any learning experience is to make it more rigorous. Less rigor signals to students that they aren't required to make a full investment in order to meet the success criteria. More rigor compels students to fully own their learning because they are the only ones who can make all the connections possible within the fabric of an understanding. If you really think about this, though, it's frightening to a lot of teachers... because the only way this kind of student ownership of learning is possible is if the teacher relinquishes control. Look again at the CRM in any cell in the DOK-4 column. If our students are thinking this way, they are in full control. You are a facilitator at that point, but it is them steering the wheel.

To know that authentic rigor must be owned by the thinker themselves has helped me to consider a different metric for high-rigor moments than I had previous to my exposure to the CRM. I now measure rigor in part through my students coming up with some evidence or connection or insight that I had never considered before because it is specific to their unique conceptual schema. It is precisely those moments in which we can feel assured that our students are so engaged that they are searching through all aspects of their identities for the relevant conceptual references. That is exactly what I think of when I say culturally responsive learning experiences bridge identities. To express what students are coming to understand in a formal academic space by drawing on the concepts they have as part of their cultural identities means that kiddos can be successful in school *because* of who they are outside of school. Their identity is an asset to their learning. These are the conscious and nonconscious elements of sustained engagement, investment, and commitment to successful effort, all of which support an authentic possession of an academic identity. Without opportunities to leverage their cultural identities in school, many students will struggle to justify the risk asked of them in academic learning because it's inherently inequitable when some kids get to draw on their cultural fluencies to prove competence and others do not.

In fact, I agree with those who argue that a focus on rigor is the best strategy for addressing classroom behavior problems. Whenever I plan for classrooms with disruptive behaviors, we plan for the highest possible rigor targets, and we get to the rigor super early too! In some cases, we've even set up the learning experiences so that the students have to watch the directions we've pre-recorded on the classroom shared web spaces so that they don't have to wait for us at all to get started. If we plan well, they will watch the video and start to get excited about the learning experience because they begin to feel the challenge and also the opportunities they will have to draw from their own social and cultural knapsacks. Students are most often likely to feel this as surges of creativity.

Earlier, I referred to Rigor and Engagement as sister or bookend themes. Rigor is the flip side of the engagement coin. True rigor is not possible without the cognitive engagement of students. In this way, cognitive engagement and rigor generate and reinforce each other. Neither is possible without the other. We can look at either as an entry point, but the consideration of one without careful attention to the other will fail to yield the consistently desired learning outcomes. In thinking about Rigor, I refer to these questions to guide me in operationalizing it as a theme into learning experiences for students: How does the instructional design encourage students to employ higher-order thinking skills beyond mere recall? In what ways are students led to construct their own meaning and interpretations from content? How does the instruction lead students into stretching their understandings of content?

What Does This Work Requires of Us?

I love to be in the presence of brilliant teachers, and in my observations, I have become convinced that these brilliant teachers have developed their mindset beyond some simple algorithm for practice. Through a great deal of hard work, focused reflection, and practiced analytical skills, these teachers whom I think of as brilliantly responsive have constructed a mindset which strikes me as equal parts expression of insight and practice of observable methods and tools. These are teachers who reflect with rigor and reason and a palpable sense of commitment to the craft. They work out their ideas and mold them into a rational form (practice). What might seem like pure intuition is actually a well-considered and finely-tuned skillset that springs from an intense source of awareness and rational focus. One of the reasons why I so frequently say that there is no checklist to CRE is that it constantly requires a creative insightfulness that draws on a deep understanding of the intricacies in successful teaching and learning, particularly as it pertains to the ways in which our most vulnerable students experience school in the local and current context. We teachers must put to rest this desire to treat complex problems with simple solutions. Checklist thinking is one of the greatest obstacles to CRE. Great teaching today is the act of constantly updating the references and methods we use to effect the rich and engaging learning we want for our kiddos. The best advice I can probably give to any single teacher is "don't get stuck!"

And please believe that teachers get stuck in their success just as easily as they get stuck in their challenges. Brilliant teachers learn from them both.

Once you've been teaching for even one week, you should realize that there is no simple algorithm for this profoundly human work! Or maybe you think there is an algorithm but you just haven't found it, in which case I can save you time and trouble with the encouragement to suspend your search. The fluid nature of the classroom is one of the most sophisticated social spaces known to humankind. With the six themes, we are adding to our vocabulary for how to create responsive learning experiences for students that thoughtfully enlist culture to support the goals of instruction. I realized years ago that teachers are more engaged in professional development about the Equity mindset when it is offered with clear direction for pedagogical implementation. The CRE themes help us to operationalize the mindset best suited for the design and delivery of learning experiences that facilitate rigorous thinking and cognitive engagement so that all students are able to bridge their identities in the most meaningful and productive ways. As I continue to say, mindset matters way more than strategies; but you can start with strategies in your effort to be more responsive. Without any doubt though, it is unavoidably true that ultimately, the *Why* of your strategic efforts are infinitely more important than the *What*. A clear knowing of *Why* you are choosing a strategy, and how it leverages the CRE themes, is a far better inspiration for the selection of instructional activities and teaching techniques. Your careful contemplation of your *Why* lends itself to a more powerful and brilliant delivery than otherwise.

Similarly, the most thoughtful teachers are unlikely to utter that altogether unproductive thought, "I already do this," because the point of CRE is not to "do" any one thing. The problems of practice which challenge us are neither simple nor even compound. They are complex and anchored in a range of dimensions of the human experience. The goal of CRE is to operationalize a mental process that yields solutions to problems of practice that are innovative and specific to the needs of your students. We never stop learning. We never reach a pinnacle. We just continue to evolve. Our capacity for growth is as infinite as our will because the circumstances and the context are perpetually in motion. This is at once what is most beautiful and most challenging about being a teacher in the 21st century. So I encourage you to reflect on your successes and also your failures – especially your failures, even though they may offend your self-esteem – because it is in these failures that you can often discern patterns, assumptions, and conventions that may be undermining your efforts. Every experience is a potential harvest of expanded understanding. Our task as responsive practitioners is to be present enough to absorb these moments as opportunities to improve.

OPERATIONALIZE THIS!

Raise the Rigor to Increase Engagement

When Mr. Vaughn and I planned the "memes for meaning" learning experience, we designed it around the premise that more rigor would create more engagement. We wanted our students to have a stronger personal investment in the different forms of government in order for them to consider the ideas more dynamically and with greater complexity than they had previously. In order to deepen the investments students were willing to make, we used the medium of memes to help Mr. Vaughn's kiddos generate content to which Mr. Vaughn could directly respond. Our students were synthesizing definitions in memes with the responsibility of presenting their meaning to the rest of the class. Memes (and gifs) have crossed over into mainstream communication tactics – especially when a language device is needed to represent big (and often witty) ideas in a concise manner. Through the memes, our students articulated themes and perspective on the various forms of government, and Mr. Vaughn was able to respond with questions, clarifications, and further connections to support students' thinking. After three rounds of meme-making, each round seeing the kiddos get more enthusiastic and creative in their designs, we shifted into a Philosophical Chairs activity so that the students could debate using some of the information they had just heard in lecture and learned in the construction of the memes to do what teenagers love to do – argue and defend their points. Mr. Vaughn and I jumped in a couple of times to keep the pace from dropping off, but it was the students at that point who were in control of the learning.

Design Learning Experiences that Compel Students to Draw from Their Social and Cultural Backgrounds

It was precisely because our students were required to draw from their backgrounds that they were able to make more and more insightful connections. The students had to leverage both their social-media literacies and their fluencies in teenager culture to decide on an image and the aligned language to communicate their shared understanding of the definition of a government type. The students' discussions were content-packed and dynamic – flowing between dialogue and searching for images to inspire and further confirm their emerging insights. Mr. Vaughn's mini-lectures were less like lectures in the traditional sense and more like a serve-and-return exchange of ideas. By basing his talking points on the ideas of students, they were much more likely to be able to channel his expertise in a manner useful for fortifying the conceptual bridges, which was the goal of our instruction.

Release Control of the Learning Experience to See More Student Engagement

The shift to the Philosophical Chairs was a handoff in the ownership of the learning experience. (I discuss the strategy of Philosophical Chairs in more detail in Chapter 5.) By providing rich prompts which could be reasonably agreed or disagreed with, the students' cognitive engagement was hitched to their vulnerability. They had to be willing to take risks in order to make their points; and each student knew themselves when they had a point but hadn't been willing to take the risk. Our task as teachers was to make our invitations to engage (behaviorally, affectively, and cognitively) enticing enough that our kiddos would not be able to resist making a salient point that drew on their own concepts and unique frames of reference. We wanted their urge to engage to override any reluctance to share.

Mr. Vaughn also had to be vulnerable in order for this learning experience to work. That required giving up control – which was a risk. He had to relinquish the centering role of teacher even in the lecture-model. I'm not poo-pooing lectures, by the way. I personally love a good lecture! But in this classroom, this particular group of kiddos needed something different to draw them into the teacher's lecture than just the teacher's expertise itself. Mr. Vaughn had to be willing to concede some of the ownership of the lecture by allowing a re-centering of perspectives on which the lecture was established. Instead of the lecture being fashioned around what Mr. Vaughn wanted his students to know, he had to offer a lecture based on what his students wanted to know given their design of memes, which defined in their own fluencies what each type of government meant to them. Though this left Mr. Vaughn feeling less in control of the direction of the learning experience, we knew if we asked the right questions and offered the right prompts at the right time, Mr. Vaughn would have the opportunity to leverage his expertise more powerfully than otherwise.

References

Adichie, A. C. (2009). The danger of thee single story. Retrieved from www.ted. com/talks/chimamanda_adichie_the_danger_of_a_single_story

Alexander, J. (2012). *Trauma: A social theory.* Cambridge, England: Polity.

Azevedo, R. T., Macaluso, E., Avenanti, A., Santangelo, V., Cazzato, V., & Aglioti, S. M. (2013). Their pain is not our pain: Brain and autonomic correlates of empathic resonance with the pain of same and different race individuals. *Human Brain Mapping, 34*(1), 3168–3181.

Bandura, A. (1977). Self-efficacy: Toward a unifying theory of behavioral change. *Psychological Review, 84*(2), 191–215.

Bandura, A. (1989). Human agency in social cognitive theory. *American Psychologist, 44*, 1175–1184.

Bandura, A. (2002a). Selective moral disengagement in the exercise of moral agency. *Journal of Moral Education, 31*, 101–119.

Bandura, A. (2002b). Social cognitive theory in cultural context. *Applied Psychology: An International Review, 151*, 269–290.

Barrett, L. F. (2017a). *How emotions are made: The secret life of the brain.* New York: Houghton-Mifflin Harcourt; London, England: Macmillan.

Barrett, L. F. (2017b). The theory of constructed emotion: An active inference account of interoception and categorization. *Social Cognitive and Affective Neuroscience, 12*(11), 18–33.

Battistich, V., & Horn, A. (1997). The relationship between students' sense of their school as a community and their involvement in problem behaviors. *American Journal of Public Health, 87*(12), 1997–2001.

Bransford, J. D., Brown, A. L., & Cocking, R. R. (2000). *How people learn: Brain, mind, experience, and school.* Washington, DC: National Academy Press.

Brewster, C., & Fager, J. (2000). *Increasing student engagement and motivation: From time-on-task to homework.* Portland, OR: Northwest Regional Educational Laboratory.

Browne, K. (2008). *Sociology for AS AQA* (3rd ed.). Cambridge, England: Polity Press.

Calarco, J. M. (2014). Coached for the classroom: Parents' cultural transmission and children's reproduction of educational inequalities. *American Sociological Review, 79*(5), 1015–1037.

Centers for Disease Control and Prevention. (n.d.). School connectedness. Retrieved from www.cdc.gov/healthyyouth/protective/school_connectedness.htm

Chiao, J., & Ambady, N. (2007). Cultural neuroscience: Parsing universality and diversity across levels of analysis. In S. Kitayama & D. Cohen (Eds.), *The handbook of cultural psychology* (pp. 237–254). New York: Guilford Press.

Collins, A. (2015). Culture, narrative and collective trauma. *Psychology in Society, 48*(1), 105–109.

Costa, A. L., & Kallick, B. (2008). *Learning and leading with habits of mind: 16 essential characteristics for success.* Alexandria, VA: ASCD.

Dearing, E., & Tang, S. (2010). The home learning environment and achievement during childhood. In S. Christenson & A. L. Reschly (Eds.), *Handbook on school-family partnerships* (pp. 131–157). New York: Taylor & Francis.

DeSteno, D. (2014). *The truth about trust: How it determines success in life, love, learning, and more.* New York: Plume.

Elliott, E. S., & Dweck, C. S. (1988). Goals: An approach to motivation and achievement. *Journal of Personality and Social Psychology, 54*(1), 5–12.

Fan, W., & Williams, C. M. (2010). The effects of parental involvement on students' academic self-efficacy, engagement and intrinsic motivation. *Educational Psychology, 30*(1), 53–74.

Fireman, G. D., McVay, T. E., & Flanagan, O. J. (2003). *Narrative and consciousness: Literature, psychology and the brain.* Oxford, England: Oxford University Press.

Fredricks, J. A., Blumenfeld, P. C., & Paris, A. H. (2004). School engagement: Potential of the concept, state of the evidence. *Review of Educational Research, 74*(1), 59–109.

Goddard, C., & Wierzbicka, A. (1997). Discourse and culture. In T. A. Van Dijk (Ed.), *Discourse as social interaction* (pp. 231–257). London, England: Sage.

Gorski, P. C. (2012). Perceiving the problem of poverty and schooling: Deconstructing the class stereotypes that mis-shape education practice and policy. *Equity & Excellence in Education, 45*(2), 302–319.

Hall, E. T. (1976). *Beyond culture.* Garden City, NY: Anchor Press.

Hanley, M. S., & Noblit, G. W., (2009). Cultural responsiveness, racial identity and academic success: A review of literature. Retrieved from www.heinz.org/userfiles/library/culture-report_final.pdf

Henry, K. L., Knight, K. E., & Thornberry, T. P. (2012). School disengagement as a predictor of dropout, delinquency, and problem substance use during adolescence and early adulthood. *Journal of Youth and Adolescence, 41*(2), 156–166.

Hess, K. K., Jones, B. S., Carlock, D., & Walkup, J. R. (2009a). Cognitive rigor: Blending the strengths of Bloom's Taxonomy and Webb's Depth of Knowledge to enhance classroom-level processes. ERIC: ED517804. Retrieved from https://eric.ed.gov/?id=ED517804

Hess, K., Carlock, D., Jones, B., & Walkup, J. (2009b). What exactly do "fewer, clearer, and higher standards" really look like in the classroom? Using a cognitive rigor matrix to analyze curriculum, plan lessons, and implement assessments. Presentation at Council of Chief State School Officers. Detroit, MI.

Hofstadter, D. R. (2001). Analogy as the core of cognition. In D. Gentner, K. J. Holyoak, N. Boicho, & B. N. Kokinov (Eds.), *The analogical mind: Perspectives from cognitive science* (pp. 499–538). Cambridge, MA: The MIT Press/Bradford Book.

Hofstadter, D., & Sander, E. (2013). *Surfaces and essences: Analogy as the fuel and fire of thinking.* New York: Basic Books.

Immordino-Yang, M. H., & Fischer, K. W. (2009). Neuroscience bases of learning. In V. G. Aukrust (Ed.), *International encyclopedia of education* (3rd ed., pp. 310–316). Oxford, England: Elsevier.

Immordino-Yang, M. H., McColl, A., Damasio, H., & Damasio, A. (2009). Neural correlates of admiration and compassion. *Proceedings of the National Academy of Sciences, 106*(19), 8021–8026.

Immordino-Yang, M. H. (2010). Toward a microdevelopmental, interdisciplinary approach to social emotion. *Emotion Review, 2*(3), 217–220.

Ladson-Billings, G. (1995a). But that's just good teaching! The case for culturally relevant pedagogy. *Theory Into Practice, 34*(3), 159–165.

Lahey, J. (2014, October 15). Get to know your teachers, kids: A new study suggests that a simple acquaintance exercise might improve classroom relationships and even close the achievement gap. *The Atlantic.* Retrieved from www.theatlantic.com/education/archive/2014/10/kids-get-better-grades-when-they-share-similarities-with-teachers/381464

Lewis, M. (2003). *Moneyball: The art of winning an unfair game.* New York: W.W. Norton.

McGee, E. O., & Spencer, M. B. (2013). The development of coping skills for science, technology, engineering, and mathematics students: Transitioning from minority to majority environments. In C. C. Yeakey, V. S. Thompson, & A. Wells (Eds.), *Urban ills: Post recession complexities of urban living in the twenty first century* (pp. 351–378). Lanham, MD: Lexington Books.

McLaughlin, M., McGrath, D. J., Burian-Fitzgerald, M. A., Lanahan, L., Scotchmer, M., Enyeart, C., & Salganik, L. (2005). *Student content engagement as a construct for the measurement of effective classroom instruction and teacher knowledge.* Washington, DC: American Institutes for Research.

McLoyd, V. C. (1998). Socioeconomic disadvantage and child development. *American Psychologist, 53*(2), 185–204.

Moll, L. C., Amanti, C., Neff, D., & Gonzalez, N. (1992). Funds of knowledge for teaching: Using a qualitative approach to connect homes and classrooms. *Theory Into Practice, 31*(1), 132–141.

Nisbett, R. E. (2003). *The geography of thought: Why we think the way we do.* New York: The Free Press.

Norton, N. (2005). Permitame hablar (allow me to speak). *Language Arts, National Council of Teachers of English, 83*(2), 118–127.

O'Connor, E. E., Dearing, E., & Collins, B. A. (2011). Teacher-child relationship and behavior problem trajectories in elementary school. *American Educational Research Journal, 48*(1), 120–162.

Orth, U., Robins, R. W., & Widaman, K. F. (2012). Life-span development of self-esteem and its effects on important life outcomes. *Journal of Personality and Social Psychology, 102*(6), 1271–1288.

Pajares, F. (1996). Self-efficacy beliefs in academic settings. *Review of Educational Research, 66*(4), 543–578.

Pierson, R. (2013). Every kid needs a champion. Retrieved from www.ted.com/talks/rita_pierson_every_kid_needs_a_champion

Putnam, R. D. (2015). *Our kids: The American dream in crisis.* New York: Simon & Schuster.

Resnick, M. D., Bearman, P. S., & Blum, R. W. (1997). Protecting adolescents from harm: Findings from the National Longitudinal Study on Adolescent Health. *Journal of the American Medical Association, 27*(8), 823–832.

Rule, N. O., Freeman, J. B., & Ambady, N. (2013).Culture in social neuroscience: A review. *Social Neuroscience, 8*(1), 3–10.

Ryan, R., & Deci, E. (2000). Self-determination theory and the facilitation of intrinsic motivation, social development, and well-being. *American Psychologist, 55*, 68–78.

Ryan, R.M., Stiller,J.D.,&Lynch,J.H.(1994).Representations of relationships to teachers, parents, and friends as predictors of academic motivation and self-esteem. *The Journal of Early Adolescence, 14*(2), 226–249.

Skinner, E., & Belmont, M. (1993). Motivation in the classroom: Reciprocal effects of teacher behavior and student engagement across the school year. *Journal of Educational Psychology, 85*, 571–581.

Spencer, M. B., Harpalani, V., Cassidy, E., Jacobs, C. Y., Donde, S., Goss, T. N., Muñoz-Miller, M., Charles, N., & Wilson, S. (2006). Understanding vulnerability and resilience from a normative developmental perspective: Implications for racially and ethnically diverse youth. In D. Cicchetti & D. J. Cohen (Eds.), *Developmental psychopathology: Volume one: Theory and Method* (2nd ed., pp. 627–672). Hoboken, NJ: Wiley.

Spencer, M., & Swanson, D. (2013). Opportunities and challenges to the development of healthy children and youth living in diverse communities. *Development & Psychopathology, 25*(4), 1551–1566.

Sternberg, R. J. (2000). Wisdom as a form of giftedness. *Gifted Child Quarterly, 44*(4), 252–259.

Stevens, T., Olivárez, A., & Hamman, D. (2006). The role of cognition, motivation, and emotion in explaining the mathematics achievement gap between Hispanic and White students. *Hispanic Journal of Behavioral Sciences, 28*(2), 161–186.

Tang, S., Davis-Kean, P. E., Chen, M., & Sexton, H. R. (2016). Adolescent pregnancy's intergenerational effects: Does an adolescent mother's education have consequences for her children's achievement? *Journal of Research on Adolescence, 26*(1), 180–193.

Tylor, E. B. (1871). *Primitive culture: Researches into the development of mythology, philosophy, religion, art, and custom* (Vol. 1). London, England: John Murray.

Wentzel, K. R. (2003). Sociometric status and adjustment in middle school: A longitudinal study. *The Journal of Early Adolescence, 23*(1), 5–28.

Wood, R. E., & Bandura, A. (1989). Impact of conceptions of ability on self-regulatory mechanisms and complex decision making. *Journal of Personality and Social Psychology, 56*, 407–415.

Yoshikawa, H. (2013). *Investing in our future: The evidence based on preschool education.* Washington, DC; New York: Society for Research in Child Development and Foundation for Child Development.

Yosso, T. J. (2005). Whose culture has capital? A critical race theory discussion of community cultural wealth. *Race Ethnicity and Education, 8*(1), 69–91.

Zimmerman, B. J., Bandura, A., & Martinez-Pons, M. (1992). Self-motivation for academic attainment: The role of self-efficacy beliefs and personal goal setting. *American Educational Research Journal, 29*(3), 663–676.

4

Planning with Equity in Mind

Planning with a Culturally Responsive Education (CRE) mindset draws on relationships with students as well as their unique identities in order to engineer moments of authentic rigor and engagement. Over time and through reflection, I've identified five guiding questions that, when centered in planning spaces, contribute to learning experiences that facilitate meaningful investments for students – behaviorally, affectively, and cognitively.

Finding the Joey

Our question was direct and yet, immensely challenging. We had been thinking carefully about rigor, and specifically we wanted to know what rigor looks like for our 3- and 4-year-old pre-school kiddos. In preparing students for Kindergarten and the primary grades, we wanted to develop the basics of literacy and numeracy, but we also wanted to build their stamina for rich thinking and problem-solving. We spent time studying the Karin Hess (Hess, Carlock, Jones, & Walkup, 2009b) Cognitive Rigor Matrix (CRM) and clarifying our shared understandings of what rigor entails for students and requires for us as the designers of their learning experiences. But the CRM felt difficult to access in this pre-school space. We needed to figure out a way to make it more inherently operational.

The Hess Cognitive Rigor Matrix combines Bloom's Taxonomy and Webb's DOK wheel so that specific goals for both type and complexity of student thinking are made evident in one tool. In the CRM, it becomes clear that rigor is neither content-dependent nor topic-specific; but rather, rigor is a function of *how* (i.e. type and complexity) students are led to think. In fact, the Hess CRM makes it easier to see that opportunities for rigor are served up by the questions we ask about content. The questions teachers ask explicitly and also embed into the learning experience are invitations to students to extend their cognitive engagement in such ways that the students themselves become the drivers of their own learning.

My ECE colleagues saw the value of Hess' CRM, but we wanted to further tailor it to our needs so we leaned out some of the language describing the targets for students' thinking – leaving key essential statements so that we could still easily grasp what the thinking might entail up and down the CRM. The teachers held onto the idea of questions as our greatest tools for facilitating rigorous thinking, so we added question stems into the CRM that we thought of as aligning with the thinking targets for rigor. A DOK-4 (extended thinking) target for Analyze, for example is: analyze multiple sources of evidence, or multiple themes. We added question stems to help us to be more intentional in the design of instruction to correspond to that target, such as: Describe how this is the same as...? What makes it different from...? How do you know that...? How would you do it differently? What would you change?

Ms. Erin was among the first classroom teachers in the building to put the revised CRM to use. She designed a week-long unit on animals to test it out. She wanted to see how many of these high-rigor moments she could build into an extended learning experience in which her students had to locate a (stuffed animal) baby joey that mysteriously went missing from the classroom. In the unit, Ms. Erin wove in speaking, listening, writing, and designing activities all as part of a storyline where the students were tasked to find the missing joey.

The unit was framed with a *Blabberize* video of the mother kangaroo asking the children, in her worried voice, to help her find her missing joey. *Blabberize* is a software program that allows the manipulation of pictures so that audio can be added to create the illusion of a talking image. Our video was short, but the kiddos found it to be powerful. A few children thought the teachers had misplaced the joey and went to the classroom area where the kangaroos lived to see if it could be found. A few other kiddos had a more pressing question: *How can a stuffed animal make a video asking us to help it find another missing stuffed animal?* This was anticipated and an important part of the learning experience for two reasons primarily: first, we wanted the students to feel empathy for the mother kangaroo; and second, in order for the project to work, our kiddos had to leverage their most valuable asset as learners – their imaginations.

Ms. Erin sold it! "Sometimes, when a mother is worried, she will do magical things to make sure her baby is safe." That was enough for the kiddos, and within minutes, every single one was joined in a chorus of Joey! Joey! Joey! as they searched the room through-and-through for any clues to the whereabouts of the missing baby kangaroo. Over the next week, they made missing posters, designed "joey-safe" traps, and developed questions to ask of the staff in the building. On the third day, Ms. Erin showed the students images from the school's "security footage" of the missing joey in various parts of the building. It seemed to be almost taunting the kiddos, listening to music in the computer room with a giant pair of headphones on, hanging out in the play-room, roaming all over the building unsupervised; but also as Ms. Erin reminded the students, in danger without the care of its mother to feed and protect it.

The students had homework. They had to collect grass (because that's what they learned that kangaroos eat in the wild) to place in the traps they'd constructed. They were guided to talk with their parents about the task while they collected the grass. In the week-long project, the search for the joey consumed the entire building. Finally, on the fifth day of the learning, new "security cam footage" showed images of the joey in a part of the building that the students hadn't previously searched. This was our chance to finally track down this little rascal! Before we went, Ms. Erin showed the students a YouTube video of a person using a shopping bag to capture a real joey in the Australian outback. We discussed the potential hazards of capturing a joey and also the fact the joey was probably very hungry and maybe even hurt given how long it had been away from the guardianship of its mother. We prepared by putting on safety goggles and gloves, we reviewed our directions for capturing the critter, and we were off.

I've been in lots of classrooms and seen lots of riveting learning experiences, but I can tell you that you have not lived until you are with a room full of 3- and 4-year-olds when they finally find and safely capture the missing joey they've been chasing for over a week. There were shrieks of joy and leaps of celebration. Once back in the room, Ms. Erin affirmed, "You guys! We found the joey," to which the students replied with an almost primal celebratory scream! It was exhilarating for me... so I know the students are not likely to soon forget it themselves.

The Five Planning Questions

Brilliant teachers choreograph rigorous and engaging learning experiences that draw richly on students' strengths and identities by building upon their assets; and brilliant teachers understand that an excellent lesson exists specifically in the context of the student audience who receives it. This understanding requires a certain fluidity because context changes over time – from year to year, semester to semester, day to day, class to class, and even moment to moment. Brilliant teachers may seem to engineer responsive experiences for their students at will, but it is abundantly clear to me that opportunities for responsiveness are conceived in planning. In order to be successful, teachers must be attentive to these varied and changing contexts. Therefore, planning is the space where teachers design the moments in which they will leverage their relationships with students and facilitate opportunities for kiddos to make powerful connections between their social, cultural, and academic identities.

Planning that yields rigor and engagement is intentional, and though it may appear that brilliant teachers are able to somehow will their students to success – and though that may occasionally be the case – it is far more likely in my experience that deeply meaningful learning in classrooms is a function of an inspired and deliberate attention to the CRE themes and the larger sense of purpose for teaching in a multicultural, pluralistic, democratic society. Of the many ways in which teachers influence the opportunities of students, planning is the high-leverage behavior that can create a cascade of positive effects for all our students, and especially the most vulnerable among them. Over many years of close study and reflection, I have identified five questions that consistently support a planning process that is likely to yield learning experiences that are engaging, rigorous, and culturally responsive.

They are as follows:

Question One: What do I want students to understand?
Question Two: What do I want students to feel?
Question Three: What are the targets for rigor?
Question Four: What are the indicators of engagement?
Question Five: What are the opportunities to be responsive?

In this chapter, I present these questions as discreet tools for planning; and I also discuss how they work together to inform our Equity mindset in the design of culturally responsive instruction.

Before I go further, please indulge me as I offer yet another obligatory caution to resist the urge to think of planning as a regimented, checklist process. If Equity were a paint-by-numbers type of project, then a lot more people would be doing it brilliantly. Planning with a CRE focus is a profoundly iterative exercise – and if you are doing it right, you should feel challenged. I am often inspired to start at different questions in the design of any given learning experience (as in sometimes the first, sometimes the fifth, or any order that seems appropriate). Ultimately, these questions must become part of one cohesive process. The questions clarify our focus relative to different elements of a learning experience, but none can be separated from the whole without compromising the integrity of the overall effort... and yet, the effort to incorporate any one of these questions where they haven't before been considered will improve any lesson plan considerably.

These questions follow in the spirit of Wiggins and McTighe's *Understanding by Design* (Wiggins, McTighe, Kiernan, & Frost, 1998) in the regard that the intent of the learning experience should be clarified before the activities are selected. Frankly, this is the most common mistake made in planning. Teachers are often inclined to plan learning experiences around activities. We teachers like to recycle activities that we have had success with in previous teaching experiences or even as students ourselves. Activities, however, should be selected not because of our prior experiences in using them but rather given how well we can predict that they support the answers to these five planning questions. When we commit to activities (whether we admit to it or not) before we conceptualize the experience we want for students, our success criteria for the learning experience – either consciously or nonconsciously – is a function of compliance. That is, we will deem the learning experience to be successful if our students *do* what we want them to *do*. If, however, we prioritize what we want students to understand and feel while carefully considering the targets and indicators for rigor and engagement and also the ways in which we can be responsive, we are much more likely to facilitate the circumstances in which students will *think* in the ways we hope for them to *think*. In terms of CRE, thinking is a far more righteous goal than doing; and thinking facilitates the bridging of identities with far greater impact than merely following the directions of activities. Brilliant teachers know this to be true. This is a critical understanding with huge implications for Equity.

Question One: What Do I Want Students to Understand?

In order to answer this question well in design, we have to get inside of the ideas that matter most. In the neuro-cognitive sense, an understanding is quite literally a physical thing. We know this because we can image how our understandings and the processes we have for retrieving them affect the physical architecture of our brains (Bransford, Brown, & Cocking, 2000; Day & Goldstone, 2012). To get inside of an idea means to understand its most basic building blocks in context. It means one should understand both the object-elements of the concept and also their goal-elements. By that I mean, a good, rich understanding can be described as a thing and also a thing that serves a certain purpose. In the former, I am describing something in terms of its characteristics, and in the latter, I am describing some-thing in terms of how it functions in relation to some goal. (In the Operationalize This! sections of Chapters 1 through 5, I have described how my colleagues and I have considered the essential understandings of the different classroom stories I've shared in this book.)

The power of teaching is in the facilitating of conceptual understandings. Many of my favorite moments in teaching are those when I am confident that my students are grasping hold of an understanding that I hoped they would comprehend deeply and with a sense of purpose. (I've learned to make time slow down for myself in those moments so I can more fully appreciate them in the there and then.) I know that many teachers share this sentiment. To share in an understanding – to grasp meaning in the same way as others – can be argued to be the very thing that most defines humanity. Human beings have the capacity to mirror each other's moods and behaviors, and we use symbols (language) to calibrate our definitions of wholly abstract concepts. No other species of life on Earth does exactly that. The sharing of understandings is the glue that binds communities. We feel most alive, we feel most like ourselves in those spaces where we are confident in our understandings.

Understandings are a function of culture, and all instruction is culturally biased. We are always advantaging or disadvantaging some cultural perspective in our teaching – the extent to which this occurs is often made clearer in the presence of greater cultural diversity, but it's always there. We learn by making conceptual connections with new understandings that build on and bridge the understandings we bring to bear. Our concepts, yours and mine and every person you've ever known, are a product of direct experience and collective experiences in the social spaces we share with others (the social spaces where we have been indoctrinated to see symbols of culture as meaningful in some specific ways). Every perception and experience in the classroom is infused with cultural meaning. We provide more equitable opportunities for students to make conceptual connections in the learning of understandings when we give them greater range from which to find conceptual associations and similarities. In the most basic sense, the way I understand it through my study of the most current published neuroscience is: Experience (the bank of individual and collective experiences from which we draw meaning) + Predictions (the estimations our brains make in the filling in of incomplete information) = Conceptual Understandings (Barrett & Russell, 2015; Barrett & Simmons, 2015; Barrett, 2017a, 2017b). Our experiences inform our predictions and vice versa, and our conceptual understandings adjust accordingly – and this is absolutely informed by our cultural identities. In fact, it is safe to say that nothing is ever learned in a culturally neutral context. The process of coming to understand anything is always supported or inhibited by our ability to make these kinds of conceptual connections either through new experiences or the symbolic representation of something previously understood.

In the UbD framework (Hess, Carlock, Jones, & Walkup, 2009b), McTighe and Wiggins describe understandings as multi-faceted and performative – meaning that once something is understood, it exists not merely in one's head but it is performed through one's being. Understandings change us. Once we understand something, we are never the same as we were prior to that understanding. I often ask teachers in planning spaces to think about what they want their students to still know about a learning experience 20 years after the fact. That thought experiment usually yields rich insight into the true learning targets for students' understanding. You might also ask yourself: *What is a deep and meaningful conceptual understanding about your content that matters tremendously for students so that they are able to think like practitioners in your field?* (Here's a clue: It's something on which other conceptual understandings hinge, as well.) *What do you remember about your own early emerging understandings of this concept? What did you figure out? How did you figure it out? How did it feel when you first understood?* In answering these questions for yourself, you are more likely to be able to get inside of the understandings you want for your students.

Another way I've found to get to the heart of the understandings we want for students is *The Dream Exercise*. I read about *The Dream Exercise* in Chip and Dan Heath's book, *The Power of Moments* (2017) in which they describe a thought experiment which they learned about at the University of Virginia's Center for Teaching Excellence. It goes like this:

> Imagine that you have a group of dream students. They are engaged, they think you're amazing, they are perfectly behaved, and they have perfect memories... Fill in the blanks in this sentence: Three to five years from now, my students still know ___; and they are still able to do ___; and they still find value in ___.
>
> *(Heath & Heath, 2017, p. 101)*

So as an English teacher in a high school classroom, I might answer these questions with regard to a piece of biographical literature like this: Three to five years from now, my students will still know that stories change the world; and they are still able to identify with literature through a preferred element (i.e. character, theme, setting, conflict, etc.); and they still find value in biographical literature for its power in providing insight into the human experience.

An understanding frames other understandings. When we know something at the conceptual level, we understand it such that we can predict how a shift in one aspect of the knowing may impact another. I might also say that understanding is a form of seeing. Persons who know and understand in any given content see better how larger patterns and networks of information work together. (I think of this as the essence of wisdom.) We could go really deep with this and challenge the perception of any one understanding as separate and apart from any and all understandings, but I'll leave you to pursue your own study of Parmenides and others. One way to think about this question is to consider what expert practitioners in your content area *see better* than others. The richest and most dynamic learning experiences happen when the focus of instruction is on facilitating students' thinking at the level of conceptual understanding because only then can they find the most authentic experiences of cognitive agency.

It's important to clarify exactly why the question, "What do I want students to understand?" is different from an easily conflated and seemingly synonymous question, "What do I want my students to remember?" I contend that these are not questions of equal merit. To remember is not the same as to understand. I often use the words *know* and *understand* as synonyms; but to remember doesn't indicate the same extent of purpose and conviction that an understanding conveys. To understand something is to know it in its conceptual context. To understand means to have some sense of the ways in which it can be applied. To understand means to have an intellectual feel for the interrelation of the idea to other significant ideas. When the story of any discipline is told, those who understand can illustrate their knowing of which elements are directly and indirectly connected to others. I think of people I know who very closely follow [insert your favorite cable television series for binge-watching] and how deeply they see the interconnectedness of the multiple storylines. They have a superior understanding of the whole, and they can much more rigorously analyze the significance of any single event or element inside of the larger context. That's much more rigorous than merely remembering the plots and sub-plots.

Understanding is deeper than remembering. I remember a lot of things that I do not understand. I could even argue that remembering is a dangerous goal for learning because it facilitates fragile memories that are more easily corrupted by our human biases every time they are retrieved. An understanding, on the other hand, is more durable because it has been more rigorously developed. When I ask students at the end of a unit, "What will you remember one year from now about [the topic of the unit]?" my students are much more inclined to talk about the activities of the learning experience. When I ask them, "One year from now, what will you still know and understand about [the topic of the unit]?" I get much richer and thoughtful responses about the skills and concepts relating to and underscoring the topic.

When I thoughtfully consider the question, "What do I want my students to understand?" in my design, I find that I can discern students' emerging understandings faster and more fluidly during instruction. I'll hear what I may have heard in other circumstances in clearer relation to the true learning targets. This facilitates my seeing better the opportunities to slow down, or speed up, or paraphrase, or ask another question, or highlight a certain student's thinking, or call for a turn-and-talk, or offer a mini-lecture or demonstration. I am more powerful in my teaching with the clarity of the understandings I hope for my students, and their sensing of my clarity makes me a more trustworthy supporter of their learning in those moments. When I am clear, they are more willing to take the necessary risks associated with the learning. In this way, my intentional support of my students' understandings is not only facilitating their learning but also affirming my relationships with them and also their relationships with the content.

Question Two: What Do I Want Students to Feel?

To start, in order to ask this question righteously – with honest integrity – we must also ask if we are emotionally invested in this work ourselves. To consider the emotional investment of others requires that we are connected to and aware of our own personal motivations and insecurities. When we consider our own feelings, we energize and activate the potential for our richest and most creative thinking. Our emotions as teachers affect our environment and the people around us just as our students' emotions affect their environments and the students around them. With an awareness of our emotions, we can more accurately associate the effects of affect – within ourselves and our students. I believe it's also true that emotions animate intentions (or it may be argued it's the other way around). Our intentions support our clarity in both design and instruction. Our awareness of emotion facilitates an awareness of intentions. With the awareness of our feelings, we are better positioned to design and facilitate learning experiences in which our students feel rewarded by being engaged; and how can we share an experience that rewards for being engaged if we aren't thoughtfully and emotionally invested in our own experience, as well?

The capacity for neuroimaging in particular has given us heaps of new insights into the inner-workings of the brain, and cognitive scientists continue to develop theories specifically about memory and learning. While I admire the work of many cognitive scientists, I would direct you specifically to the work of two – Mary Helen Immordino-Yang and Lisa Feldman Barrett – whose writings I find it helpful to draw from in the application of neuro-cognitive discoveries to our understandings of and practices in teaching and learning. I would not pretend to be able to comprehensively cover either of their research, but I'd like to make an inference based on a single thread in each of these academician's bodies of work. Let's focus on the idea of "concepts" and Affective Thought. The process of new learning entails the recruitment of existing neural networks in order to modulate and facilitate further construction of neural networks that support the development of skills and concepts. This process is not merely *cognitive*, it is also social and emotional. As discussed in Chapter 1, concepts are interrelated object- and/or goal-focused constructs that comprise our understandings of the world around us – and the extent to which they have meaning is massively influenced by culture (Barrett, 2017a, 2017b). Neural network functioning is an active agent in the construction of our concepts, a process that lives at the intersections of our biology and our sociality.

The many recent advances in cognitive science illustrate the connections between emotion, social functioning, and decision-making. We now have a great deal of neurobiological evidence that "suggests that the aspects of cognition that we recruit most heavily in schools – namely learning, attention, memory, decision-making, and social functioning, are both profoundly affected by and subsumed within the processes of emotion" (Immordino-Yang & Damasio, 2007, p. 3; Immordino-Yang & Fischer, 2009; Immordino-Yang, 2011a; Barrett & Russell, 2015; Immordino-Yang, 2011b; Barrett, 2017a). In the words of Professor Immordino-Yang: "Emotion forms the rudder that steers learners' thinking, in effect helping them to call up information and memories that are relevant to the topic or problem at hand" (Immordino-Yang & Fischer, 2009, p. 313). In short, Affective Thought represents the understanding that the thinking we most value in learning comprises the cognitive processes which live inside the overlap of "reason" and emotion. I often refer to a cognitive process like creativity in my work with teachers as an example of this, and we consider together what that really entails. When we are being creative, we are leveraging both reason (i.e. rational thought) and emotion to construct something that draws on multiple parts of ourselves and some unique combination of concepts, experiences, and affect. If we aren't bridging these different parts of our selves, we may be mimicking the creativity of others or pointlessly puttering around with concepts for which we have little to no understanding; but there is no way to reasonably claim creativity if we aren't employing both reason and affect. Creativity is a desired cognitive function that draws on both our capacity for reason as well as our emotion, but the same can be said about decision-making or interpretation – or basically, any human cognitive function. Our emotions color every thought we have. It is central to our humanity (Immordino-Yang, 2010; Immordino-Yang, Chiao, & Fiske, 2010; Barrett & Russell, 2015; Barrett & Simmons, 2015; Barrett, 2018). Mary Helen Immordino-Yang defines this interplay of biology, culture, and emotion as "Affective Thought" or "the platform for learning, memory, decision-making, and creativity, both in social and nonsocial contexts" (Immordino-Yang & Fischer, 2009, p. 314).

Many teachers, myself included, were indoctrinated socially and professionally to believe that our minds essentially have two dimensions: a rational brain-based dimension and an emotional body-based (or heart-based) dimension (Nielson, Zielinski, Ferguson, Lainhart, & Anderson, 2013). We were further taught that the rational is somehow a regulator of the emotional (at least in the case of the most self-controlled persons), and the emotional functions of the body were somehow subservient to the rational functions of the brain (Immordino-Yang & Fischer, 2009; Barrett, 2017a). This is, scientifically speaking, inaccurate. In fact, it isn't even accurate, in the scientific sense, to say the body and brain are operating on different planes – with the body coordinating our physical and emotional being while the brain manages our thinking. In fact, the body and the brain are in a constant state of co-regulation (Barrett, 2017a). Your mood, for example, is determined by both your body *and* brain. Your body sends signals to your brain that are processed through cognition to create a perception of mood. Similarly, what you experience as pain is not determined by your body alone. That too is a function of a co-regulated process. There is no single thought or awareness that is ever solely a function of either the brain or the body in isolation of the other. Our thoughts and emotions are always developed within a web of social context, cognitive activity, and biological interoceptions (Barrett & Simmons, 2015; Baer, 2017).

The question, *What do I want students to feel?* guides us to better discern how learning experiences can leverage our students' full humanity. When students are affectively engaged in their learning, they are much more likely to find the conceptual connections that are most meaningful for them. The emotional investment in their learning makes it more likely that they will be able to bridge, combine, and recombine the ideas in ways that best align with their conceptual schema. Further, students who are emotionally engaged are more likely to feel the reward of learning in ways that incline them to stay engaged. To feel rewarded for an investment – an investment that isn't initially guaranteed to yield a specific return, no less – is a critical aspect of participation in any endeavor. When students are affectively engaged, they are more likely to trust the people and spaces in which others also are likewise invested. Those spaces becomes authentic learning communities for them.

Asking the question, "What do I want students to feel?" in my planning has better allowed for the intentional engineering of affect that yields the richest and most productive engagement for my students, but it also makes me better attuned to the emotional economy of the classroom. By giving forethought to how I want my students to feel, I am better able to recognize during instruction when my students are owning their learning in the most profound and appropriate ways. In my own teaching, I have come to recognize that the knowing of when to release control is a critical aspect of my effectiveness. The shift in the onus of responsibility for the ownership of the learning isn't solely a function of my students' content understanding. It is often wise to relinquish control before my students understand the content and concepts we are learning if they are demonstrating the kind of emotional investment that I feel confident will sustain their work through their evolving interpretations. In fact, I know many students who have learned to minimize the risk in their cognitive engagement by relying on their teachers to over-manage the emotional investment for students. I would much rather design a learning experience that compels their affective investment than maintains their dependence on the teacher's.

The asking of this question in the design of units and lessons requires us to recognize our students' humanity, particularly as social and cultural beings who bring a wealth of experiences and understandings with them to the classroom – even if these differ culturally and qualitatively from our own. Though the anticipation of what our students will feel is inexact, we should make an effort to place ourselves in their skin and imagine their affect without rejecting their values or projecting our own onto them. We must also remember that emotion is not a single instance – meaning there are many ways to experience happiness or sadness or excitement or concern (just to name a few emotions). Emotion is a population of instances so the question, *What do I want students to feel?* compels us to consider our students in more dynamic and multidimensional contexts than we might otherwise. I think of this as the height of emotional intelligence in teaching.

When asking this question in my planning, I think deliberately about the emotional journey on which the learning experience takes students (which is why I find the unit, and not the individual lesson, to be the most effective level at which to plan). The richer the emotional environment and the greater the sense of emotional agency for students, the more likely that students will be able to make conceptual connections. In general, I always want my students to feel inspired and empowered, but sometimes I bring them through a bit of frustration or confusion along the way in order to enhance their sense of purpose. In the final analysis, the most useful emotions for a student to feel depend on the targets of the instruction. We as teachers must ask ourselves, *What are the goals for the learning experience and what affects will most powerfully support them?* As human beings, we are more likely to feel like our needs are being met when we experience some kind of positive affect. When students feel as though they have the tools and support to be successful, their feelings will be a contributing factor to their successful learning. Relatedly, when I am working with students to improve their engagement, after a successful learning experience (and sometimes during), I like to consider with them what the success felt/feels like. I want them to understand their emotional agency in engineering their own engagement. In many cases, my more vulnerable students will lack the language to describe the feeling though they know it to be positive. My work in those moments, giving them the language and tools to be able to describe with greater specificity their feelings and the emotional ownership they felt of their success, can be identity-shifting for students. After all, how can anyone justify the risk of investing themselves in a space in which they regularly feel as though they are not in control of their emotional well-being? This planning question encourages a more deliberate co-construction of a social and emotional environment that benefits a palpable sense of classroom community. You, the teacher, contribute to the co-regulation of the emotional economy. Thus, in very real ways, your students' emotions are impacted by your own.

Question Three: What Are the Targets for Rigor?

If engagement is the moneyball of CRE, rigor is the virtue; and I have found that it is unlikely that rigor can be achieved for students in the classroom if it isn't first embraced in the design spaces. It's important for me to be abundantly clear in making this point: If you are unwilling to think rigorously in the design of a learning experience, it is highly unlikely that students will experience what you have designed as rigorous. In Chapter 3, I defined the CRE theme of Rigor. When I think about this question regarding the targets for rigor in instruction, I'm thinking in the performative sense, as in, *How can students perform their rigorous understandings of a concept?* As John Dewey (1933) explained, to understand something "is to see it in its relations to other things: to note how it operates or functions, what consequences follow from it, what causes it" (as cited in Wiggins, McTighe, Kiernan, & Frost, 1998, p. 46). When we understand something, we go beyond the facts, dates, and measurements to make inferences, connections, and associations. The understanding takes form inside of larger theories and suppositions. Powerful and insightful thinking is possible at this level of understanding. We can bind together seemingly disparate segments of information into a coherent, comprehensive, and illuminating account. We can predict how these understandings might apply in imagined scenarios.

When we consider the question, *What are the targets for rigor?* we are planning for those moments when students will demonstrate cognitive engagement to the point that they own the learning experience so profoundly that we, the teachers, are no longer in control – and that is, of course, a wonderful thing. We as teachers lose control whenever our students are leveraging their own assets and capital in building their own unique conceptual connections in their developing understandings. They are analyzing and synthesizing and creating in ways that we could not have predicted – because it is impossible to fully anticipate how another human being will come to truly understand something.

If there is a single tip I can share with you, it is to plan to get to the high-rigor moments as early as possible in the learning experience. The high-rigor moments represent the treat in the thinking. The longer students feel as though they must defer to the thinking of others before they can more fully own the thinking for themselves, the more likely it is that our instruction will lose the attention of our most vulnerable learners. Some teachers are afraid of true rigor precisely because it means that they will have to relinquish control of the learning, and they might have to deviate from their lesson plans to support the affective and cognitive engagement of their students; but planning for Equity requires that we are intentional about designing more high-rigor moments in the learning and not fewer.

I literally use the CRM to chart out the high-rigor moments for the learning experience. I think of high-rigor moments as those DOK-4 targets of the learning experience in which students are extending their understandings by making conceptual connections with content. Think about it like you would if you were producing a movie by building the entire script from one climactic scene. You learn a lot about what the audience needs to know in order to fully engage in the movie through a close study of the culminating scene; and even if a high-action scene comes at the start of the movie (in the style of, for example, the James Bond franchise), you are clearer about what must be back-filled in order for the viewer to have a full appreciation of all the meaning of the pivotal moment. To know what thinking is necessary to support the high-rigor moments for your students, you need only to look back down the row at DOK 1, 2, and 3. I have been part of high-rigor moments in pre-K classrooms all the way up to advanced-placement high school courses. Some think that our younger kiddos aren't capable of rigor. I disagree. In fact, I can confidently make the argument that high-rigor moments are more easily developed in the classrooms with our youngest learners because they are less wedded to the concepts they bring with them into the learning experience. (Some of my most difficult students are adults whom are so locked into their concepts for teaching that they have very little intellectual room for growth. The ideas they have about instruction crowd out new ideas which could be helpful to their practice... *but that may be a topic for another book.*)

I am firmly convinced that the critical variable in students being able to engage in high-rigor moments is the teacher's capacity to plan well for them. I am also a proponent of planning high-rigor moments for my especially rambunctious groups and my reluctant learners, as well. I have found that students experience high rigor as much more interesting than they do the rote, mechanical learning experiences to which they are too often exposed. When I have a classroom that isn't predisposed to compliance (i.e. a rowdy group), I plan learning experiences that introduce rigor at the very outset. The earlier I can get my students thinking, the sooner I have the opportunity to meet them deep in some meaningful thought. It is in those spaces where

I can prove myself to be a capable and trustworthy thought-partner to them... because everyone wants to be understood as they are making some effort to work toward a challenging understanding.

Rigor doesn't harm students. The damage of low expectations, however, is extensive. I've never met a teacher who admits to their low expectations of students, but I have known a great many to resist the planning effort to move students toward high-rigor moments for some very professionally stated desire to manage a productive learning environment or to give the students "what they need to be successful." I, just like every teacher reading this book, want the very best for all of my students; and yet, it is unreasonable to expect any student to truly commit to a trusting relationship with any teacher who doesn't demonstrate the belief in their ability to be successful with effective effort. (Personally, I think kiddos are wise to resist the authority of people who see them as incapable of rigor.) Planning for rigor means planning with the clarity for how we want students to think. Planning for rigor means giving careful consideration to the trajectory of students' thinking with clear and intentional sight on the type and complexity of the thinking we most value in any given learning experience. The clarity with which we set targets for rigor makes us more dynamic facilitators of students' thinking in learning experiences. We are better positioned to push their thinking with our questions and feedback. If our learning experiences are well-designed, we are able to support our students in advancing their capacity for complex thinking even as they are becoming more familiar with the foundations and baselines of the content.

Question Four: What Are the Indicators of Engagement?

There is no one single right way to describe engagement. In Chapter 3, I have outlined some of the defining principles of the theme. Most importantly in support of our planning, we are wise to clarify the nature of the engagement we are seeking at any given time in terms of behavioral, affective, and cognitive targets. In my thinking about engagement, I also like to refer to the work of Mihaly Csikszentmihalyi on the subject of *Flow*. Professor Csikszentmihalyi, a psychologist, describes *Flow* as the "zone" in which we are at the perfect intersection of challenge and skill (Csikszentmihalyi, 1990). It's the mental space where time seems to stand still, and where we are most likely to feel deeply connected to a meaningful sense of purpose. A Google search of Mihaly Csikszentmihalyi and *Flow* will bring up a link to a TedTalk he gave on the subject which explains the concept better than I am able to here (Csikszentmihalyi, 2004).

However one might conceptualize engagement, what is most important to know is that when we ask the question, *What are the indicators of engagement?* we are making predictions as to what engagement may look like in the learning experience, and we are prioritizing when and how we might yield some expectations for engagement in favor of others. We are essentially seeking the pathway to *Flow* – the perfect intersection of challenge and skill that will sustain students' self-driven investment in the learning. The key for teachers is to anticipate what those indicators for engagement might be so that we can authentically coach students along to even greater investment in the learning experience.

I like to make a sports analogy when describing the intent of this question in planning spaces. I (like many of you reading this book, whether you acknowledge it or not) am a former athlete. I was once an athletic person, but I no longer have the explosiveness that was such an essential component of my athleticism. I measure explosiveness in athletes in terms of time, and I define it as the difference between the instant of recognition that a play can be made and one's physical ability to make the play. That would mean that "explosiveness" is a function of both physical ability and conceptual understanding of the game. Gifted athletes may not see the play before a more experienced one, but they are able to leverage their physical abilities to execute even before others can complete the play. More experienced athletes, on the other hand, can often out-compete more physically talented players given their depth of understanding of how to play the game. We might, however, say that an athlete is in their prime when they have both the capacity for fast recognition of the potential plays that can be made and a heightened physical ability to make those plays. That is how I define explosiveness in athletics. (Many athletes are able to extend their competitive prime by being able to perfect their capacity for recognition, and many physically gifted athletes never learn the techniques for better recognition and are ineffective when their athleticism begins to diminish.)

The best way to regularly be explosive in the practice of teaching is to pre-load instances of engagement in your mind before the commencement of the actual learning experience. In doing so, we are clarifying our concepts for engagement and aligning them with look-for's in instruction. If you can give thought to what the engagement might look like – including but also beyond mere behavioral engagement – you are much more likely to recognize it quickly and provide a fluid response. When you do that in your teaching, you are being explosive.

Planning with the indicators of engagement in mind has also helped me tremendously in managing my response to behaviors during instruction. The attention I give to this question in my planning makes it less likely that I might conflate bad behavior with affective or cognitive engagement – because, as we've noted, when students become deeply engaged in a learning experience, they tend to take ownership. This student ownership can manifest itself in many behaviors, and if I am not careful, I may misunderstand the meaning of some behaviors and respond poorly. For example, when I give my high school students something rich and interesting to think about in small-group conversations, they will often ignore my first attempts to bring their attention back to the full group. In that instance, if I am not able to recognize the slow return to our full group conversation as an indicator of their affective and cognitive engagement in their small-group discussions, I may undermine the trust and relationship affirmed by the rigor and engagement they are experiencing. In that instance, if I prioritize behavioral engagement over affective and cognitive engagement, I am signaling to my students that I value their mindless compliance over their mindful participation. As teachers, we have to know the difference between productive noise and that which is unproductive, but affective and cognitive engagement are more likely to be noisy than otherwise. After a particularly rigorous and engaging Design Challenge learning experience in a fourth-grade classroom recently, one student – who had been splendidly engaged for the entire learning experience – looked at me and said: "This classroom is a mess!" I mimed a look of shock as I clutched my imaginary pearls, and responded: "Well, what would you expect with all the thinking you've been doing?" We agreed that the mess was, in fact, a perfect illustration of our engagement. I will gladly take a mess like that any day.

Question Five: What Are the Opportunities to Be Responsive?

I have planned entire units for one objective moment in which I can be sitting down on a carpet, *criss-cross applesauce* in front a kiddo while they effort through an emerging understanding (because thinking is hard work). In those moments, I feel like everything slows down, and the entire universe is centered on this exchange between teacher and student. When I can be present for that meeting of the minds, I am able to affirm my student's sense of their academic self by giving them the support and encouragement they need to bridge their social and cultural identities through the construction of their own uniquely defined understanding. Whether this happens on the carpet in a second-grade classroom or in a Socratic Seminar in a high school AP Literature course, I always – every time – emerge from that interaction just a bit more trustworthy in the eyes of my student than I was before it began. That coming together of minds to construct understandings is the essence of responsiveness; and if I am prepared for it, I can, by design, be my most powerful teacher-self in those interactions. Often times, after such moments with students, as I move away and tend to other elements of the learning experience, I think to myself, *Now I can teach that kiddo anything!*

In considering the question, *What are the opportunities to be responsive?* we should focus on our most vulnerable learners. Here is where we are deliberate about how we will incorporate meaningful protective factors into the fabric of the learning experience. If our lessons are planned well in terms of targets for understanding, rigor, and engagement, a focus on the most vulnerable of our students will not disadvantage any other students in the process. In my experience, this is when the positive-sum impact of well-designed instruction is most palpable. My less vulnerable students benefit from an environment in which all of my students are engaged. My support of them in those instances is more focused. It is also my perception that all students see the learning environment as more trustworthy when everyone is receiving the support and direction they need to sustain their engagement and advance their understandings. These are the moments when the sense of agency and inclusion of the learning community come together powerfully for everyone.

This question provides a rich opportunity to consider the ways in which my identity in the role of teacher as a cultural being may be limiting the expression of my students' competencies. We should be deliberate in our thinking about how we imagine our students to be capable and creative thinkers. Here is where I can consider what I have learned previously about the protective factors that have proven to be most meaningful in the support of my students' engagement. In the answering of this question, we as teachers should be forthcoming and honest with ourselves about what we believe to be possible for our students so that we can prioritize their needs over our habits.

Consider how you will confirm that your students are perceiving the experience as responsive. When planning, I like to predict specific moments when I can be positioned to listen and respond to my students' thinking. Serve-and-volley exchanges of ideas are some of my favorite times to be a teacher. What's more, these moments of responsiveness support students in developing greater agency and a detailed sense of what they are feeling – which are the essential ingredients of emotional intelligence. It is a powerful thing for a student to give a learning experience their serious attention and have a teacher, the more experienced thinker, acknowledge, support, and validate that effort. Building in opportunities for students to reflect on their engagement is important because it helps them to put language to their investment and be accountable to themselves for their choices and effort. Some of the most important opportunities to earn students' trust are when they are making an effort to come to know something that is meaningful to them.

Have you ever noticed a student who is deeply engaged in one classroom and equally disengaged in another – on the same day? I am convinced that those students have had more responsive moments, either with the content or people, in the spaces where they are more willfully engaged than in the spaces where they are resistant. I do not claim that responsiveness is easy work (in fact, there is very little about teaching that I would ever claim to be easy), but in my experience,

I have seen one cogent responsive interaction change a student's entire sense of themselves in relation to a teacher, classroom, content, or even the idea of school altogether. These are the interactions that students remember their entire lives and often propel them to see themselves differently than they had prior. Responsiveness is an identity-shifting experience.

And these responsive moments don't have to be over-the-top dramatic performances. Most can easily go unnoticed to the untrained eye. I like to try to position myself so that I can be there with an affirming fist-bump or an encouraging word at the very moment of the critical synapse when a student has come into ownership of a pivotal understanding. If understandings truly change us, I think of those moments as my opportunity to be the first one to introduce myself to the new and improved version of that kiddo. I literally have pictures of those moments that I share with students' families and the other adults whom they trust in school. When I share them, I am figuratively (and sometimes literally) saying, "Hey! Look at how much this kiddo has grown! This is who they are now! They are not the same person as they were before they had this learning experience! *How awesome is that?*"

How Do the Planning Questions Work Together?

Now that we've considered each of the five CRE planning questions in isolation, let's further flesh out how they work together. The questions are only effective in closing Equity gaps when we commit to a vision for brilliant teaching that entails reaching both the heads and hearts of our students. Let's first confirm, in fact, that this is a righteous target to pursue – otherwise, we might mistakenly believe this conversation to be frivolous and unnecessary.

I have a thought experiment I like to use to help clarify our thinking on the intersections of the five planning questions:

Think of something that you understand. It doesn't have to be particularly profound on its face; it can be a more or less technical understanding. But we are searching for a specific type of understanding so it's important that we clarify. In terms of this understanding, it must fit certain criteria:

You have to use this understanding. Using this understanding means that you reference it in some material way. By that I mean, you have to draw on this understanding in support of making an argument or completing some task. You have thought about it. The very fact that you have regularly returned to this understanding to make use of it means it has likely expanded and evolved (or I may counter that you don't really understand it).

You have to remember when you were first introduced to this understanding. On some level, you have to be able to recall not having this understanding; and you should be able to recall the person(s) with whom and the space(s) in which your earliest incarnations of this understanding began to clarify in your mind. This understanding must be meaningful and not some trivial reference. This is an idea that matters because of its purposefulness.

I'll give you an example of my own. It wasn't until my sophomore year in college that I developed the understanding of how to use commas with coordinating conjunctions in compound sentences. Dr. Gladys Heard taught me that in a composition class for English majors at Norfolk State University. It was under her tutelage that I realized why a comma along with the words "and, but," or "or" together clearly signaled the reader that a sentence had two related ideas and that each was significant enough to warrant its own independent clause. This understanding was a critical step in my own developing voice as a writer, and it led to my use of more sophisticated grammar conventions like semi-colons and dashes. Dr. Heard was a tremendous mentor and teacher to me while I was an undergrad. In addition to writing, I learned a lot about grace and dignity from her, and she also gave me my first opportunity to teach a college course. In a way, I pay a tribute to her every time I compose a compound sentence. More germane to this discussion, though, this initial understanding I developed as a student lives in my current identity as a writer. A compound sentence represents a choice for the writer. It's a choice in how to use one's tools to express the relationship among the ideas in one's writing. It offers opportunities to add pace and form to one's writing that are not possible without a firm conceptual understanding of compound sentences.

Your understanding may be either skill- or content-based. It can basically be anything. Trace the insight or reasoning that was the initial handle on a concept, and if you tell the story of that discovery, there is affect that underscored your initial understandings. You felt something when you learned it, and you may experience the feeling again even just in re-telling the story. In my many discussions using this thought experiment, one thing has always been true: our big understandings always have some emotional context. The emotional context is sometimes a relationship, or it may be a remembrance of a particularly significant time in our lives. In other instances, the affect is the first inkling of our passion for a particular topic or area of study. The affect may show up in any number of ways, but our most durable understandings have strong emotional anchors; and the fact that these understandings evolve over time is even more evidence of the significance of affect. Understandings that evolve do so because they extend beyond the initial and limited neural networks so that they become embedded in other experiences and understandings. When we understand something deeply, it has become a part of our being in innumerable ways; and thus, it can be said to be accessed through a multitude of neural pathways.

When I first started teaching, I was excited to show my students how to use commas with coordinating conjunctions. I didn't fully understand it then myself, but I was sharing an intimate experience with my students that came in the form of a grammar lesson. I wanted my students to feel the command of their ideas in their writing through the understanding that some thoughts, though they are strong enough to stand alone, can be brought together to create dynamic and flowing compound sentences. And this superpower could be unleashed with a comma and a coordinating conjunction. My students used to look at me like I was crazy when I would explain to them that a compound sentence could change their entire lives, but that's what it felt like to me.

In terms of your thought experiment, think about how this understanding defines you. If it's significant enough to have continued to stay relevant in your consciousness so that you can recall the story, it must be meaningful. We are, a philosopher might say, the sum total of what we understand. Isn't it interesting how rich the story is of even this one understanding?

Now let's imagine that we are teachers planning a unit or single lesson that is intended to teach us this very understanding. The

CRE planning questions could support a lot of the most powerful connections we retain from the experience. Let's spell it out just a bit. As we discussed in Chapter 1, your understandings and mine are conceptual in nature – either in the objective, descriptive sense, meaning we use the concepts to define something perceptually, or in the goal-focused sense, meaning we understand the concepts in terms of accomplishing some goal (Barrett, 2017a). Our understandings have emotional anchors. We remember what we were feeling when we learned it, and sometimes, those feelings even come back to us when we retrieve the understanding. These understandings are rigorously developed. We've learned how to extend these understandings beyond our recall and working memory. We were engaged behaviorally, affectively, and cognitively as our understandings took form. We were not merely passive participants in the learning process. And finally, there was an element of responsiveness in the learning experience for us personally. Some part of our identity was leveraged and it bridged into other parts of our identities. The experience may have given us a further sense of belonging in some local or discipline-specific community so that a part of ourselves is birthed in these moments.

You can't reduce a complex and large-scale issue such as Equity to any one single variable, but I firmly believe that planning is a high-leverage behavior that can directly and indirectly address much of what contributes to the opportunity gaps in American public education. The five CRE planning questions allow us to get inside of the concepts we want to teach with greater focus and clearer intentions in order for us to facilitate more powerful understandings. When we plan with these questions – with our CRE lens – planning for understandings that entail the deliberate attention to both the skill- and content-based understandings we want for students and also the affective context in which they learn, we are more likely to develop lessons that honor the full humanity of our students in ways that invite their identities and cultural fluencies to the table. This, again, is what I mean by teaching our students in ways in which they can be successful not in spite of their cultural identities and backgrounds, but precisely because of them.

Equity work requires more elegant conventions for planning. You have to see design as something deeper and more profound than mere *lesson planning*. A vibrant and visceral experience is more likely to engage *all* of your students. You must have good habits for planning if you want to regularly design learning experiences that work for *all* of your students. We have to think boldly in our planning to close Equity gaps. A more integrated and seamless perspective allows us to better facilitate an overall dynamic conducive to the richest learning experiences possible. Regularly reminding ourselves of the overall purpose of our work allows us to *see better* the opportunities for responsiveness. Just like the themes, these planning questions should be thought of as a synergetic whole. These questions, taken together, (re-)introduce a perspective in our planning spaces that can further develop habits and behaviors that close Equity gaps by giving *all* of our kiddos meaningful opportunities to bring vital parts of themselves into the learning experiences where they are actively constructing their academic identities.

Your own capacity for imagining is critical – just as a character in a novel will come to life for a reader if the author has given the appropriate attention to vividly imagining the detail of that character. The writer doesn't need to literally lay out all of the details, but the reader will feel it and will intuit the level of research that went into the creation of the work. If you can feel the essence and life-force of the learning experience in planning, you will be able to more consistently express it in your teaching. (This is the difference between teaching the mechanics of compound sentences or the delightfully challenging experience of pairing related ideas for a powerful concoction of meaning.) We want our students to have empowered learning experiences from which they emerge with understandings that will live with them forever. These understandings, like yours, will evolve over time, but they can be defining.

I could argue that with practice and higher understanding, one sees these aren't even five separate questions but rather multiple and interconnected variations of one. *How do I want students to feel?* isn't a different question from *What do I want students to understand?* as much as it's a different vantage point of the same question – because we know now that reason and affect are part of a whole and symbiotic cognitive process and not two different functions of processing. *What are the targets for rigor?* isn't a different question from *What are the indicators of engagement?* because cognitive engagement is rigor in its highest form. It's Mihaly Csikszentmihalyi's notion of *Flow*. The question, *What are the opportunities to be responsive?* essentially asks, *What is my role as a teacher in facilitating for students a happy and productive co-regulating (in terms of affect and reason) learning experience?* This is the culmination of everything we would want to be in the recollection of our students when they retrieve their transformative understandings in the way we did in our thought experiment. Thoughtfully answering any one of the five CRE planning questions requires that we consider some aspect of them all. If we expand our thinking inside of the vital behavior of planning, I have found that there is potential for an exponential impact on the other parts of our practice. *It's just good teaching.*

Give yourself time to think about how you can marry these CRE planning questions with the six themes I discussed in Chapter 3. The six themes help me tremendously in nurturing the space and energy that is most likely to draw my students into the learning experience. Neither the themes nor the guiding questions tell us what to do exactly... but they set a course. The course isn't limited to any one single delivery model. The CRE themes facilitate differentiating the learning experience relative to cultural identities, relationships, vulnerabilities, and students' assets. With this mental model, I've been able to craft authentic learning experiences in a manner best befitting any given student audience without compromising the learning targets for understanding.

OPERATIONALIZE THIS!

Build Learning Experiences Around Problems that Students Can Solve

Ms. Erin's 3- and 4-year-olds learned a lot about literacy and numeracy as they sought to find their missing joey, but they learned it in a way that carried over through the rest of the school year. One of the earliest indicators of engagement in the learning experience was a phone call from a concerned parent who was more than a little anxious that a child, some poor kiddo named Joey, had somehow gone missing from the classroom! That means that one of our little ones brought their learning experience home in an emotional way to share with their family members, albeit with a slight glitch in the communication. Think of what's happening there. That is the epitome of bridging identities. When the learning goes home like that, the students are inspired to bring their home identities into the understandings we are prioritizing in school.

We wanted our kiddos to understand that we had a problem, our missing joey, and the problem needed our focused attention. Some problems require a multi-faceted and coordinated effort that draws on an entire community to solve. In the solving of these problems, we have to use our reading, writing, listening, speaking, design, and number skills. In the solving of this problem, we wanted students to feel empowered. We wanted them to feel as though the solving of this urgent problem was directly related to their ability to focus in on a sustained solution effort. I can only surmise that this was accomplished from the sheer exuberance we all experienced together once we had located and safely returned the joey to its place in the classroom.

Design Units with a Focus on the Questions You Want to Be Able to Ask Your Students

Over the course of these several days, students were confronted with rich, open-ended questions about their thinking. The information they were learning about the characteristics of kangaroos was enlisted in service of a higher purpose. In this way, the students were rigorously working with concepts, which is much more productive and rewarding than working with isolated facts and loosely connected information. Each day's learning leveraged the memory traces of students (and the teachers) so that the community was building a shared narrative around a learning experience.

The teachers knew that engagement in this learning experience would be noisy and have lots of movement. One of my favorite moments was when literally every student was calling out, "Joey! Joey! Where are you!" as they opened every cabinet and looked under ever surface in the classroom. And yet, even with that kind of emotional investment, we wouldn't have hit our goals for understanding if the strategies and activities we used didn't match well with the type and complexity of thinking we wanted for our students. With that kind of investment by the students, there were countless opportunities for all of us to ask our kiddos questions like, *So what do you think we should do?* or *What do you think will happen next?* or *What would happen if...?* Our kiddos' brains were so ignited that we were able to sustain their attention for long stretches of time in challenging activities.

Which brings me back to the question of strategies... I have lots of strategies. I keep a curated collection of what I call my "super toolkit." It's over 200 pages of strategies, but even more important than the strategy is a clear sense of purpose. Purpose is more powerful than even the best laid plan. Purpose gives meaning to a journey; where a plan gives direction to the next step. The emergence of certain obstacles or opportunities, however, may render a plan null. It is only purpose that guides the journeyer onto another appropriate course without compromising the intent of the journey. Purpose-driven, in-course adjustments are much deeper and more profound than mere strategies.

Frame the Learning Experience for Affective and Cognitive Engagement

One more technical note: Let's talk briefly about the idea of "framing." There's a fantastic book called *The Skillful Teacher* written by Jon Saphier and colleagues (Saphier, Haley-Speca, & Gower, 2008). It's basically an encyclopedia of classroom pedagogy. I've been using it as a reference for years. In it, Saphier (and his co-authors) discuss the idea of framing. Often when I initially use the term "framing" in planning spaces, some well-meaning soul will say something like: "Oh, you mean the hook!" But that isn't exactly what I mean, nor do I mean anticipatory set. By framing, I am drawing on the work of Jon Saphier in reference to something different, and frankly more robust than hooks or anticipatory sets. These are related ideas for sure, but the design of a frame is, in my view, more intentional and calculated to support a long-term learning goal for rigor and engagement.

Saphier defines "framing" as providing opportunities for students to understand the objectives, general itinerary, big ideas, criteria for success, and the reasons why the activities are worthy of the students' interest and investment at the outset of a unit. The more creatively this is done the better. In the *Finding the Joey* unit, one shouldn't underestimate the significance of the *Blabberize* video for framing the unit-long learning experience. That emotional draw, established straight-away in the learning experience, infused a certain energy and attention that was essential to the success of the unit. It was a rational and emotional reference point to which we could return and re-set the focus for our learning. Everything that we did subsequently could be framed by what we saw and heard from the concerned mother kangaroo in a 15-second video. It allowed us to ask, "Remember when we saw the mother kangaroo's video?" You needn't always use *Blabberize* to create the compelling conceptual context for the learning experiences you plan, but the framing is an anchored and purpose-driven tool for re-calibrating both ours and our students' engagement throughout a learning experience. If you can channel your thinking from the five CRE planning questions into a rich framing experience for the students, nearly everything that follows in the unit will flow much more smoothly than otherwise.

In order to consistently plan these types of experiences well, we must fully abandon the false premise that emotion (affect) and reason are distinct entities. Even if that were true (and the neuro-cognitive evidence is increasingly drawing out the shortcomings of this *classical* view of affect and reason as separate elements of learning), a pedagogical perspective of the sort is immensely limiting. It also profoundly disadvantages any student who doesn't (either because of preference or indoctrination) consent to methodically and linearly building an understanding without emotional connection or conceptual familiarity – as if that were possible for anyone. The human brain is not a battleground between reason and affect. Emotion and reason are in a state of perpetual co-regulation. Emotion doesn't hijack cognition and somehow lessen it. Emotion and reason are threads of the same fabric; to remove one compromises the integrity of the other.

References

Baer, D. (2017, March 6). This psychologist is figuring out how your brain makes emotions. *The Cut*. Retrieved from www.thecut.com/2017/03/what-emotions-really-are-according-to-science.html

Barrett, L. F., & Russell, J. A. (2015). An introduction to psychological construction. In L. F. Barrett & J. A. Russell (Eds.), *The psychological construction of emotion* (pp. 1–17). New York: Guilford.

Barrett, L. F., & Simmons, W. K. (2015). Interoceptive predictions in the brain. *Nature Reviews Neuroscience, 16*(1), 419–429.

Barrett, L. F. (2017a). *How emotions are made: The secret life of the brain.* New York: Houghton-Mifflin Harcourt; London, England: Macmillan.

Barrett, L. F. (2017b). The theory of constructed emotion: An active inference account of interoception and categorization. *Social Cognitive and Affective Neuroscience, 12*(11), 18–33.

Barrett, L. F. (2018). You aren't at the mercy of your emotions: Your brain creates them. Retrieved from www.youtube.com/watch?v=0gks6ceq4eQ

Bransford, J. D., Brown, A. L., & Cocking, R. R. (2000). *How people learn: Brain, mind, experience, and school.* Washington, DC: National Academy Press.

Csikszentmihalyi, M. (1990). *Flow: The psychology of optimal experience.* New York: Harper & Row.

Csikszentmihalyi, M. (2004). *Flow, the secret to happiness.* Retrieved from www.ted.com/talks/mihaly_csikszentmihalyi_on_flow

Day, S. B., & Goldstone, R. L. (2012). The import of knowledge export: Connecting findings and theories of transfer of learning. *Educational Psychologist, 47*(3), 153–176.

Heath, C., & Heath, D. (2017). *The power of moments: Why certain experiences have extraordinary impact.* New York: Simon & Schuster.

Hess, K., Carlock, D., Jones, B., & Walkup, J. (2009b). What exactly do "fewer, clearer, and higher standards" really look like in the classroom? Using a cognitive rigor matrix to analyze curriculum, plan lessons, and implement assessments. Presentation at Council of Chief State School Officers. Detroit, MI.

Immordino-Yang, M. H., & Damasio, A. R. (2007). We feel, therefore we learn: The relevance of affective and social neuroscience to education. *Mind, Brain and Education, 1*(1), 3–10.

Immordino-Yang, M. H., & Fischer, K. W. (2009). Neuroscience bases of learning. In V. G. Aukrust (Ed.), *International encyclopedia of education* (3rd ed., pp. 310–316). Oxford, England: Elsevier.

Immordino-Yang, M. H. (2010). Toward a microdevelopmental, interdisciplinary approach to social emotion. *Emotion Review, 2*(3), 217–220.

Immordino-Yang, M. H., Chiao, J. Y., & Fiske, A. P. (2010). Neural re-use in the social and emotional brain. *Behavioral and Brain Sciences, 33*(4), 275–276.

Immordino-Yang, M. H. (2011a). *Embodied brains, social minds.* Retrieved from www.youtube.com/watch?v=RViuTHBIOq8

Immordino-Yang, M. H. (2011b). Implications of affective and social neuroscience for educational theory. *Educational Philosophy and Theory, 43*(1), 98–103.

Nielson, J. A., Zielinski, B. A., Ferguson, M. A., Lainhart, J. E., & Anderson, J. S. (2013). An evaluation of the left-brain vs right-brain hypothesis with resting state functional connectivity magnetic resonance imaging. *PLOS ONE*, *8*(8).

Saphier, J., Haley-Speca, M. A., & Gower, R. (2008) *The skillful teacher: Building your teaching skills* (6th ed.). Acton, MA: Research for Better Teaching, Inc.

Wiggins, G. P., McTighe, J., Kiernan, L. J., & Frost, F. (1998). *Understanding by design*. Alexandria, VA: Association for Supervision and Curriculum Development.

5

PROMISING PRACTICES

The belief that strategies alone make one culturally responsive ignores the humanity of Equity work and absolves the teacher of their inherent responsibility to be a lead learner. To prioritize strategies over beliefs is the opposite of responsiveness because it expects students to conform to pedagogy when pedagogy should always be planned with intentional consideration of the students' needs and assets. If, however, strategies are used in the larger context of the Culturally Responsive Education (CRE) mental model, they can support dramatic shifts in teachers' practices and the experiences of kiddos. As I present these tools, I will describe some key actions, but I am more interested in highlighting specifically how one's beliefs and attitudes might inform the successful implementation of the strategy.

Productive Struggle

I'd known most of Ms. Allen's students for two years before they were in her fourth-grade classroom. Toward the end of the school year, after having been inspired by reading Jo Boaler's book, *Mathematical Mindsets* (Boaler & Dweck, 2016), we decided to design a learning experience that focused on teaching our kiddos how to leverage their growth mindsets to navigate the challenges of learning mathematics. Ms. Allen is a gifted architect of relationships. She and I put together a week's worth of learning with two primary targets: First, we wanted students to work with multi-step word problems just beyond their comfort zone; and second, we hoped students would use their math strategies to work through the moments in which they felt most challenged so they would consciously make decisions that allowed them to stay engaged – behaviorally, emotionally, and cognitively.

We began by defining growth- and fixed mindsets using a *Star Wars* metaphor. (The rebel forces and the Jedi had a growth mindset based on hope and perseverance while the dark side was driven by fear and negativity.) We used an activity we learned about in Boaler's book to develop the idea of synapses so that our students could better understand the science of how the brain grows when it struggles though a difficult learning experience.

In *Mathematical Mindsets*, Jo Boaler shares an account of how one of her students (a teacher herself) illustrated in experiential terms the concept of a synapse. I've used it, as well, with great success. In order for students to be able to develop their own personal and functional concept of growth mindset (meaning an understanding that kiddos can refer back to in challenging circumstances that can help bolster their sense of efficacy and commitment to the task), they have to be able to draw on a tangible understanding of why the struggle is valuable. If there is no value in a struggle, then it is hard to justify the discomfort that struggle invariably brings. To support this understanding, we have each student take a blank piece of paper and carefully fold it twice so that it has four panels. We then open the paper up and have the students trace the fold lines with a pen or marker. (It's important that the lines are pronounced.)

At this point, I like to show students a visual image of a brain. I'm very careful to pick an image with lots of wrinkles and folds because I point out to the students how each one represents a great deal of cognitive and synaptic activity. Sometimes I'll project multiple images admiring each for the length and depth of the folds, which indicates a tremendous amount of thinking: "Oh, look at these wrinkles on this brain, everyone. This person must be a great thinker!" We explain to kiddos that a synapse is the point at which tiny electric signals in the brain called neurons leap across miniscule gaps to connect with other neurons, and each time a synapse happens, we

get a little smarter and move a little closer to understanding something important. We then call their attention back to the neat lines
on their papers, which we explain are like the synapses that result in
their brains when they solve a problem in only a few simple steps.
Then we have the students take those same papers and crumble
them up as tightly as they can. Sometimes, we even ask the kids to
take their papers and throw them up against the wall. Now we open
the papers and trace the lines again, but this time it takes longer
because the folds are everywhere! It's important to give kiddos time
to invest themselves in the tracing of the lines because with every
coordinated movement of the hand and eye, the idea of synaptic
activity is more firmly developed. As they trace, we tell them that
this is what their brains look like when they struggle through a difficult math problem. If they aren't challenged, their brains won't accumulate as many folds and wrinkles as they will if they work through
the difficulties… *and this is super important because we want our brains
to have lots of wrinkles!* This, we told them, is what their brains will
look like after a productive struggle. I've had students trace and cut
their line-filled papers in the shapes of brains so we can save them
and decorate the classroom walls with the images of their wonder-
fully wrinkled masterpieces.

The students are then given differentiated problems, each written in
such a way that every student would struggle regardless of their math
ability level because it's inside of struggle that they can best manage
their own growth and sense of agency. They also receive tools in the
form of guiding questions, and they are instructed to refer to those
tools as a first attempt to manage their struggle. The guiding questions
we give them are:

- What is the problem asking you to do?
- What part of the problem makes sense? What part of the
  problem is confusing?
- What do you need to do first? Why?
- What do you need to know to begin your productive struggle?

After using the guiding questions as the first attempt to get unstuck,
the students are directed to use their tablemates as resources in their

processing of the questions. We want our kiddos to experience the questions as tools.

> When you feel like you're stuck, you have to first ask one of your tablemates to help you to use one of the guiding questions to get unstuck. That means you have two jobs: You have to ask for help if you get stuck so you can figure out how to get unstuck, and you have to be willing to think with a tablemate about what they can do to get unstuck.

Only then are they permitted to ask the teacher for help, and we are resigned to support the students by allowing them to struggle – so we are very careful not to give too much away in the support of our kiddos' thinking. We are hyper-mindful of our role – that we are facilitators and thought-partners and not solvers of problems. Anything more intrusive than that and we would undermine this opportunity for them to build their capacities for internal- and peer-supported resolve and resourcefulness.

The students struggled with problems on the first day. Imagine the surprise of those few who thought their problem wasn't very challenging at all when we served them another, even more challenging problem following their rather routine solving of the first. Then, the kiddos do a think-pair-share to discuss what it felt like to struggle before recording a reflection of the experience. We chose reflection questions that led them to look internally at how they responded to the challenge. On day two, the kiddos picked up where they left off the day before. They struggled through their problems, using their tablemates' ears and ideas to help them find a strategy. There was a beautiful buzz of math talk. *It was so dope.*

We differentiated our supports – manipulatives for some, an encouraging fist-bump for others, coaching for others on how to take deep breaths and re-center themselves; and by the end of the third day, all of our students completed their problems. The energy was high. There were lots of smiles, and a strong sense of accomplishment (and also more than a few metaphorical "bruises" from the struggle in various stages of recovery). The kiddos then recorded another reflection to speak to their insights having now gone all the way through the struggle. To cap off the three-day experience, we had the students do an "inside-outside circle" so that each kiddo had the chance to speak and listen with three peers about the steps they took to solve their problem and what they learned about what it means to struggle productively. Afterward, in group discussion and in individual interviews, the students themselves recommended that every teacher teach their students about the productive struggle, because as Tara said: "I really, really hope that you will teach your students this because this productive struggle is really good for your students and the struggle is kind of helping me; and it makes your synapses grow bigger even if you get the wrong or right answer."

One kiddo, an emerging bilingual student and one of our more reluctant mathematics learners, even proposed that this is an experience students should have often. In his words: "Many kids should get struggle, like maybe 100 times a year. And that will make you better and better, so that when you grow up, you can be way smarter than you were when you were a little kid."

The How Is More Important than the What...

If you have come straight to this section of the book without giving your attention to the context presented up to this point, you might be a horrible person. (I wouldn't know for sure, of course; but it's worth your attention.) You should definitely take that personally, but don't @ me. Just stop being horrible and read at least one (basically any one) of the previous chapters so that you can consider the essential premise of this entire book, which is that no single teaching strategy alone will make you culturally responsive. In fact, in planning spaces where I feel a tug toward strategies without the authentic contemplation of mindset and context, I like to introduce a thought experiment by asking: *What would it look like if this strategy doesn't work?* That mental exercise helps us to see that when any strategy seems to be working well for students on the surface, there is always a great deal in place supporting the observable practice that is outside of the view of the casual observer. *But it's never just about the strategy!* So, if you've skipped to this chapter and you don't yet feel sufficiently guilty to go back and read the earlier context, you are probably incorrigible, and thus, I will say to you what I say to our most challenging students: *I am annoyed with your behavior right now, but I will not give up on you.*

But, I get it. I totally get it. (Most) teachers want to be successful with all of their students. Some are willing to explore every part of their practice in order to do just that, while others want to keep beliefs and attitudes out of it; except, that's impossible. But, I really do get it. I too have had major challenges in my life at various times, and I have often (okay, every single time) wished for a simple solution to a supremely complex problem. But once my tantrums have passed, I've always found that my most productive and fulfilling response to the challenges – personal, professional, or otherwise – lives in the process of my thoughtful, reflective presence, and specifically in those high-leverage behaviors (like planning)... *And you know I'm right!* In the classroom, the way any single strategy is received by students (because remember that responsiveness is a student-centered measure, as in *perceived* responsiveness) is a function of a highly fluid incorporation of perceptions, fluencies, predictions, and past experiences. One great lesson isn't going to interrupt a longstanding pattern of disconnect and discontent, but the best thing to do when in the midst of an unproductive cycle is to start a new pattern; and the conscious effort to expand one's mindset should be aligned with some shift in behavior in order to make the change-effort more durable.

Brilliant teaching always begins with clear vision and a sound purpose. The teacher who deeply understands this is often able to evoke brilliance from even the most mundane of strategies. Planning for culturally responsive learning experiences requires a feel for the complete picture of the learning, and it entails having a sense of an overall strategy. The best instructional designs are planned with built-in flexibility because, as we know, there is much about teaching that cannot be anticipated. Plan with the knowing that a rich learning experience is often commandeered by the students' engagement, meaning you must be prepared to make shifts in the interest of the highest-value goals you have for your students' understandings. It's also important to develop a thorough sense of the space(s) in which you teach. You should have a feel for each part of the classroom. Think about your students' assets. What are their tools? Planning with a CRE mindset draws on the relationships and unique identity markers of students in order to engineer moments of authentic rigor and engagement. Consider how you will signal to students that they are empowered to use their tools in achieving the goals of the learning experience. Your planning should never be wedded to any specific teaching strategy or student activity until you have clarified the true learning targets in the five CRE planning questions. In this way, the five planning questions are the metric for the selection of activities. By that I mean, a good activity is one that best allows your students to think richly about the understandings prioritized in your planning (because as the neuro-cognitive axiom goes, memory is the residue of thought). A good activity is one that provides the affective context you want for your students. A good activity is one that leads them to the type and complexity of thinking you have targeted in your planning for rigor. A good activity is one that will support the engagement you hoped to see, and a good activity is one that allows you the opportunity to be responsive in the ways that build relationships and affirm identities. The strategies in this chapter are just a handful of those with which I've had great success. There are countless variations of each of these, and there are literally thousands more. Give yourself permission to be vulnerable by pushing your own comfort zones. Allow yourself to be stretched in thoughtful experimentation. See these strategies as merely suggestions for the instructional experience. Don't let anything you read here stifle your own brilliance.

These are all strategies used by many teachers that can span across a range of content areas and ability levels, but when they are used with a CRE lens, they have enormous potential for elevating the rigor and engagement for all students. I do not intend to be exhaustive in my description of these strategies nor do I claim authorship or ownership of them. Even the ones that I've had more of a creative hand in developing can't be reasonably said to be my own intellectual property because all teaching is informed by the countless generations that have preceded us. I believe all of these strategies can be successful in different variations. I seek here to identify the essence of the strategy (i.e. what the strategy most intends to do and the most essential elements of its form) with a clear goal for responsiveness. I am certain there are myriad ways that each of these strategies can be used successfully, and I celebrate any use that embodies the spirit of Equity in an authentically culturally responsive context. The best questions to ask oneself when reading these are: *What would this look for my kiddos? What does the strategy most intend to do? What are the most important parts of it? How does the strategy support students' rigorous thinking? How does the strategy allow for responsiveness?* Finally, I would suggest that teachers plan to use these strategies in a larger thematic or project-based context. Ideally, teachers should plan (and even teach) in teams and reflect carefully about what their students' engagement looked like, and further, what that engagement required of them as teachers.

Method Acting

In Chapter 1, I described how Ms. Allen and I used the method-acting technique with her fourth graders in a writing unit in which we wanted students to understand that they could create a clearer and more engaging reading experience for their audience if they *show* their meaning with their words rather than just *tell* it. Through the method-acting technique, we first developed the conceptual understanding of "show, don't tell" with method-acting exercises to get our kiddos used to performing some activity that they could otherwise just describe. With the performance-related definitions of the terms histrionics, concentration, and imagination in tow, our students practiced those understandings in a rather silly community experience – an experience which challenged them to be both creative and vulnerable.

Your preparation for the moment when your students do the method-acting exercise is critical, and you should not launch into it without the thoughtful consideration of your language and pacing. Doing the exercise with them, slightly off to the side but coaching them along with your voice, can help to alleviate some of their anxiety (and yours too). You should be careful not to be front and center because then many of your kiddos will be inclined to mimic you – which isn't how we want them thinking. We want them to have to translate a concept like "looking in the mirror" into something that can be demonstrated through action. You can also assume the role of coach, but you should first introduce them to other famous acting coaches like Lee Strasberg or Stella Adler (or another famous coach who will relate to your students) so that they can know that you too are playing a role as you move them through the exercises.

As you perform the method-acting exercises with your students, commit to the moment. Let them see you invest yourself in the performance of your imagination. You can coach as you perform. You can create your own exercises too! A good method-acting exercise is any mundane activity not typically described in rich detail but just carried out often without much comment or thought at all. So for example, "the breakfast drink" is a great method-acting exercise. You have to prepare how you will give directions so as not to infringe upon your students' creative expressions. This is how I do it. On a screen, I'll project the following while I read it deliberately and with vocal affect:

> The purpose of this exercise is to experience all the sensory aspects of a breakfast drink. You can choose to drink anything: either a cold fruit juice, or a hot drink like tea, cocoa, or cider.
>
> This performance should be done slowly. Deeply explore all of the sensations. The more time devoted to exploration, the more beneficial the exercise is for you. The idea is to be entirely focused and completely concentrated on the breakfast drink.

When I'm describing the beverages they can choose to drink, I like to playfully "forbid" them from drinking an imaginary cup of coffee because if our method acting becomes "too real," I say, "your parents might hear about it and think we served you real coffee, and kids shouldn't drink coffee, and then I'm going to have to assure them we didn't, and I just don't feel like going through all that!" You will know you have engagement if any students push back against that. (It's great in this instance to hear one student whisper to another: "I'm drinking coffee anyway." If a kiddo defies you and drinks an imaginary cup of coffee in their method-acting exercise without telling you, that is actually an awesome indicator of affective engagement!)

Then, I coach them further by saying:

> First, just imagine the drink you will have for breakfast.
>
> Now, take the cup or glass in both hands and concentrate on your five senses one at a time.

See the color, size, and shape of the cup.

Breathe in the smell. Concentrate on the aroma.

Feel the heat, steam, or cold of the cup. Explore the cup with your hands. Is it heavy or light? Is the cup hot or cold? How hot? How cold?

Listen to the liquid as you stir it or swirl it.

Now... taste the beverage. Be aware of the temperature, texture, and flavor. Concentrate on what it feels like to press the cup against your mouth.

It's best if all of your directions for the students are given explicitly with little ad-libbing so that you don't inadvertently restrict their creative choices. I project the directions as I'm reading them on a screen so that students don't have to turn and look in my direction as I move around the room and from one exercise to another.

There will be giggles and awkwardness, and your kiddos will also be amused and uncomfortable too. Think of this as a perfect transition into the "Mirror Exercise."

Now imagine a full-length mirror in front of you. Look at yourself in the mirror. Concentrate on your reflection.

Fix your hair... Style it just the way you like it...

Wait! What's that smell? Something smells bad! OH MY! It's so *stinky!* What is that terrible smell? Something smells awful!

By now, your students should be getting the hang of it. We really want them to commit to the acting because the recordings they make of their own writing must be performed with histrionics – boldly and dramatically. The "Shoes and Socks" exercise is a great time to bring up histrionics again:

Imagine that you are bare-foot. Wiggle your toes, and feel them against the ground.

Put on a pair of socks and shoes, and concentrate on what it feels like.

Wait! There's an irritating pebble inside of your sock! Do you feel it? It's uncomfortable... Take it off, remove the pebble, and try it again.

Your students should have already completed a first draft of writing before doing the method-acting exercises. This strategy works well with narrative writing, but it fits other genres too. With the momentum of the method-acting exercises providing the force and motive power for your collective sails, have your students get in front of their own devices to make their first attempts at recording themselves performing their own drafts. Find a space where students can spread out. Let them bring their drafts and record their performance pieces without interruption. Think of it as a creative experience in a studio shared by many artists. Your task at that point is to provide creative consult to any students who may feel stuck in their ability to craft a performance that is an authentic match to their draft; though, the whole point of this exercise is that they see the limitations of their writing so they can build their own understanding of the concept of showing and not telling.

Through their performances, students are better able to identify discrepancies between what they've composed and what it is they mean to convey. Students learn that revision is not merely an exercise in "correcting" what's wrong – but rather a reconsidering of their use of tools to more clearly communicate the intended meaning. The different scenarios are exercises in precision. With each one, you want for your students to be more creative and committed in their expression.

This strategy targets several types of rigorous thinking. I can cite from the fine arts version of the Cognitive Rigor Matrix in the *Perceiving, Performing, & Responding* row and the DOK-4 column:

> Analyze more than one performance or product (same composer, time period, theme, etc.) drawing from multiple source materials for the analyses (e.g., different treatments of same theme); Perform an 'old' idea in a new way.

The rigor in this activity is the opportunity for students to immerse themselves in a text, from the perspective of a reader, so as to get inside the ideas they want their writing to convey. This level of analysis will help to expand their perception of how they can use their language tools to develop ideas to compose more dynamic and illustrative representations of the sentiments they wish to express.

Once students are starting to record dramatic re-enactments of their drafts, you will pause the activity and give a brief mini-lecture and demonstration of how to compare their video recordings with their first drafts. *This is the critical teaching moment.* Your students will have to learn how to look for the evidence of confirmation and discrepancy in order to construct their understanding of what to do next... because once they understand that there is a difference between what they intended in terms of meaning and what is showing on the screen, they are truly the only ones who know most clearly what revisions are needed. If they don't identify that something should and could be done to better (i.e. more accurately or with more detail) convey their meaning, then they will resist learning how to develop their tools as writers.

Revision is one of those things where if it isn't self-directed, it will never be rigorous. If a young writer is merely taking directions from more experienced writers, rather than being creative in their expression through words and conventions, they're not likely to develop a strong identity as a writer. And that isn't to say that there's no value in following directions to learn some writing tools. But our goal is to develop writers with composition skills and the intact identities to match, and not just students who write, even if they are respectful and dutiful when asked. Your mini-lecture has to provide the tools for students to develop that sense of agency in becoming writers. Your most powerful moments of responsiveness using this strategy will be when you can show a student that with some revision, you now clearly understand what it is they are trying to say – because being understood through our words is the greatest joy of the writer. *Responsiveness is guiding our kiddos to that joy.*

At the conclusion of the first day of method-acting activities, you want to include time for the students to reflect. In order for them to take this activity seriously as a tool that can support them in becoming a better writer, they should have the opportunity to think about how this can potentially help them to improve as writers. In a think-pair-share, you can have them respond to the following questions:

- Do you think this is going to help you become a better writer?
- How is this going to help you edit and revise your writing?
- What do you think will be the hardest thing about this learning experience?

As a very last step you might ask them to leave themselves a short note with an important tip to remember that they can review before they continue the lesson the next day.

After a few days (but your timeline will be dependent on your reading of your students' needs), we also had our kiddos, as an additional round of revision, exchange their second drafts with a classmate so that a peer could perform a reading of their piece. In this way, the students had yet another tool to confirm or disconfirm if/how their piece was sending the message they hoped the audience would receive. This is also a terrific way to build on the shared sense of community by leveraging the vulnerabilities of everyone in the room in the interest of improved writing. In very short order, the novelty of performing the drafts fades such that the exercise of acting out one's writing on screen becomes normalized within the classroom. It becomes an expectation that we are vulnerable in our writing, which then opens opportunities later in the unit and throughout the year for students to give each other supportive and critical feedback when reviewing each other's work.

Memes and Gifs

In Chapter 3, I shared how Mr. Vaughn and I used memes and gifs to get our students to define different forms of government. I would encourage you to think of these images as opportunities to create buy-in so that you can respond with mini-lectures that build on the key points your students are making about the topic. Students are often able to very cleverly bring into the discussion some aspect of the content that you can more explicitly expound on with their more captive attention given that your points are directly related to their creative thinking. With this activity, students' brains are more likely primed to make meaningful conceptual connections because they have had to incorporate their own insights into a multimedia representation of the content. When using this strategy, I have found we have a much more attentive audience from some of our reluctant learners.

A meme is an image (often drawing on some person or event of cultural significance) paired with language to yield a clear, succinct, powerful meaning. The majority of the memes we see on our various social-media platforms are captioned photos that are intended to be funny and/or thought-provoking, often as a way to publicly ridicule human behavior. A gif essentially serves the same purpose as a meme but it utilizes moving images (in either short video or a rapid succession of multiple still-frames). The Memes and Gifs activity is an opportunity for students to leverage the communication devices of social media, a venue with which many have developed tremendous fluencies, to convey meaning. The goal of this activity is for students to explain their thinking, which allows for the teacher and peers to offer responses relating to some specific element of the meme in its relation to the larger academic concept.

I am most likely to use this strategy in upper middle- and high-school classrooms. I think any more than four students per meme-creating group may make it less likely that all students will stay engaged. This technique can be used in many content areas, but I generally use it in activities where I want my students to construct their own working definitions of terms that we as a class will further clarify. What is most important is that the students are given an idea or a key term for which they have some general (or even more extensive) background. They are then given a specific amount of time to create a meme in order to explain the idea or term to someone with no familiarity of the concept. The strategy compels students to synthesize their best thinking to create their memes, which they will have the opportunity to present and explain to the entire class.

I've gotten push-back from adults when presenting this strategy at times, and it does carry a certain risk. (I can argue that there is no strategy worth bringing into a 21st-century classroom that does not carry some risk because we assume risk the instant we put the tools for learning in the hands of our students. I can also argue the greater risk is *not* putting the ownership of the learning experience in the hands of our students.) The specific risk with this activity is that your students will select inappropriate images, in which case you need to be prepared to offer a thoughtful and reasonable response (beyond mere frustration). You will, of course, have guidelines for what is and is not an acceptable image to use. Specifically, this is a great strategy for talking with students about the importance of avoiding any images that "punch down." I like to find the opportunity with this strategy to make the case to my students that a good point doesn't require that someone is derided or in some other way made to look deficient. I usually say something like:

> If you need to make fun of someone in order to make your point well, I would like for you to consider if your point is as strong as you might think it is. Good arguments don't require that others are made to look foolish. Good points can stand on their own merit, and they don't require the denigration of others to be heard.

In classrooms with more reluctant learners where there hasn't been a lot of engagement, a thoughtful response to an inappropriate image can actually be an effective on-ramp to more rigorous thinking and an opportunity to build a relationship where it has previously not existed.

Your key as a teacher is to give careful attention to how and what you want your students thinking about and prepare your own language and response to deepen or redirect their thinking accordingly. In my experience, when the activity is linked to something worth thinking about, the students have engaged responsibly. When the students are able to handle the activity responsibly and they find that you are willing and able to fashion your lectures after their lead, this becomes a wonderful way to further develop a meaningful sense of trust and community. (It is self-evident that this strategy won't work unless you have a deep relationship with the content and the concepts you want to teach, without which you'll be exposed as not having a meaningful understanding yourself.)

There are several websites that can generate memes and gifs. I don't want to endorse any specific sites here, but if you ask any teenager who is on social media (i.e. 98% of the teenagers you know), they'll be able to give you excellent consult on the matter. If you aren't comfortable having students search out images themselves, you can pre-load a stockpile of images or have them clear any image with you before showing it to the whole class. Stockpiling images that you give to your students can be limiting in some ways, but it can also be helpful if you want to focus their thinking in a specific direction. I have, however, always been happy I did not pre-load my students' images because they end up surprising me with the memes they make that I couldn't have anticipated but end up working so well as a launch-point for my responsive lecture.

The memes activity is able to spark students' thinking in many personal and specific ways to support even more rigorous engagement as a follow-up. In terms of rigor, I can look to the Apply, DOK-4 target in the *Historical, Social, & Cultural Contexts* row from the Social Studies/Humanities CRM, which reads:

> Integrate or juxtapose multiple (historical, cultural) contexts drawn from source materials (e.g., literature, music, historical events, media) with intent to develop a complex or multimedia product and personal viewpoint.

Like many of the activities I describe in this chapter, this is a strategy that is most effective when used in tandem with others. In Mr. Vaughn's class, we used the memes activity as a lead-in to a Philosophical Chairs activity. This is students' opportunity to make connections and conceptual analogies that deepen their personal relationship with the academic content. In addition to leveraging students' social-media fluencies, this is also a great tool for expanding our own fluencies as teachers. Our students have a way of giving their memes context and explanation that affords us greater insight into how they understand some of the more important concepts in our content. We are also profoundly more responsive in serve-and-volley dialogue when we are engaging with language that translates their thinking into academic terms. I would encourage you to begin your use of this strategy by focusing on memes exclusively, but your students, with confidence and practice, will eventually be able to handle using gifs too. Gifs may require a bit more time to develop but with thoughtfully designed prompts/topics, it can be a richly engaging experience for an entire classroom community.

And one more thing, the debate of how to pronounce gifs has long been settled. You joyless people who insist on using the hard "g" to say gif probably also hate kittens! *You're monsters!* Can we all just finally agree that the "g" in gifs is a soft "g" because the inventor of gifs told us that's how he intended for it to be pronounced; and yes, I know just because he invented it doesn't mean he gets to declare how it will be called – but if you ever invented anything as cool as gifs, I'd feel inclined to pronounce it however you thought appropriate because you would be an incredible person, and that seems like the least I can do. Also, every pre-K, Kinder, first-, second-, and third-grade teacher knows that (except in the case of specific exceptions) anytime an "i," "e," or "y" follows a "g," the "g" by rule takes the soft sound! If you know this and yet you still continue with the hard "g" pronunciations... *you are a savage.* Just stop it, and be a better human being. Just say (soft-g) gif.

Philosophical Chairs

Philosophical Chairs is a type of debate in which students are given prompts which compel them to either agree or disagree regarding a position on the topic. In the Philosophical Chairs, students debate with each other on issues by making points in order to persuade others to see some argument from their perspective. Students are able to physically demonstrate understanding, insight, and agreement through the changing of their position. In planning for the Philosophical Chairs, the most important thing to keep in mind is that to sustain a good debate, the prompts have to be written in such a way that they can be reasonably agreed or disagreed with, otherwise your kiddos won't think rigorously.

There are lots of protocols on the Internet for you to find. I'm a fan of AVID (www.AVID.org), and I referenced a lot of their guidelines when I first began using Philosophical Chairs. These seven rules can be shared as an (re)introduction to the activity.

RULE #1: Make sure you understand the statement before you decide to agree or disagree.

RULE #2: Face each other across the center of the room depending on your response.

RULE #3: Think before you speak, and organize your thoughts and ideas.

RULE #4: Briefly summarize the previous speaker's points before stating your own comments.

RULE #5: Address the ideas, not the person.

RULE #6: After speaking, wait until at least two students from your side speak before speaking again.

RULE #7: One speaker at a time; others are listeners.

I've experienced faster starts to the activity when I give students a visual so that, as they learn the rules, they can understand it in a physical context. I like to show them a clipart image of two rows of chairs, facing each other, and leave that image projected while I describe the spirit of thoughtful argument. In the Philosophical Chairs, the students will get the opportunity to do one of their favorite things – debate! But too many kiddos (and adults, as well) have conflated debate with mean-spirited altercations. We want students to understand that good points in debates don't have to be made in hostility, and a really good measure of a good point is how convincing it is to reasonable-minded others. With the image of the chairs ordered into two rows on the screen, you want to explain that if a point is made that is especially compelling then they should be willing to move to the other side. They should take that decision seriously, but this is where I try to help my students to see themselves as the kind of thinkers who can be independent and fair-minded. If they, I tell them, can't be reasonable enough to concede when someone who disagrees with them is making a good point, they aren't debating, rather they are defending; and it's really hard to have an honest debate if people are being defensive. (That's probably also good relationship advice to somebody. You're welcome.) If you change your mind all the time, however, you probably haven't been thinking very seriously; but a good indicator of thoughtfulness is someone who can change their mind once they are presented with compelling evidence.

I like to give students a handout with rules on one side and sentence stems on the other to support their use of academic language and logic structures. Have a discussion (at the beginning and then as needed throughout) about how they can use sentence stems to make particular types of points. For example, you can categorize responses in terms of "To build on..." or "To challenge...". A stem for building on a point might be "I want to add on to your point about..." to encourage students to incorporate other good ideas into their own. (Otherwise, you might have a situation where the students respectfully wait for each other to speak but don't talk *to* each other but rather just *at* each other.) A good sentence stem to use for a challenge might be "Another way to look at that might be..." Or "Although... makes a good point about..., I think... because..." Time and again I have found that many kiddos who don't speak in whole-class forums have good rich thinking that they don't know how to share. The sentence stems are helpful for giving those students greater confidence to start their statements, which is often just what a lot of them need.

Unlike Socratic Seminars, the students aren't only being asked questions in the Philosophical Chairs but rather we can also give them statements to which they can agree, disagree, or in some cases, take a neutral position though I don't generally prefer to have a neutral position for my students to take. I think it's smart for our students to learn that taking a position on a matter doesn't mean that one isn't still considering, and the stakes are low enough in the classroom that they won't be branded forever by taking a less than fully informed position that they may later find to be unsatisfying. A good prompt is one that can have reasonable positions taken on either side, pro- or con-. If, in fact, you see that the positions are overwhelmingly one-sided, you have two choices: If you think that students have revealed a shortcoming to your prompt, meaning that everyone thinks one way, just move on from the prompt to the next one. If, however, you think students aren't giving fair consideration to one side of the debate, you jump in there yourself or plant an idea in a kiddo's head! I know that sounds a little disingenuous, but if you believe that your kiddos would benefit from digging into a debate for which only one side is strongly represented, give the counter-argument some life by whispering in a kiddo's ear, "Okay, I see why a lot of people think…, but I wonder if they're thinking about…, *ya know.*"

Be ready to dramatically perform your responses to students' points. It's especially important that while your kiddos are learning the rules and format for the Philosophical Chairs, you are able to give them rich affective context for it. You want to show the authentic exaggeration of your listening so that your kiddos will see what it looks like to engage deeply as they are also thinking about what the experience of the Philosophical Chairs requires of them. It's important to show reverence for the skill of making good points. The honoring of good points is essential for the Philosophical Chairs to be a meaningful experience for your students.

Let's get inside of the moment for a kiddo who might be a little uncomfortable sharing their thinking in a classroom but whose interest is also piqued by this notion of being able to make a really good point. In thinking about our opportunities to be responsive, there are a few things we can do to make it easier for this kiddo to engage. It's important to keep the prompt projected on a screen so that students can see it while it's being debated. When I introduce the prompt, I ask my students to take a full minute for private reasoning time. I think it's very important to honor a full minute of time because I want my kiddos to value the opportunity to think before they speak. I will remind my students when I can that my first thoughts aren't always my clearest so it's good to take the full 60 seconds to work through my own position. And given our familiarity with the strategy or the needs of the kiddos, I'll sometimes do a turn-and-talk before we get up and take positions. I like to move around when kiddos are processing, and listen in a little myself. That way, I can offer an affirming fist-bump or a paraphrasing response (e.g. *So what I'm hearing you say is…*). Any opportunity to help kiddos find some confidence and clarity in their thinking is almost always rewarded with more thoughtful and engaging discussions. So if we're thinking about our kiddo who is nervous and also curious, I can give them several steps to prepare before the relatively higher-risk effort of sharing with the whole class. Any of these can be the critical support a kiddo needs to take the plunge.

The art of the Philosophical Chairs is in the design of the prompts. In a third-grade classroom, in a science unit on adaptations, a teacher offered up this gem that really exemplifies the value of this strategy while showing two pictures, one of a North African Fennec Fox with its extra-large size ears and the other of a Sand Grouse, the species of bird that is capable of carrying water in its wings: "Which adaptation would you prefer if you lived in the desert, and why?" This question compels students to apply something that they have learned about the concept of adaptations with what they know or can learn about specific animals. In this case, the students had just visited the zoo, and their experience was fresh with these two animals. There is no right or wrong answer to this prompt, but it can be approached from many different perspectives. The opportunities for rigorous thinking are rich. In looking at the Writing/Speaking CRM, and specifically the *Evaluate* row in the DOK-4 column, the description that best conveys the goals for students' thinking is: "Apply understanding in a novel way, provide argument or justification for the application."

Inside/Outside Circle

The Inside/Outside Circle is an activity that organizes students into two circles – one inside the other – so that students can face each other in order to listen and respond in either explaining or summarizing their thinking in a structured manner. In the Inside/Outside Circle activity, students practice clarifying their thoughts and the language they can use to explain their thinking. Their circle partners are able to exercise their capacity for intentional listening. Through this strategy, students are better able to understand that with multiple efforts, they can become clearer communicators by increasingly refining their language and the delivery of their ideas more precisely.

One half of the students stand and form a circle facing outward. The other half of the participants form a circle around (outside) the first group facing inward so that each participant is facing a person from the other circle. (If there is an odd number, you can jump in yourself – just make sure you don't lose touch with your role as time-keeper.) Before you form the circles, you should explain to kiddos what you want them talking about. The topic should be either an explanation or the providing of evidence of something (e.g. strategies used to understand the math problem, or evidence to support their interpretation of a theme in a shared text), but be explicit about the amount of time they have. In the first round, when the students are initially getting familiar with the activity, you may want to give them a 15 second warning so that they can get a sense of how long a minute is. It is a hugely useful cognitive skill to be able to estimate in one's mind how long of a statement a minute allows for. When you call time, the listener takes 30 seconds to summarize what the speaker said. After those 30 seconds, the first speakers become the listeners, and the process repeats. When both students have each been speakers and listeners/summarizers, a round has been completed. The students switch by having one of the circles move to the left or right one position. Then commence the next round.

The Inside/Outside Circle strategy needs pace and rhythm to work well. The time to talk, listen, or respond cannot feel interminable. It is better for students to feel a hint of rush than to have a fraction of a second of purposelessness. This activity fails if students lose the direction of their conversations and begin to talk about other things. (Though with every round, you are able to re-set the sense of commitment.)

The Inside/Outside Circle helps to illustrate that a listening community is an essential element of learning. This is as true for kiddos as it is for adults. Many times, I've had colleagues who were writing pieces for publication, and they've come to me to talk through their thinking. Sometimes I've given feedback, but other times, I've just been a listening observer as they basically talked themselves into a deeper understanding. In my summarizing what I've heard them say to me, they themselves discover an insight that is a breakthrough for them. The Inside/Outside Circle makes that same sense of community available to our students. When they can see their peers as resources that can help them work through difficult understandings, they then identify other pathways and strategies for growth that are not dependent on the teacher. This is another key for our students in developing an authentic academic identity that can be sustained through challenging learning experiences.

We want students to have the experience of sharing an understanding in a way that allows them to feel further understood. It's wise to give students a minute or two to think about what they can say in the first round. It's good to have them write down a few key ideas that they know they will want to cover. In my coaching between rounds, I will often say things like: "Think about something you've said that you think really works for clarity and directness." Or I may say, "If you've found a really clear way to say something, can you challenge yourself to see if there is other language that you can try too? There may be more than one really good way to get your meaning across." Or I might just unabashedly celebrate their effort by saying, "Wow! I'm feeling like I really understand what you guys are saying as I'm listening in. Be bold in your delivery. I think you are making your points very clearly!"

The Inside/Outside Circle is an excellent transitory activity to stir those emerging understandings and concepts in a shared experience with peers that gets them up and moving. But be forewarned: If this activity works well, it should get noisy. You might see your little ones bouncing with enthusiasm as they share their thinking. As such, there will be many excellent opportunities to be responsive as you support specific kiddos in rehearsing their thoughts and finding language that most clearly captures what they want to say. When a kiddo really nails it, you can perform your understanding with a dramatic stroke of your chin and a slow, meaningful nod indicating that you see what they are making the effort to say. I don't often serve the Inside/ Outside Circle as the entree of any learning experience, by itself, but it can prepare the pallet for rich and enticing learning by priming the cognitive connections that students are making in their developing understandings.

Think about the cognitive activity that's involved with putting language to an emerging understanding in a way that someone else will be able to see what you see from a vantage point that you co-construct with them. There is a lot of rigor in this kind of dynamic back-and-forth. I could pull from many of the CRMs but in terms of targets for rigor, I look to the Writing/Speaking CRM in the *Apply* row in the DOK-4 column: "Select or devise an approach among many alternatives to research and present a novel problem or issue." In this exercise, your students will be thinking about how they can most directly and succinctly convey their meaning to an attentive peer. Your first few times using this strategy with your students will likely feel clunky and awkward, but if you make the in-course adjustments and give the proper clarifications, your students will begin to feel more confident in expressing their thinking and responding to the thinking of others in clearer, more specific terms. To support your kiddos in developing their agency, it's a good idea to have them reflect before ending the lesson. Asking the students to reflect on a question like, "What do you understand now about [some key element of the conceptual understanding] that you were unsure of before today?" is a good way to get them to better see the value of both repeatedly putting language to their thinking and listening and responding to peers.

Design Challenges

Design Challenges are some of my favorite learning experiences to bring to classrooms because with just a bit of preparation on the front end by their teachers, I have been able to be super successful even with students I am only meeting for the first time that very day. Design Challenges require only a small amount of physical preparation, and they can be fun and effective community-building exercises which also support conceptual understandings. A Design Challenge is an open-ended, timed project that encourages students to ask questions, take initiative, and think dynamically in order to create and evolve their plan in the process of design. Every Design Challenge follows the same basic format: Introduction of the task, time to plan, first attempt at a design, test of the design, and then a second cycle of the same steps.

All of the activities listed encourage the design mindset and support basic engineering principles. There are many challenges that you can use with your students. I haven't created any of the ones I mention here. In each case, no additional materials are allowed! A few of my favorites are given in the following sections.

Book-bag Challenge

In the Book-bag challenge, students are tasked with creating a "bag" that can hold a textbook (which you show at the start of the challenge) and be worn on any part of a student's body. Any kind of contraption that can hold the book is acceptable as long as both hands are free. I am careful about how I name the task. For example, I used to refer to the "Book-bag" challenge as the "Back-pack" challenge; but I modified the description of the task because the bag needs to hold a book and not necessarily be worn on your back. Most groups figure that out, but our language as teachers can unnecessarily stifle their engagement if we aren't mindful about the implicit images we project onto their thinking. The students have two design cycles (planning, design, and testing equals one cycle) of 10 to 15 minutes with a runway-style demonstration of their book bag at the end of each cycle.

Materials for each group: Two feet of butcher paper, one pair of scissors, and one foot of tape.

Rules: Students have two design cycles; the first is 15 minutes long and the second can be the same amount of time or slightly shorter. A book bag is successful if it can hold a book while affixed to a team member's body while they move a distance of 20 feet with their hands free of the book bag.

Results: The groups that are successful may not necessarily design a functional book bag in the two cycles. I reward groups who are ambitious in their design and also cohesive in their teamwork. As with all of the Design Challenges, students should be given the opportunity to reflect on their individual engagement and contribution to the success of the team.

Paper-link Challenge

The goal of the paper-link challenge is to design the longest chain using the materials provided. One of the most important things to remember in this activity is that you have to be precise with your language as you are introducing it to your students. This is so important because your students will be listening and looking for language that will cue them to a particular vision of the final design, and that could potentially limit their creativity in the process. So be careful not to say that it's "like the chain that holds the swing-set together in the playground" or make a comparison to some other link that the students are familiar with because then they will try to re-create a paper chain of that style of link. Instead, talk about what links do. Plan your language and don't deviate, or you risk taking the design out of the challenge and turning it into a more elaborate effort to copy their sense of what the teacher wants to see.

Materials for each group: Five pieces of 8 × 11 construction paper, one pair of scissors, and one foot of tape.

Rules: Students have two design cycles; the first is 10 minutes long and the second can be the same amount of time or slightly shorter. With the younger grades, I'll often have students send a team member to observe the other team's designs halfway through the first cycle. When I do this, I typically don't let groups send more than one kiddo to "spy" on other groups because I want the groups to have to rely on the communication within their group as a means to develop the ideas that will be most helpful to them. This becomes an excellent opportunity for students to reflect on how well they were able to listen, discuss, and adjust their process based on the information they received.

Results: Have the students line their links up and measure them to see which is the longest. With the older students, you can also discuss which groups most efficiently and effectively used their resources, which can be measured by assessing how much of the construction paper is utilized at the conclusion of the Design Challenge.

Spaghetti Marshmallow Challenge

The goal of the Spaghetti Marshmallow challenge is to build the tallest tower possible that will support a marshmallow.

Materials for each group: 20 pieces of dry Spaghetti, two feet of tape, one pair of scissors, and two feet of string.

Rules: Students have two design cycles; the first is 15 minutes long and the second can be the same amount of time or slightly shorter.

Results: I typically don't allow students to look at the designs of other groups until the end of the first cycle at which time the entire class can follow you around the room as you measure the towers. The winning team is the group of kiddos that creates a tower which hoists the marshmallow the farthest distance from the surface of the table.

Index Card Tower Challenge

Create the tallest index card tower that remains self-supporting for at least one minute after time ends.

Materials for each group: 25 index cards, one pair of scissors, and one foot of tape.

Rules: Each pair or group will have 15 minutes to build. The cards may be cut or folded as desired. The tower will be declared successful only if it can remain standing for a minimum of 1 minute when time ends. Height is determined by measuring the highest point of the tower from the surface of the table. The towers don't always remain standing for very long so the measurements should be collected simultaneously. You can designate measurers to record the official tower heights to assist you in doing so.

Results: After time ends and the towers have been measured, record the results. I like to make an impromptu "leader-board" and rank the groups by the height of their towers. As with the other Design Challenges, I like to provide the students with the opportunity to reflect on their groups' ability to work cooperatively and also their own individual contribution to the team's success.

Whatever the specific challenge you select, be careful not to give too much modeling and direction. If students see an especially compelling image of the final product, for example, it may hijack their creative process. I also like to set up a timer and project it so that all the groups can look to see how much time is remaining in the design cycle.

I've also had success framing Design Challenges with mini-lessons on growth mindset like the one Ms. Allen and I used in the Productive Struggle learning experience. It's important for students to know that their brains grow by working through challenges, and that every step in the Design Challenge process represents a synapse (in terms of understanding the problem, testing solutions, and improving the prototypes).

When it makes sense, I also like to bring the Habits of Mind into the learning experience – especially for elementary-age kiddos. I've customized a PowerPoint with a cool gif to visually represent each of the 16 Habits of Mind so that students can read, hear, and also see illustrations of the definitions. I use the Habits of Mind to help students conceptualize their strengths as learners and also commit to goals for their own growth – goals which we will be mindful of in the Design Challenge.

Most importantly, students come to understand that re-design is an essential aspect of the design process. Design Challenges offer so many opportunities for kiddos to build on the merit of ideas, and the groups that are the most successful are the groups that are more focused and generative in their design. That means you shouldn't panic when a group seems to have a doomed idea in the first round because they will be able to improve on their process and their designs in a second round. When the time limit for the first round is up, stop the students and have them showcase their prototype to the rest of the class. (Two indicators of engagement, by the way, are when they count down out loud to the end of the first design cycle, and when they cheer when you inform them that they will have another round to design.) The showcase is also an opportunity to add a little levity to the learning experience. In the book-bag challenge, for example, I like to give a straight-face explanation for why they need to pick the person who has the best model walk in order to show off their prototype because a runway-worthy modeling of the design may be the winning stylistic difference if all the book bags function equally well. However you do it, it's important to have some fun and be a bit dramatic in setting up the showcasing. If you're measuring how high the groups have been able to lift the marshmallows above the table surface with their spaghetti sticks, for example, you want to take deliberate measurements – twice! – for accuracy's sake. Or when measuring the index card challenge prototypes, I will very resolutely request that everyone stand back five feet from the table so that their breathing doesn't interfere with the measurement – and then for added emphasis, I will usually claim in mid-measurement with the suspense mounting that I can feel someone's breath on the back of my neck. (I've even gone so far as to suggest that a group is trying to illegally breathe its way into victory by interfering with the measuring of the other groups' prototypes.)

Resist the urge to give feedback during the design cycle other than to praise collaboration. If you comment on any specific strategy, your students are likely to abandon their own creative inspirations to try to indulge your observations. Be careful to give students a dedicated time before and between the two design cycles to plan. Ask them to not touch the materials in the planning time, but rather develop a strategy. The success of any team requires that they be able to draw out the strengths of their collaborators in order to maximize the likelihood of completing the task. The Design Challenge offers a purposeful and paced opportunity to find those talents in each other. Our instruction to students at the front end of the challenge is critical in supporting quality collaboration. The goal of the Design Challenge is for students to see that they are better designers when they are able to maximize and rely on every person's capacity for contributing. We hope for a mixing of concepts and a collective design of strategies. We want students to feel that with more collaboration, the smarter they all get. Design Challenges can effect highly rigorous learning experiences for kiddos. I tend to look to the Career/Technical Education CRM in the *Apply* row in the DOK-4 column, which states the target for rigor as: "Conduct a project that specifies a problem, identifies solution paths, tests the solution, and reports results."

I've also seen Design Challenges used expertly to support the sense of community with students. Mrs. Wolfgang, a fifth-grade teacher, had her students read several mission statements from successful companies before their Spaghetti and Marshmallow Design Challenge. As a reflection activity, she had her students first develop categories and then a rubric that they could use to describe and measure the qualities of effective teamwork. To get her students thinking, she asked: "What is it that good teams do?" Her kiddos came up with targets like #AllVoicesMatter, Mix Ideas with Ideas, Construction Zone, Invite Your Courage, and Elephant Ears to set their goals for teamwork throughout the year. As her kiddos constructed the categories, they were not only collaborating in building the norms of their community, but they were further clarifying and internalizing the lessons learned in the Design Challenge. By using the Design Challenge as a framing experience for the articulation of classroom expectations for teamwork, Mrs. Wolfgang and her kiddos were able to develop a tool that both captured the spirit of a rigorous and engaging learning experience and also charted a course for collaboration going forward. The students saw it as a living document which they would use to further develop their tools for success in the classroom.

Question Formulation Technique

There is an entire book written specifically about the Question Formulation Technique (QFT) by Luz Santana and Dan Rothstein which offers a comprehensive description of the method. I would suggest you read *Make Just One Change* to get the authors' first-hand and full perspective on the QFT (Rothstein & Santana, 2011). I've been using the QFT for several years, and I have found it to be a great resource for expanding students' concepts of questions and their own roles and responsibilities in creating a question-rich environment that is designed to meet their own learning interests and needs.

Broadly speaking, the QFT is an explicit step-by-step process that facilitates the asking, categorizing, and prioritizing of participant-developed questions. Students are led to "Q-storm" a rich list of questions in a high-energy generative phase where every question is recorded just as it is stated. The students are then led to review their questions, marking them as either closed- or open-ended, before converting a sample of their questions from one type to another.

Finally, students prioritize their questions according to criteria given by the teacher that further focus their thinking into a more specific direction. Most importantly, through the use of the QFT, we have the opportunities to:

- center students' questions in learning experiences that follow;
- provide tools for students to generate questions most likely to get at the heart of what is most important to understand; and
- develop a spirit of democratic participation in the classroom learning environment.

I've had many successes using the QFT, and there are a few key insights I share with teachers whenever I get the chance. The first is focused on the closed- and open-ended question conversations. The QFT gives us the opportunity to enhance students' understandings of the power and purpose of questions, and one specific way to do this is by expanding the well-travelled notion that a closed-ended question is one that yields a "yes or no" response while an open-ended question is "open" to longer and further interpretations. Logically speaking, that definition doesn't fully account for the nature of the response that a question is likely to yield. In my role as a researcher, the paramount focus of the design of a question is on clarity from the respondents' perspective – as in, can the answerer clearly understand what is being asked of them and does the questioner ask the question with an informed understanding of what type of answer is likely to be forthcoming? We have to be precise in our definitions or we will fumble over this critical distinction and leave kiddos confused and left to fill in their own understandings.

In my QFTs with students, I slow the experience down when we are considering what is a closed- versus an open-ended question. I'll bring the students to the front of the room and guide them through a discussion of intent, as in: "What kind of information is this question seeking?" A closed-ended question, I tell students, is one that seeks a fact-based response. A fact-based response is either right or wrong and there is no room for debate because we can confirm the correctness of our response through research with credible sources. We may not know the information when the question is asked, but we can find it. An open-ended answer is one that asks for an opinion, and the answers we get don't have a simple right or wrong answer because they depend on what the person answering the question thinks, feels, or has experienced. After providing these definitions, I then have model questions I use to test our understanding. With the little ones (grades K through 2), I ask, is this question closed- or open-ended:

1. Does Spongebob Squarepants have a friend named Patrick?
2. Is *Spongebob Squarepants* the best show on television?
3. Is there a blue Power Ranger, a yellow Power Ranger, and a red Power Ranger?
4. Who is the best Power Ranger? The yellow Power Ranger or the red Power Ranger?

The students know well that the first question is closed-ended because anyone can confirm by watching just one episode of *Spongebob* that he does, indeed, have a loyal and trustworthy friend named Patrick. The second question is a bit more challenging, but they can get it. With just a little prompting, if any, they can deduce that not even everyone in their household, much less the whole universe of television viewers, are of the opinion that *Spongebob* is the best show of all shows. We can agree with some discussion that the second question is open-ended because it can be answered differently by different people, and everyone can be right in their answer. I've had some pretty strong reactions to the third question, but maybe not for the reason you might assume. By now, many of the students can agree that this is a closed-ended question (but I have had strong student reactions to the fact that the question fails to mention that there is also a pink Power Ranger, a white Power Ranger, and a black Power Ranger). Finally, we also find agreement that the fourth question is open-ended because the matter of which Power Ranger is the "best" requires some interpretative analysis drawing on the opinion of the viewer in question.

I ask kiddos in grades 3 and up a similar list of questions, which I invite you to modify to work with the interests and context for your instruction. In Colorado, where I have done much of the work outlined in this book, the Denver Broncos are a sacred topic that one should handle with great respect and care. I've used these questions successfully in much the same way that I make use of the Spongebob and Power Ranger questions for the younger ones to help support the conceptual understanding of open- or closed-ended intent in questions:

1. When did the Broncos most recently win the Superbowl?
2. Who was the best player on that Superbowl winning team?
3. What year was the city of Denver founded?
4. Why has the population of the Denver area grown so much in the last 20 years?
5. Are the people of Denver nice?

The exercise in defining fact and opinion helps to clarify the investigative nature of open- and closed-ended questions and strengthens the students' questioning mindsets. As a qualitative researcher, questions are my greatest tools, and I want my students to be able to use those tools well which starts with knowing which type of tool we need to excavate the type of information we are hoping to uncover… And then you send them off to practice converting their own questions with this freshly defined understanding of closed- versus open-ended questions in tow.

It's also important to be thoughtful in the selection of your question prioritization criteria. A good criterion gives focus and direction so that students can pick out the questions that will most directly support the big ideas the teacher hopes to further develop in instruction. For example, in a second-grade science unit, I used this language for the prioritization criteria: "What are the three questions that a marine biologist would most want to answer?" The added benefit of that criteria is that the students will want and need to know what it is, in fact, that a marine biologist does. (Though it seems that there is always at least one kiddo who knows exactly what marine biologists do!) Your prioritization criteria is a lens through which information is sought and understandings are constructed. Keeping that in mind, I've been a part of many successful QFTs where the students finish inspired and ready to dig into an upcoming unit.

Selecting the Q-focus is the art of the QFT. Again, I would encourage you to look to the direction of the original architects of the QFT to hear directly from them what they have learned and advise in mastering the skill of the Q-focus. Anything that inspires thinking can be a great Q-focus including text, short videos, and images. I like to use images, particularly with the younger kiddos. I have found that "less is more" in the sense that a busy image doesn't always lead to clearer questions as often as the simpler and more direct images do. With less to process in the actual image, I've found that often students are more dynamic in providing context and conceptual connections, which is where the most rigorous thinking occurs.

I've also seen the QFT developed into a community-building instructional tool not only within but also between classrooms. Once your students in the fourth and fifth grades on up have become familiar with the processes and protocols of the QFT, they can be taught to facilitate the process for younger students, which can richly benefit both the older and younger students. You will want to have the older students reflect about precisely what elements of the QFT they found to be most engaging and most challenging – because this kind of intimate understanding of their own engagement will best translate into powerful coaching of younger students. After your older kiddos have had multiple opportunities to experience the QFT themselves, introduce the possibility of their teaching the QFT to a younger group of students. Ask them to consider the importance of younger students having the opportunity to Q-storm and prioritize questions, and their own potential role as more experienced learners facilitating that kind of experience. I've found that, if introduced properly, students are willing to take on the role quite seriously.

I've done this several times, but one of the most memorable was with a group of fifth graders. This was one of those rowdy classrooms. (I use the term "rowdy" here with a great deal of appreciation and affection because (1) rowdy classrooms offer the most growth potential to us educators, and (2) the kids who are rowdy when you first meet them are almost always the most loyal and dutiful once you earn their respect.) These kiddos gave me a serious run for my money! The first time I met them, they made me work really hard to maintain the order of a fairly productive learning experience. We did a Philosophical Chairs, and it was a difficult teaching experience for me. It wasn't unpleasant, but it was challenging to keep all of the students engaged. At the end of that learning experience, however, the most amazing thing happened. Before dismissing the class to proceed to the next part of their day, I gave them some honest feedback about their participation – including a reminder that they, as fifth graders, have some responsibility in asking for clarity when they are confused about what to do. I was able to deliver the feedback in a way that they heard me without feeling attacked, and as I looked to their classroom teacher for the direction of where to send the kiddos next, the students gave a spontaneous round of applause. I was shocked. I didn't think it was a very strong teaching moment for me, but apparently, something did work for the class – so I decided that we should have a follow-up experience together. On my next visit we did a QFT, and the kiddos were all brilliantly engaged. (That's one of those redemptive teaching moments I live for...) Everyone – the teachers who were present, the students themselves, and certainly me – were all excited about what happened. We huddled up together in the front of the room and decided that they wanted to do the QFT again, but I offered up the challenge that they could also teach the QFT to a second grade class too. We had to practice, and it didn't come together the very first time we tried; but we eventually created a masterpiece with our fifth graders independently guiding the younger kiddos through a rigorous and engaging experience of generating and clarifying their own questions that would drive a unit of study.

When I asked the fifth graders why should we have older students lead learning experiences like the QFT with younger kiddos, Juan said:

> We can talk to younger students... like if we're in a higher grade in middle school, and if there's a kid that's going on... they can trust us. You can talk to them so if they start acting up then they have somebody to talk to, so any kid that's making a lot of mistakes – and they'll be helping them. It's saying to him that even if you do make mistakes... that's a big difference in your life... So if we can communicate with little kids from different grades... and we can help them with their mistakes, and then they can trust them – the teachers that are in their grade – that they're not alone in that [situation].

Like Juan, I also think of the QFT as a strategy that can help build trust within and between classroom communities. It is a powerful thing to be heard, and any academic activity which can incorporate authentic opportunities for students to feel understood and supported in their effort to think through challenging tasks is much more likely to feel connected to those spaces.

In guiding the fifth graders through their role as facilitators for second graders, we came up with a couple of tips for preparing students to lead the QFT. First, define the concept of "explaining," which is, of course, more than just telling; but this is a significant shift in understanding for the older kiddos and an opportunity for them to draw on other parts of their identities – particularly those who are older siblings at home. Our fifth graders came to understand the task of explaining as bearing a certain responsibility for supporting other kiddos in their effort to feel engaged in a meaningful learning experience. Second, make space and time for the explicit practicing of students giving the QFT directions. It's important to give students multiple opportunities to practice explaining the rules of the QFT so they can feel comfortable in speaking and looking for the signals of understanding. Our fifth graders had many opportunities to practice giving the QFT instructions, each time searching for the clearest language for communicating with younger learners.

The targets for rigor draw from several of the CR matrices in terms of creating opportunities for students to *Create, Synthesize, and Evaluate*. Most importantly, we want students to be able to think dynamically in terms of the purpose and nature of their own self-guided inquiry into the discovering of new understandings. Through the structure of the QFT, students have a free and fair opportunity to download any and as many questions as they choose, but they are led to think rigorously about what types of information the questions seek while determining the merit of some questions relative to others (i.e. merit in terms of which questions are better designed to get the information we seek) and also having the space to collapse multiple questions into clearer and more effective ones. Each of these targets represents an important cognitive capacity that supports our kiddos' engagement at every stage of their academic learning.

Interview Yourself

The Interview Yourself strategy is an activity in which students are responsible for both crafting and responding to questions relative to a central theme, skill, or topic. I like this as an option for summative assessments, especially for my middle- to high-school-age kiddos with a multimedia production skillset. (There are lots of budding YouTube talents out there who would be able to provide rich representations of their learning on screens.) Most of your adolescent kiddos will be familiar with the Vlog format (which is basically blog content but in video form). Or maybe you would rather think of it as a video podcast. In any case, it's a conversation captured on video featuring the students themselves as both the interviewer and the guest conversant.

The video podcasts cannot be simple restatements of factual information, and the format itself will support that understanding for students. They will recognize that in interviewing themselves, they are dreadfully boring if they are only recalling information from memory. The more compelling interviews are those that provide analysis of the more complex and interesting elements of the topic. In order to demonstrate their points well in the interviews, students will have to consider both the most important elements of an understanding and the best questions to uncover those understandings. First, have the students design their questions (maybe in a QFT activity). A big part of the learning lives in a rich, generative process where questions are refined with focused attention given to what type of information the questions are likely to yield. We want students thinking deeply about their wording and the ways in which the questions may be leading (or misleading). This is also an opportunity for you to clarify understandings with students through your support of their developing questions. Short conferences with individual students to unpack the logic of one or two questions can be tremendously helpful in directing students toward more rigorous engagement.

Establish a time limit for the video podcasts so that students will be compelled to make choices about what makes the final cut. (This also saves you the trouble of having to endure an hour-long video podcast of kiddos who are infatuated by the sight of themselves on screen.) In this way, students have to consider their text from the position of both producer and viewer. Editing is valuable for practicing the ordering of understandings. In some cases, students may decide to re-arrange the sequence of the questions in their editing; in others, they will abbreviate their responses or cut some out altogether. Their production decisions reveal a great deal about what they see as centrally important to their learning. Without clear guidelines and support in editing, however, your kiddos may be employing video production skills without having to think critically about the content itself.

In assigning the Interview Yourself activity, you can give your students one meta-question that everyone must consider as a starting point for their individual productions. It can be something as simple as "What more do you need to know now?" or something more specific to the content which you want students to investigate. You can also give your students the opportunity to come up with one question and response as a mid-unit formative assessment. In terms of our targets for rigor, I'm thinking about the *Analyze* row in the Writing/Speaking CRM at DOK level 4: "Analyze complex/abstract themes, perspectives, concepts."

In addition to submitting the video podcasts to a shared folder where other students can view them, consider a World Cafe style activity in which students can present and discuss their video podcasts with their peers in more focused conversations. Among many matters that they should consider together are the logic and direction of the questions. I think of the question *Why did you answer the question this way?* to offer up rich opportunities for thinking and responsive reflection; but it is even more rigorous for kiddos to consider *Why did you ask that?* Those opportunities to think with their teachers and peers about the strategies for uncovering the essence of what we most want to know push the students to articulate even further what they think of as the most significant underlying issues.

Human Barometer

The Human Barometer strategy is an activity that allows students to place their perspectives relative to the positions of others in response to a problem or question posed to the group. A key to using the Human Barometer strategy well is students have to be given a question that requires them to consider carefully where they stand on a matter so that they can quantify (with their movement) their point of view (i.e. where they are on a perspective continuum in relation to others). Our opportunities to be responsive with this strategy show up in the form of one of my favorite prompts for students: *Tell me more.* Getting kiddos to talk in small groups at different segments of the line is an excellent opportunity to build a sense of community in which every student's input matters, not just to them but to others as well. In this learning experience, any one kiddo's clarity about where they fit on the line also adds to the clarity of every other kiddo.

In a third-grade classroom, we were learning about persuasive writing, but our students were not quite grasping the concept. They continued to write in the style of opinion pieces, which had been our previous unit. They were telling us quite convincingly what their preferences were, but they were not making an attempt to connect with an audience beyond themselves. The concept of audience is, of course, a key conceptual understanding essential in the writing of strong point-of-view pieces. Students have to understand that they need to be aware of the motivations and preferences of their reader in order to make a compelling argument. But our 8-year-olds (much like many adults I know) had a hard time imagining that someone else might have a different perspective than their own.

So we decided to go on a field trip... right there in the classroom. We had the students cram together within a few feet of the interactive whiteboard so that we could all together virtually go on a roller coaster ride at a theme park! We found a short video on YouTube of first-person footage of two friends riding a rollercoaster using *Go-Pro* camera technology with lots of dramatic twists and turns. Our kiddos squealed and shouted as if they were on the roller coaster, until the ride ended – and then we posed our question: *Now that we've all been on a roller-coaster ride together, would you be willing to get on that roller coaster again in an actual theme park?*

Enter the Human Barometer. The task, we informed our students, was to find out exactly where they fit on our line. We told the kiddos that they should go to the far left if they couldn't wait to get on this roller coaster again. This was for the people with the point of view that roller coasters are amazing! The higher they go and the more twists and turns, the better! We asked the students to go to the far right if they absolutely, unequivocally, no way, no-how would even think about getting on that roller coaster because roller coasters are terrifying! Only two students would be at the far extremes of either left or right, of course – so everybody was going to have to talk to their peers to find out where they should be on the line. The question of,

Am I to the right or left of my peer? could only be determined through some discussion in which each kiddo's willingness or lack thereof was calibrated relative to the willingness of others.

We wanted our students to see that though we all had shared the same experience, we were also likely to have differing opinions about how much we enjoyed (or not) the same experience and if we would want to do it again. My co-teachers, Mrs. Davis and Mrs. Venzara, had committed in our planning to use the words "perspective" and "point of view" as often as possible during the discussions, as in: "Well that is an interesting perspective. I hadn't thought of that." Or, "From your point of view, are roller coasters really, really fun or just kinda fun?" As our students were thinking about the concepts we'd prioritized in the context of the roller-coaster ride, they were increasingly ready to match our academic language with the ideas we were exploring together. In terms of our targets for rigor, I can draw on the *Understand* row in the Social Studies/Humanities CRM at DOK-4: "Explain how concepts or ideas specifically relate to other content domains or concepts (social, political, historical, cultural)." The students were each constructing their own concepts for fun and their tolerance for danger (real or perceived) as they were determining where they fit on the Human Barometer line. In order to explain their own point of view, the activity compelled them to recognize the differing perspectives of others.

I heard some great stories from kiddos that day. Maritza, who was way toward the right-side of the line, told me about a time she was on an actual roller coaster with her cousin, but once their carriage reached the peak height just before the ride was to start with one initial dramatic drop, she called the whole thing off and had the attendant come and get her down! *Weren't you embarrassed?* I asked. "NOPE!" She emphatically told me. "I knew I didn't want to do it. I was gonna throw up!" Beyond that being a rich teaching moment to illustrate the concept of perspective, it was a bonding moment for Maritza and me. Moments like that are opportunities to show our trustworthiness by not shaming students but instead offering a compassionate and understanding response. I helped her to understand perspective by letting her share hers with me. (By the way, the only reason Maritza wasn't at the very far right end of the line was because Jay was adamant that no one had as much objection to a roller coaster as he did. He was quite convincing.)

After a lively conversation and jostling back and forth, every kiddo found their final place on the line, and then we all looked around.

> Okay, everybody. So I want you to think about something. We were all just on the same roller coaster, and even though we had the same experience, we have different perspectives on the question of if we would want to go on that ride again.

We then had several students tell us why they were where they were on the line. We prompted them to use our key academic terms in their reporting – and then we gave them thinking maps to help them capture the big ideas for a writing exercise. While the Human Barometer is a great strategy to get kiddos moving, talking, and thinking, it should be followed up immediately with another strategy that allows them to further capture their ideas into a format which they will be able to retrieve later and continue to expound. When students have the chance to chart their thinking against the thinking of others, every opinion and perspective becomes a text which can be used to inform the understandings of others in the group. This is one of the essential elements of an authentic learning community.

Socratic Seminar

The Socratic Seminar is a structured discussion of a text and its related topics emphasizing evidence-based contributions of discussants. It's different from the Philosophical Chairs in that it isn't intended to be an exercise in debate. Rather, it is a strategy useful for building students' capacities for citing evidence in making reasonable claims. Socratic Seminars look different in different spaces, but it's a concept that I've used with students as young as first grade. When we set it up well, students can feel a great sense of agency in supporting their positions by making references to a text. All kiddos can appreciate the mental exercise of "I think [blank] because the text says..."

A powerful understanding lies within the Socratic Seminar format for students. When a Socratic is done well, and students feel successful in their participation, they can begin to more deeply understand the value of informed dialogue. In order for the participants of any social group to co-exist in a community (classroom, local, regional, national, or global), reasonable-minded people must be able to have an informed conversation with other reasonable people centering on some objective text(s). A text is anything that can be interpreted, so the ability to participate in an informed text-centered dialogue does not mean that all will necessarily agree. It means, though, that all will participate in good faith with the same facts and objective text. In the Socratic, arguments that are compelling are evidence-based, meaning they draw from texts to justify themselves. We want our students to understand that evidence-based arguments drawn directly from objective texts can be subjectively different from the opinions of others and yet still reasonably based in fact; and thus, while everyone is entitled to their own opinions, no one is entitled to their own facts.

The success of the Socratic Seminar depends on the students thoughtfully listening and responding to each other in ways that affirm the participation of everyone in the discussion. This is something that many adults struggle to do well, and it is a skill that we should practice with and model for our students. Hand signals are useful tools in this regard. Teach your students the universal signals of agreement. This allows others to participate in dialogue even as they are listening. Other signals can be incorporated into the format to be used by both speakers and listeners to further add to the clarity and engagement of the conversation. (I learned that in Ms. Smith's class where her deaf and hard of hearing fourth-grade students along with the rest of the kiddos use some sign language to communicate their thinking in the Socratic Seminar.) Once students have some experience with the Socratic Seminar format, talk with them about what other hand gestures can be useful in supporting the conversation.

Many students may feel intimidated by the Socratic Seminar format when they are first becoming familiar with it. (I actually think of that as an indicator of engagement because it means on some affective level that they are anticipating what the investment is going to require of them in terms of their own vulnerability and preparation.) In order to support these students, when I project the question and twice read it through, I like to build in one minute for students to first collect their thoughts. I literally have us all sit silently, maybe taking a note, maybe leafing through a text – but all of us thinking about how we might answer the question. In some cases, I'll even have my students do a short turn-and-talk after our think-time to steady their confidence and prepare their language. The important thing is that we want the students to develop the habit of thinking first before they offer up statements. Otherwise, they may start to conflate uninformed confidence, loudness, or even rudeness with making points effectively – which is the opposite of what we want them to understand.

My Socratic Seminars generally consist of two rounds. A round consists of one group participating in the inside-circle discussion while another group participates as outside-circle, back-channelers. I like to plan two rounds by splitting the classroom in half with four questions for each group, and then I sometimes introduce a video text after the second question in each round to re-focus the discussion. Each question levels up on the rigor matrix. For example, my first question will be focused on memory and recall using a sentence stem like: *What is…? Where is…? Which one…?* With each successive question, I raise the level of the rigor in the question. For the second question, for example, I may use one of the following sentence stems: *How would you explain…? Can you give an example of…? Can you tell me what… means?* For the third question, we wade into deeper waters with question stems like: *What facts or ideas show…? How do you know that…?* And finally, the fourth question of a cycle is the most rigorous in that it seeks students to stretch their thinking by asking them to make further conceptual and contextual extensions. For that purpose, I use stems like: *What facts or ideas support the conclusion that…? What do you think will happen when/if…? How might you change…? Is there another way to…?* I'm hoping that there will be opportunities for kiddos to extend a text-based reference with some knowledge gained through their cultural fluencies. Those are the moments when identities are bridged.

The first time you have a Socratic Seminar with your students, you will have to spend extra time going over the rules. I like to give them a handout with the rules for participation on one side and sentence stems on the other. (I'll say more about the sentence stems shortly.) But after our kiddos are familiar, I usually only review particular rules that I think need our attention or one or two that I want to give extra focus if we're working on a specific skill. The rules I use are:

- Speak so that all can hear you.
- Listen closely.
- Speak without raising hands.
- Refer to the text.
- Talk to each other, not just to the leader.
- Ask for clarification. Don't stay confused.
- Invite and allow others to speak.
- Consider all viewpoints and ideas.
- Know that you are responsible for the quality of the seminar.

As with any time that I introduce behavioral guidelines for an activity, I ask students to consider which of the rules will be the most difficult to follow and why. Thinking about why a rule might be difficult to follow helps to engineer students' agency in accommodating the norm. I've found that to be a helpful way to clarify our expectations and understandings of the expectations for behavior.

I've made a video montage of very serious-looking adults on cable news talk show programs talking over each other and yelling without any evidence of listening to others as an example of what we do NOT want for our Socratic Seminar. I'll show the video and ask students what they think. One third grader once said to me: "I feel stressed out just watching them!" To which I reply, *Exactly, our conversation isn't going to be anything like that.* When I am first describing the concept of the Socratic Seminar, I read and project this definition so that the key elements of a successful experience can begin to resonate with everyone:

> The Socratic Seminar is a formal discussion based on a text. The leader asks open-ended questions, and students on the inner-circle respond. During the discussion, students listen closely to the comments of others, thinking critically for themselves, and articulate their own thoughts and their responses to the thoughts of others.

The inner-circle is the space where students are speaking aloud and listening to each other. If your class is small enough, you won't need an outside circle, and everyone can be an inner-circle discussant. I take the role of lead facilitator in the first attempts at the Socratic, but my primary task is to keep the conversation flowing according to the rules of the format. I do not contribute my own answers to the questions, but I can encourage the engagement of students and their attention to the texts. If, for example, I see a kiddo shuffling through pages before stopping to re-read something and then making a statement without making it clear that they are referencing the text, I can say: "May I ask? Are you basing that statement on evidence from the text? It seemed like you were re-reading something just a moment ago." (When that's confirmed by the kiddo, I may reach over for a fist-bump with an admiring tone and say: "Nice use of the text there. That's impressive.")

I think it's important to provide and review sentence stems so that students can practice using tools of language to support particular types of points. Sentence stems can help students sort and synthesize their comments, which boosts their confidence for participation.

I give my inner-circle discussants these sentence stems though they are not obligated to use them:

- Can you clarify what you mean by "…"?
- I'd like to piggyback/add-on to _____'s statement about…
- In my opinion…
- I believe that…
- I respectfully disagree with _____ because…

With most classrooms, there are too many kiddos to have everyone attempting to speak in a Socratic at the same time. Generally, I've found that anything more than 15 discussants becomes difficult to manage. In order for your Socratic Seminar to be successful, students can't feel bored. We have to give them some outlet for their thoughts even if they aren't able to speak while they actively listen. To keep everyone engaged, I like to set up a virtual message board for back-channeling in an outside circle. Your technology coaches or your more tech-savvy colleagues can help you with this if you feel like this isn't your strong suit. It is not terribly difficult to do. It has never required any additional software and can usually be developed using your school district's web-enabled platforms. In principle, you need a space where students can record their thoughts and reactions to the inner-circle dialogue. I've known many teachers who've managed to insert the sentence stems on the message-board page so that students can copy and paste them with their comments. I've had third graders do that successfully. Just as with the inner-circle sentence stems, review them with your students and describe them as tools to not only help with language but also the logic of their statements. (As in, "So if you want to agree with someone's point, you can use the sentence stem "_____ made a good point about _____ because..." That shows that you agree, and then you can add on additional evidence that you think also supports the point.")

I give the back-channelers these sentence stems:

- _____ made a good point about _____ because...
  - made connections to...
  - used evidence from the text...
  - gave examples like...
  - used an expert's words like...
  - added details to justify her/his statement about...
  - added her/his own thoughts about...
  - spoke from the heart about...

- _____'s statement about _____ could have been stronger if s/he...
  - made connections to...
  - used evidence from the text...
  - gave examples like...
  - used an expert's words like...
  - added details to justify her/his statement about...
  - added her/his own thoughts about...
  - spoke from the heart about...

Keeping the outside-circle participants engaged is a major key. I read the room to make my determination of when it's a good time to pause the inner-circle discussion so that I can switch the screen from the questions to read some of the comments on the back-channelers message board. By read the room, in this case, I'm looking for any evidence of the outside circle's interest beginning to fade, or a dip in the inner circle's conversation, or if my outside circle seems to be so engaged that they may burst if I don't provide an outlet for their voices. But at some point, I switch the screen away from the questions and project the back-channelers posts. I read a few of the comments with strong academic inflections while editing in my reading any misspellings and/or awkwardly stated phrases so that I can best capture their meaning in a competent, academic voice. The point here is to not hold students hostage to their typographical errors but to speak their intent with purpose and enthusiasm. It isn't necessary to read all of the comments, but if your more vulnerable kiddos have made a reasonable comment, it's wise to put those on the spoken record. That's an important memory for kiddos to have as they are constructing their concepts of the Socratic Seminar.

My favorite moments of a Socratic Seminar, and it happens often, are when students reach out to others by saying: "[Kiddo's name], we haven't heard from you yet on this question. Will you share what you are thinking with the rest of us?" Celebrate when students share talk-time. I'm a fist-bump guy myself. When I have a student invite another into the conversation this way, I try to make my way over to the inviter and give them warm eye contact and a fist-bump. I want them to understand the gesture to mean, *You just did a really good thing, kid! Thank you.*

In some cases, you may have students who have struggled to engage productively in discussions with their peers. To commemorate those instances, I like to do a "play-by-play" style review of their engagement following the Socratic. It usually goes something like this:

> Hey, remember when you said…? Well did you notice how your comment led to [another student] saying…, and then that led to [another student] saying…? I really thought that was a very important part of the conversation. Your comment kind of set the whole thing in motion. What do you think? A huge part of what we accomplished today in our Socratic Seminar happened because you made the important contributions that you did.

When the Socratic Seminar is working well, it's an exciting experience for students because they get to feel in control of the discussion. I think kiddos like it because it feels impressive to be so responsible with their own engagement individually and also as a community of learners. These seminars can be very rigorous, and there are lots of ways that we can use the CRMs to describe the targets we set for students' thinking. One of many ways I could describe the goals from rigor can come from the Reading CRM in the *Create* row and the DOK-4 column: "Synthesize information across multiple sources or texts." If we think of each kiddo as participating in a shared conversation that centers a text and making contributions in the form of statements and observations that then become elements of a cohesive dialogue for the whole class, synthesis in a Socratic Seminar is the ability to pull from the many inputs in a discussion to add in significant ways so that the conversation continues to move forward.

It isn't always easy, but I look for opportunities to be responsive when a vulnerable learner is looking through a text and then – either at the invitation of another kiddo or of their own volition – makes an evidence-based contribution. I make it a point to come back to that kiddo and replay what I saw and how it added to the substance of our Socratic Seminar. I want to be able to hear from that kiddo how that specific moment of engagement made them feel so that I can use it then and in the future as a reference for how their academic identity was performed successfully.

As with just about any strategy, momentum is a key element of the success of the Socratic Seminar. Once your students begin to understand the form of the Socratic, they will exhibit more independence and confidence in their engagement. See if you can step back without the students noticing and let them take over the flow of the conversation, and please enjoy it when this happens no matter how fleeting it may be. Even 30 seconds of student-directed learning is to be celebrated. Notice what the engagement looks like and feels like for your most vulnerable learners. If possible, take a picture of them at the height of (or as near as possible) their engagement so you can share and review it with them later. It is with highlights like these that you can further build the trust necessary for you to continue to facilitate even more rigorous learning experiences with your students in the future.

Eventually, your students will be able to take on the role of leaders in the discussion. The student Socratic leaders are still required to participate in the discussion, and this can be a challenge. Ultimately, however, it is beneficial for students to take as much ownership of the learning experience as possible; and of course, you are looking for the opportunity to give the leader role (or at least a co-leader role) to your most vulnerable learners as an indication of your trust in them as thinkers and responsible members of the learning community.

Success Reflections

Success Reflections is a strategy I use with students in Kinder through the fifth grade who are struggling with behavior. It incorporates technology to capture students' reflection of a success from the day. This strategy is designed to have kiddos document themselves talking about and making sense of a personal success. The keys to this strategy are that (1) students can personalize their definitions and understandings of success in the most local and immediate contexts possible, and that (2) they log evidence of these successes so that it can be used as a text to support further discussion and celebration for growth.

I find that there's something special about a small, inexpensive tripod that adds a certain sense of theater to the chronicling of a Success Reflection. Many of us have an old smart phone (maybe with a cracked screen) that doesn't have an active cellular plan, but it can still access the Internet through Wi-Fi. That's actually perfect. The whole strategy revolves around students responding to three prompts:

- Today I was successful when...
- I was successful today because...
- When I was successful, I felt...

Today I was successful when...
It's important to be intentional in our understanding of each prompt. A big part of selling this to your students is going to hinge on how you co-construct the definition for success. For your purposes, what matters most is that the success will be able to be linked back to some choice (to do or not do something) on the part of the student that led to some positive outcome. For some of our kiddos, that's going to initially mean walking down the hallway without pulling down something that's posted on the walls. *Cool! Yes, kid! That was amazing how you walked down the hallway and didn't rip down any of those announcements! Wow, you must have really been focused on our appropriate hallway behaviors! That might be a Success Reflection you can record?* (Some of you might chuckle at that. Others are thinking of a specific kiddo that you could 100% say that to and mean it from the bottom of your heart.)

I Was Successful Today Because…

A success is anything that is productive (moving us closer to a goal) and good (benefiting the student and the classroom community). In this way, a Success Reflection for a Kinder student whose explosive behaviors have made them a less than ideal playmate might be based on a great game of tag with their classmates at morning recess. Your job is to help the student think through the choices they made that allowed the game to go so well. *What did you do?* is what you want the kiddo thinking about. You want to isolate the success down to a few discrete choices so the kiddo can feel an intellectual ownership of the experience. Maybe they decided to find another place to hide when their favorite hiding spot was taken instead of yelling at another kiddo. Or maybe they decided to tell the truth and admit they were actually tagged when they really didn't want to be "it." You want to be able to provide less direction and more support with clarifying questions as you push your student to construct their own concept of success in school. We want that concept to be underscored by an awareness that their choices go a long way toward ensuring the greatest likelihood for success.

When I Was Successful, I Felt…

But the most important question you want your student to consider is: *How did it feel when you were successful?* This is the critical element of the strategy that allows for your students to develop greater emotional intelligence and more nuanced emotional granularity, meaning they can explain their emotions in more detailed terms. When your students first record their successes, they will often use more or less general terms like "happy" or "proud." But through their reflections they are able to come up with even more refined language which will add to their command of their emotional well-being. So when your Kinder kiddo who feels successful for playing with their peers during recess says they are "happy," you will have an opportunity to introduce the concept of "confident," or "enthusiastic," or maybe even "encouraged." I promise you that if you have a clear working definition for terms like these, and if they match emotionally the context of the students' experience, a student as young as five can develop an emerging understanding for each. You can also use emojis to help the kiddo remember what emotional territory you've already covered. I like the idea of having a dedicated part of the classroom where the success reflections are recorded so that you can also capture the growing list of emotion words the student has used to match with their successes. In many cases, they will search for a word by remembering how they felt in a previous experience. That's again another opportunity for you to deepen their understanding of emotional concepts by searching with them for how this feeling is like one before but different in some specific way.

There are so many opportunities to be responsive with this strategy. I find that even the little ones only need a few days to get the hang of success reflections. I advise teachers to set an alarm reminder for themselves toward the end of the day to prompt the student to think about their success and record it; though, of course, you should be coaching your student all day. "Oh, that was impressive (kiddo's name). That might be a success you can reflect on later." But it's important to let the kiddos define the successes for themselves. Coach gently in that regard. Think of each success as a text that you can return to later when you need material to remind your student that you know they are capable of good, productive choices. A good problem is when kiddos feel torn between more than one success when it comes time to reflect. One simple solution is to have them record more than one success, but an even more rigorous solution is to have them share with you or a thought-partner which success required the most impressive choice, and then to make a recording based on that discerning metric.

But I advise you to go even further in your responsiveness. The video texts give you a chance to share the reflections with others to build on trustworthy spaces and relationships for your kiddo. With the permission of the student's guardian, you can easily set up a private YouTube channel, and literally with a few clicks, you can post the reflection and automatically send emails notifying the invited subscribers that a new success reflection is available for their viewing pleasure. I like to invite any family member with whom the student talks regularly about school. That could basically be anybody. I also like to share it with a school administrator, possibly a counselor, maybe a past teacher — basically anyone that the kiddo sees as trustworthy. The videos are almost always less than 90 seconds long, and they create these amazing opportunities to tell a kiddo, even in passing: "Hey! I saw that success reflection about playing tag at recess. That was awesome! I think I probably would have felt excited too! You made some excellent choices! Nicely done." I think it can be worth the investment of time and energy, especially early on, to march the kiddo around and commandeer a few people's time – even just a random passer-by in the hallway to say: "Excuse me, but I have to show you something. My student [kiddo's name] made an amazing success reflection yesterday, and I want you to see it." Every time that kiddo has to add some further explanation or re-tell the story of their success, it becomes more deeply embedded in their schema for school. With this strategy, we want to (re)wire their brains to know that their positive choices in school lead to success for themselves and others. This is a much better narrative about school than the ones some of our kiddos bring to bear.

If your students are older than nine years or so, they can probably teach you how to access the video recording app, and how to save the video when they are finished with their reflections. Students shouldn't be allowed to post before you've viewed the video, and though I think there is something significant about the ceremony of students coming to you to retrieve your backup smartphone to make their recording (plus it also gives you a quick opportunity to hear a preview of their idea for a success reflection topic), you can just as well have students record on tablets or classroom laptops. And for some kiddos, you won't be able to wait until the end of the day before you have them consider and record their success reflection because, well, some of our kiddos struggle to make it to the end of the day with one success intact without other behaviors dominating the attention they receive from others. So in some cases, you may have to call out a success at any point in the day and ask the kiddo if they are okay to go and capture a reflection right then and there.

Here is a critical caveat: You must continue this method even on the days that the kiddo presents the most challenging behaviors – and if that means your student has pushed your buttons to the point where this is difficult for you (as our kiddos sometimes do), you're going to have to have another trusted adult help your student to get something recorded. These are the moments when they are testing the boundaries of our trustworthiness. You have to operationalize your commitment to never give up on this kiddo in these instances. You are showing your student that even when you make unproductive choices, *I'm going to be here for you.* You might not be as happy with their choices as you would be in other circumstances, but you are committed to supporting them through it all.

Whatever your technical implementation, the strategy must essentially do the following to maintain its integrity:

- provides students the opportunity to own their successes as a function of their choices and behaviors;
- creates spaces in which students can use language to express their feelings relative to a success that is directly attributed to their choices and learn emotional granularity through the discussion of their feelings, i.e. emotional intelligence;
- creates a structure in which students can literally see themselves (on screen) as successful;
- teaches students how to manage their behavioral and affective engagement;
- compels students to tell the story of their successes.

Many middle- and high-school students will balk at recording themselves in a video reflection, but this strategy can be adapted for secondary students through the use of text messaging. Simply use the prompts and have students send their responses to you from their phones. You can either set up a group text or get the kiddo's permission to forward the text messages to other trusted adults. The spirit of the strategy is the same, delivered through a different digital medium.

Once, a principal asked me to spend some time speaking with a kiddo I've known for a few years who was struggling with behaviors in his fifth-grade classroom. When he came to talk to me, his shoulders were drooped, his glance was downward, his pace was slow. He had just freshly disrupted the classroom environment and been disciplined for it, and I read his body language to mean he was anticipating another negative response from me. (I also read his body language to mean that he viewed me as trustworthy because he wasn't projecting hostility toward me but rather regret.) I sat him down, and told him that before we speak about why he had been pulled from class, I wanted to give myself a minute to de-escalate because I had been having a rough morning myself. I opened up my laptop, and I pulled up some footage of him talking about his success in a math experience that challenged him. I watched the video without letting my student see the screen. He could only hear himself speaking. In it, he talked about the feeling of accomplishment he felt for having a growth mindset instead of a fixed mindset, though he acknowledged it's really hard to do in math. By watching the video, I reminded him that I know who he is when he's making productive choices. The video also recreates a much more textured affective memory of the experience; it's like we were both transported back to its emotional context. After watching the few minutes of footage, I closed the computer and said, "Okay, I'm ready to talk. I just needed something to lift my mood a little bit." We then had an honest and forthcoming conversation about his behavior, the choices that were leading to his behavior, and then we developed a strategy to help avert similar situations in the future. I feel like I let him know in no uncertain terms why this was important and that my expectations were that he followed through on what we discussed. I was not easy on him. I say I feel like I was clear because I did wonder for a split second when, as we were ending the discussion, as he got up from the table to walk back to his classroom, he turned to me and said: "That was a good talk. We should do this again sometime."

The Success Reflections strategy draws from several of the CR matrices in terms of *evaluating and analyzing*. Most significantly, the images of students speaking to their own agency in a successful school experience compels them to analyze the inner-workings of those successes as a function of their choices. It allows them to evaluate their own emerging fluencies in academic spaces so that they will be able to better predict how their choices can contribute to successes in the future. The record of the students' reflections becomes a text that should be returned to because, like all rich and sacred texts, their meaning is deepened through our own expanded experience. When students are able to evaluate and analyze their own engagement, it demystifies the school experience and makes the likelihood of their future success much more realistic than it would be without the texts to support our conclusions.

The Bat Phone

It's important to redirect behaviors that are disruptive to instruction, but we have to find ways to do so that restore (and not tear down) relationships so that students can feel as though they have meaningful opportunities to experience connection to teachers and the school community. I like the Bat Phone strategy as a way to signal to students that we teachers recognize and appreciate their appropriate engagement (behavioral, affective, and cognitive). It's simple. You need a device (i.e. cell phone, tablet, or laptop) with texting capability. I like to let students know what kind of engagement I am prioritizing for the day, as in: "I'm looking for connections today. If you can impress me with a thoughtful connection or extension of one of our big ideas today, you're gonna get the Bat Phone."

With the Bat Phone, students send a text message to whomever they choose to let know that they got caught being engaged in the learning, and that the teacher wanted them to know. The students fire off a quick text in their home language (and there are platforms that can translate the messages into the languages you select). I've found that kiddos try to keep a cool visage when they get to use the Bat Phone, but inside, they're excited for the chance to share good news with a family member. But the coolest thing about this strategy is that the family members often text back, not realizing that the student has given back the Bat Phone to the teacher once they've hit send. You get to see these warm, congratulatory return messages. I will often tell a student privately at the beginning of class: "Let's send a positive text message home today, okay? Give me something good so I can pass on the Bat Phone." (And I can't think of a reason why I wouldn't give the bat phone to the same kid every day if they were giving Bat-Phone-worthy engagement *every* day.)

In addition to building trust with the student, the Bat Phone strategy makes your voice more credible with a family member when you need to make contact about an inappropriate behavior (though that shouldn't be the purpose for the strategy). Think of this as a strategy to support the momentum of engagement. It is most useful to immediately acknowledge the choices and engagement of students as close to the experience as possible, particularly for our most vulnerable learners. It is in these instances where they begin to better understand just how they are leveraging their assets in support of their successful engagement in school. We position ourselves to earn their trust when we can be there to validate the moment.

OPERATIONALIZE THIS!

Provide Your Students Tools for Engaging with Both the Content and Their Emotions as They Encounter the Inevitable Struggles of Learning

Though the "Productive Struggle" learning experience was developed in the context of mathematics content, what we most wanted our students to understand is that it is good to struggle. Productive struggle supports learning, and you can't be your best self if you don't struggle – because struggle yields growth. In this way, our students can better own their feelings and reaction in the midst of struggle as something that is a routine part of the learning process, and thus, struggle is not something to be avoided but rather welcomed because it is an opportunity for and indicator of growth. In order to truly understand the value of struggle you have to experience it beyond the abstract. In the midst of the experience for struggle, you also need spaces for safe reflection and the consideration of your next steps. You have to have a problem that challenges you, and the solving of the problem has to be important to you, and you have to feel agency in solving it.

We wanted to see students use their tools to stay engaged through the struggle, and we wanted them to see their engagement as a function of their choices. Instead of following a narrative of, *This math problem is challenging, and I can't do it successfully*, we wanted students to develop a new narrative of, *I have tools that can help me persevere where I may otherwise think I have no hope of being successful.* The tools for getting unstuck and the calibration of the difficulty of the problems for each kiddo are major keys in this project. Ms. Allen had to know which problems would provide challenges to which kiddos because this project would potentially do great harm to any student who *did not* feel struggle. We wanted students to analyze the math problems that challenged their mathematical understandings – which could only happen in any authentic way if they weren't immediately able to solve the problem. We wanted to think critically beyond, *What is the answer?* toward a more rigorous understanding of *How is this problem challenging me?*

Differentiate Without Compromising Rigor

A kiddo who *doesn't* experience the challenge of the multi-step math word problem is more vulnerable in the future when they inevitably encounter the struggle because it can represent an existential crisis to their identity as a math learner. They may reason with themselves that they've never before struggled even though they are aware that others have... so maybe *this* problem represents the limits of their mathematical abilities. In that moment, the most effective strategy is the awareness that tools can be used to support their continued effort. The only question is to identify the steps – but they can be certain that there are strategies at their disposal that can help.

Though there were different mathematics problems for students based on their skill levels, we had the same goals for rigor for everyone. We wanted students to be able to *evaluate* at a DOK-4 level, which is defined in the Math CRM as students "gathering, analyzing, and evaluating information to draw conclusions." Similarly, we also had the target for students to *create* at the DOK-4 in the "design of a mathematical model to inform and solve a practical or abstract situation."

Ms. Allen and I used the Inside/Outside Circle as an exercise for students to reflect on how they came to realize which strategies were most useful to them with the multi-step math word problems. This is also an important opportunity to allow students to draw from their cultural fluencies inside of the concept of struggle because the ways in which we engage in difficult times has a lot to do with our cultural indoctrinations relative to larger narratives of challenge and difficulty. We were hoping this exercise would really help to confirm for each of them that their learning was the product of their thoughtfulness and sustained effort. In the Inside/Outside Circle, they got to own their victory by giving account for how they remained vigilant in a challenging experience. Staying engaged until you can figure out a better pathway in the effort to solve a problem is an excellent definition of "productive struggle," and once students experience it for themselves, they know for sure that they have the capacity to rise above difficult learning challenges. When students are able to track their progress and their effort, they learn enormously valuable lessons about mathematics and their own self-efficacy. In this experience, we generate a specific and individual text of each student's success through a challenging learning experience which we can use for celebration and reflection. Essentially, we will be able to say whenever a student feels challenged: "I remember when you were productive in your struggle with that math problem…"

Stay Engaged Yourself

Equity work has both an emotional and logical structure. The logical structure of Equity work is anchored to questions about practice. These are what are often colloquially referred to as the *Now what?* questions… as in, *How do I organize a culturally responsive learning experience?* At times, I've found in my work with teachers that these questions are asked inauthentically as a way to undermine the commitments required to challenge mindsets that may be directly or indirectly limiting the opportunities of our most vulnerable students. At other times, these questions are honestly asked with the intent of operationalizing shifts in attitudes in alignment with strategies to improve access for all students to meaningful opportunities to learn.

The emotional structure of Equity work entails the difficult tasks of evolving one's own thinking in ways that may be immensely personal. It requires us to be accountable in the most profound sense. Humans are emotional beings, and emotional thought gives context to our perceptions of ourselves and the world around us (Immordino-Yang, 2011b; Barrett, 2017). What I think of as Equity work is powerfully emotional, and is only accomplished with a sustained commitment to the task of seeing oneself in the (sometimes) unflattering gaze of our students (Delpit, 1995). As such, none of the strategies will help you if your mindset is not properly calibrated; but it is possible, I believe, to develop one's mindset through our focused and intentional attention to the logical structures of CRE.

So, as an example, if you are a person who believes it isn't appropriate to discuss race and identity as it pertains to your pedagogy, the strategies in this chapter will not yield the richest harvest in your practice; but they'll probably help you to be better than you would have been otherwise. If, however, you are willing to be vulnerable in giving consideration to how your own racial and cultural narratives may be influencing your view of what's possible for *all* of your students, and in particular, your racial- and ethnic-minority students, you will find that these strategies have potential to unlock both yours and your students' brilliance in ways you may not have seen before.

References

Barrett, L. F. (2017). *How emotions are made: The secret life of the brain.* New York: Houghton-Mifflin Harcourt; London, England: Macmillan.

Boaler, J., & Dweck, C. S. (2016). *Mathematical mindsets: Unleashing students' potential through creative math, inspiring messages and innovative teaching.* San Francisco, CA: Jossey-Bass.

Delpit, L. D. (1995). *Other people's children: Cultural conflict in the classroom.* New York: New Press.

Immordino-Yang, M. H. (2011b). Implications of affective and social neuroscience for educational theory. *Educational Philosophy and Theory, 43*(1), 98–103.

Rothstein, D., & Santana, L.. (2011). *Make just one change: Teach students to ask their own questions.* Cambridge, MA: Harvard Education Press.

6

IMPLICATIONS AND NEXT STEPS: WHERE DO WE GO FROM HERE?

I've referred many times to concepts throughout this book. If you accept the premise that concepts are the substance and building blocks of shared understandings, then we can extend that premise to a larger observation that these shared understandings taken together become the organizing framework for our social reality. But let's consider even further that concepts evolve, and therefore so do social realities. School is a concept – as is the role of both the teacher and student. We have to evolve our concepts so that educational opportunity is relevant and available to *all*, which means we have to evolve with greater attention to and intention for supporting fairness and Equity... or the great and honorable concept of American public schools may perish on our watch.

There are no hidden secrets that, once revealed, make the work of Equity in education easily accomplished; nor is there anything programmatic about brilliant teaching. In fact, in writing this book, I'm hoping to convey the opposite. I am not attempting to tell teachers what to do; but I do want to tell them what they can do. And there's a lot that isn't even addressed in this book! Rather than to try to be exhaustive (which is impossible), my goal is to point teachers in the direction of a particular kind of adventure. Ironically, it's the adventure most of us imagined when we first entered the profession. I am aware that there are many teachers who know much more than me about what it means to do the work of Equity day-in-and-day-out with our kiddos – and to those teachers, I salute you. I respect and appreciate you so much. Thank you, thank you, thank you... for all that you do. Sometimes, when I'm in your classrooms, I'll quietly ask one of your students if they know how lucky they are to have you as their teacher, and they always do. Even though they don't always cooperate, our kids know when they are in the presence of brilliance. I had my own great teachers too. I still wonder, even after having told them, if they truly realize how much they've helped me. I don't think they do; but I know.

In my work with teachers, I am often asked for answers to problems of practice; but the process of problem-solving is most effective when it's consistently capable of generating the right questions. We must ask the right questions to support our design of strategies (and combinations of strategies) to address novel circumstances in ways that align with our values and core beliefs about Equity and opportunity. Among the most harmful inclinations in this work is the search for shortcuts. If there was a simple checklist to Equity, I feel certain that I would have found it by now – and I would happily share it on every platform I have. Rather, what I've found is that the desire to reduce complex matters to bite-size solutions can corrupt the search for truth. I hope that in reading this book you have come to (re)consider some of the many ways that you can more consistently operationalize your intentions in order to be more responsive in your practices; and for most teachers I think of this as less a matter of complete reinvention than one of re-patterning and re-tooling. We re-pattern our mindset so that we can see better. We re-tool our practice to be consistently clearer in how we serve the purposes of Equity work. Our focus should be on bringing our theory into alignment with our beliefs and further into our practice because, in truth, there is no separation of theory from practice. Practice is the illustration of theory; theory is the seat of practice. Neither exists in sovereign designation irrespective of the other.

OPERATIONALIZE THIS!

Think Like an Artist

Having presented a defense of Equity as a goal-focused concept for teaching and learning consistent with the original purposes of

American public education, the six CRE themes and the five CRE planning questions, along with strategies that can be employed to operationalize the CRE mental model, I want to step back and re-state some simple truths about the mindset necessary to be brilliant with all of our students and particularly our most vulnerable learners.

I think of teaching as an art that is based on scientific principles. Thus, I think every teacher is an artist, and we work with the medium of "experience." We create with our choices, or one might say, creativity in our practice is expressed through choices that are inspired by our sense of purpose. In this way, teaching is much like performance art. The brilliant teacher is the brilliant performance artist. The goal of the performance artist is to create a powerful and enlightening work of art. Performance art, done well, is a pure and authentic form of engagement with one's audience. For the artist, it requires a release from one's fears and insecurities. It is that sense of liberation that invites the audience to find similar freedom. And yet, performance art, unlike a scripted experience of theater, is real. Performance art is a function of a full, human presence that connects with the humanity of others. Performance art is done for the audience. Without the audience, the art doesn't exist because performance art doesn't have any meaning without the audience. So I ask: *Can we teach with more artistry?* Teaching with an Equity mindset means accepting the challenge of the artist.

Aim for Brilliance, Not Mastery

The teacher-artist's contribution to the world is to inspire insight and understanding. The brilliance of the teacher-artist is dynamic and illuminating. I prefer the term *brilliance* to *mastery* because it reminds us that the brilliant artist is more or less brilliant given their presence and attention to their purpose and the skillful use of the tools of the craft. Teaching is emotional work. It requires a lot of us. It is emotional for both teachers and students. In fact, the most reliable indicator for any teacher that their time to leave the classroom has come is the precise moment when they realize that there is no longer an emotional draw in the work for them. If it isn't emotional, then it isn't being done well.

When I observe brilliant teachers, I study their maneuvers, how they move about in their classrooms – so as to understand their performance and results. But a brilliant teacher is not merely the sum of her maneuvers. She has a highly complex and fluid interaction with her environment, and it doesn't merely imitate a single prototype of brilliance. In fact, the only consistent characteristic that I have seen in brilliant teachers is that they evolve. Brilliant teachers evolve by asking good questions in the effort to understand if and how our instruction is effective and how we might improve! (One can't be both brilliant and also stuck in old habits and patterns!) I believe firmly and without equivocation that any teacher with the will to evolve and humility for the craft can improve their capacity for teaching even their most reluctant learners – but you must suspend your belief that there is a trick that you must find to be effective. There is no such thing. We all have to do the work, and the work is hard. Design your instruction with your performance-artist mindset, and always remember that the learning experience can't be said to be successful unless it engages your students. No one can claim to be successful in their teaching/art unless the audience for whom the performance is planned can reasonably be said to have been engaged – because without engagement there is no learning.

The Issue of Assessments

While there are many critical Equity issues in American education, it's important to devote some attention to the topic of assessments, and more specifically, the way high-stakes, standardized tests are used currently to broadly measure the quality of instruction. I have come to believe it is unrealistic to think we can evolve our mindset and practices in the direction of Equity without re-conceptualizing our paradigm for assessments. Assessments frame how we discuss and reward the work of schools, and our paradigm for standardized testing holds great consequences for the future of American public education.

In Chapter 1, I defined Equity as the notion that fairness and opportunity are ultimately measured as performance and achievement outcomes. That means that the whole point of assessments is to track data that informs and instructs our capacities for closing Equity gaps.

What does it mean to close Equity gaps? In terms of pedagogy specifically, closing Equity gaps means developing meaningful learning experiences for students that allow them to draw from a range of conceptual understandings in order to support greater process- and content fluencies with the skills and understandings we prioritize in school. Doing so fairly means, by definition, that what is the same (equal) is decidedly not fair.

Therein lies the assessment challenge. We want to measure Equity, and we want to do so without compromising the integrity of any group's quality of opportunity, but the execution of fairness means that students will be getting what they need, which is different than an expectation that they will receive the *same* thing as everyone else. This is potentially a slippery slope because it can lead to lessened expectations for some students relative to others, *but I don't think it has to…*

The Goals of Assessments in Terms of Equity

I want to make two larger points here about our use of assessments: the first is that teachers with an Equity mindset must more explicitly incorporate an element of action-research as a matter of general practice. The teaching cycle is incomplete without evidence of students' growth. In fact, I can make the argument that our best efforts to close Equity gaps will be thwarted until we teachers are better about more systematically defining the indicators which are most meaningful and instructive to our practice. The performative meaning of Equity requires that we consider the goals (outcomes) and tools of our teaching as part of a whole and ongoing deliberation, and if we aren't intentionally measuring our progress, we are susceptible to the interpretations of outside entities which are profoundly less informed than us because they don't know our kiddos in the ways that we do. As a classroom teacher, I learned that the assessments which were most helpful to me and my kiddos were the ones that allowed students to show their understandings of the biggest and most important ideas in some meaningful context or exercise. When I plan with an emphasis on measuring students' growth toward conceptual understandings through performative tasks beyond quizzes and tests that highlight the capacity for recall, I am much more likely to capture meaningful and specific evidence that instructs me on how I might improve my teaching.

Just as our creativity in instruction is a function of our pedagogical choices and our personal and professional beliefs about Equity, our assessments are choices about how we will collect the evidence of our students' knowing. No matter how well we think we are doing in offering equitable learning opportunities, the spirit of the Equity construct requires valid metrics that can confirm or disconfirm the effectiveness of instruction. Assessment independent of instruction is inherently invalid. An assessment that is not designed in alignment with the context and goals for learning is at most a proximal indicator. More often than not, however, it becomes a woefully mismatched measure of learning.

The Dangers of High-stakes Standardized Tests

My second larger point is that we need better assessment strategies for standardized tests. I understand and agree why it is important to measure within and across districts, and I agree that we have a responsibility to know how and what students are learning in schools and which groups are performing better or worse relative to others. I do not think, however, that the way we use standardized tests now does that effectively. We need a much more innovative, performance- and portfolio-style approach to capturing the evidence of students' growth toward the critical skills and conceptual understandings we value as learning outcomes. I am not an assessment expert, but there are many people who have thought carefully about different approaches to measuring the authentic learning outcomes of students. We have more and better options than the ones we currently employ.

All performance measures exist to enrich our understanding around the question of *How do we know if we are doing well?* Measurement is an integral part of the change effort and, done correctly, it informs and drives behavior. These, in fact, are the essential rules of psychometrics in the social sciences: Assessments, in order to be considered valid, should be designed to most directly measure what is most desired to be known; and assessments should provide insights and direction that may be used to direct improvement. The way we use standardized tests in the United States today accomplishes neither. The high-stakes, standardized tests that we use now track and measure one thing and one thing only: the performance of students on that single high-stakes, standardized test. The test itself is neither a definitive nor generalizable measure of anything else. It certainly can't be said to measure the quality of instruction nor necessarily the quality of student learning, nor the quality of the learning environment, or basically anything other than the score the student received on the assessment itself.

Worse even than the fact that the standardized tests we use now provide no helpful data for closing Equity gaps, many teachers see the standardized tests as an obstacle to CRE. I've heard teachers say countless times (maybe you've even thought it yourself while reading this book) that yes, we should all be teaching with a CRE mental model, but *Will the evidence of this kind of teaching and learning show up in the standardized tests?* Or more bluntly: *How's this going to affect my students' scores on the standardized tests?*

My answer to these questions is always the same: If we teachers can confirm that our methods are effective with our students, then the standardized tests – if they are valid measurements – should corroborate what we see in the classroom. If it doesn't, that is much more likely to mean that the standardized tests are not measuring the effects of good instruction but rather something else. I further argue that if the tests are the center of the assessment paradigm (as I would contend they are now), instruction will respond to it because the standardized test scores are seen as the most credible and valued evidence of effective instruction; but that should make us deeply uncomfortable. Students' learning should be at the center of the assessment paradigm, and whereas the CRE mental model requires us to be responsive to the needs and identities of our students as a baseline expectation for Equity, so too should the standardized tests center the context for our students' learning.

Reimagining the Assessment Paradigm with an Equity Lens

Imagine with me a world in which there is no such thing as high-stakes, standardized testing. If we were today considering for the first time ever how we might design a model for standardizing the assessment of the quality of students' learning and the efficacy of teaching on a national scale, we would reject a proposal of our current paradigm because it wouldn't give us the kind of data we need to support improvement, and we would be able to foresee its potential for discouraging culturally responsive teaching. Yet, it's standardized test scores that are presently discussed and rewarded as the most highly regarded outcomes for schools which, I would argue, is something different than Equity. Our philosophy and approaches to standardized testing should be grounded in what we believe about instruction that's good for kids. Standardized tests should not drive instruction. Instruction that serves the needs of our students should drive our design of assessments.

I agree that standardized tests should be a variable in the larger Equity assessment environment, but we are over-invested in them as it is now; they are the wrong variable to prioritize! I understand how and why the tests have come to such prominence (including the role of corporate greed in elevating their status), but the size and influence of the testing industry is not by itself corroborating evidence of its correctness. The measure of a measure to accurately report on and contribute to the mitigation of the problem is its actual influence. If there's a chance that the very process of measuring results might misrepresent the issue or drive the wrong behavior, then the measure is fundamentally flawed. Which brings me to the conclusion that we need to reimagine the way we assess students' learning and specifically in ways that provide meaningful feedback to teachers and students so that they can have a clearer sense of what is and is not effective in the practices of schools.

Unfortunately, some of the people who do subscribe to the validity of these measures are teachers in schools where the social and economic advantages are so overwhelming that the children are virtually teacher-proof! The high-stakes, standardized test results, however, it has been shown time and again, are most reliably a correlative indicator of zip code. Again, I am not arguing that we should not seek to measure, but I do mean to assert that teachers should think with specificity about how they might more accurately capture the evidence of their students' learning. Reliable evidence of learning is always calibrated with the goals of the instruction; a measure is meaningless unless it is designed to match the specific targets for teaching and understanding. Anything other than that is a proximal measure of learning at best.

Though I am opposed to the ways we currently use standardized tests in the United States, I can say that one positive outcome of their use is the problematic and persistent patterns of underperformance that are predictable along racial, ethnic, language-background, and socioeconomic lines have been brought to the attention of the public. I don't think we can take our objective analysis beyond that because of the flawed character of the tests and the vast expansiveness of inequity in our larger society. We don't really know from standardized tests, in my opinion, the true nature of the gaps or what we can do to redress them. Clearly, the achievement gap is a hugely variable phenomenon. The term "achievement gap" itself includes a wide spectrum of symptoms that undoubtedly have multiple, complex causes. A range of data points is necessary anytime we are seeking to understand complex situations. To use any metrics that would imply that the effects of inequity are reducible merely to classroom instruction is intellectually lazy and dangerous.

What Should You Remember?

One of my favorite spaces in the world is Room 41 at the National Gallery, London, the largest of the four gallery spaces dedicated to the permanent exhibition of Impressionist paintings. On four magnificent walls, one can regularly view Manet's, Monet's, Cezanne's, Pissarro's, Matisse's, Degas', Renoir's, and Van Gogh's – all on display for us to learn from and admire. In that space, one can realize that the brilliance of each artist isn't in competition with the others; but rather, each is an element of a larger, inspired movement. When we study the context of these masterpieces, we see the threads that extend throughout the collective portfolio. Pissarro and Cezanne were friends who painted landscapes together, as were Manet and Monet who painted each other's families. Renoir and Matisse are also considered pioneers in the genre of French Impressionism (though Matisse resisted the label), and one can see the influence of Pissarro, Cezanne, Manet, and Monet in their every brush stroke. The energy of the Impressionist movement stretched across the globe reaching the likes of Picasso, Rothko, and Basquiat – each of whom crafted their own individually brilliant styles, informed though not restrained by the brilliance that preceded them.

I attended the same high school in New York City as Jean-Michel Basquiat. I can vividly remember one of my own brilliant teachers grieving his death and telling me about her sweet, thoughtful student who had gone on to become one of the more famous and important artists of his generation. As a child, Basquiat's mother would regularly take him to see Picasso's Guernica, which was then exhibited at the Museum of Modern Art in New York. Basquiat said that Guernica inspired him to imagine the potential for the power of the artist, and it helped to free him of any false notions of the limitations of his craft. Guernica didn't merely influence Basquiat, it became part of the DNA of his artist-self; he never created anything that lived separate and apart from his experiences as a young impressionable person standing in the presence of Picasso's most historically significant masterpiece.

In a lot of ways, I think we are living in a golden era of Equity work. I see so many who offer brilliant, unique contributions under the broad banner of fairness and opportunity. Similarly, in classrooms across the country, I've seen brilliant teaching create opportunities for kids that inspire them to be brilliant themselves. Every time I see it, I feel inspired myself. The cool thing about brilliance is that we can learn to be brilliant by studying the brilliance of others – and it really doesn't matter in which arena that brilliance manifests itself. Brilliance is always an excellent reference for brilliance – and remember, there is no single expression of brilliance... Our task is to stay engaged in the discovery of how brilliant we can be.

Index